Journal of the
Plague Years

VOL. I: END NOTES

John Rember

Journal of the Plague Years

VOL. I: END NOTES

MARCH 2020–MARCH 2021

John Rember

Stanley, Idaho

Rember, John.
Journal of the Plague Years, Vol. I: End Notes / John Rember.

ISBN (Print): 979-8-9995968-2-6
ISBN (Ebook): 979-8-9995968-3-3

Library of Congress Control Number: 2025921033

Publisher's Cataloging-in-Publication Data

Names: Rember, John, author.
Title: Journal of the plague years , vol. I : end notes , March 2020 – March 2021 / John Rember.
Description: First Grand Mogul Books Edition | Stanley, ID: Grand Mogul Books, 2025.
Identifiers: LCCN: 2025921033 | ISBN: 979-8-9995968-2-6 (paperback) | 979-8-9995968-3-3 (ebook)
Subjects: LCSH: Rember, John. | Authors, American--Biography | COVID-19 Pandemic, 2020-2023--United States--Personal narratives. | BISAC: BIOGRAPHY & AUTOBIOGRAPHY / Memoirs | BIOGRAPHY & AUTOBIOGRAPHY / Literary Figures
Classification: LCC RA644.C67 .R36 vol. 1 2025 | DDC 362.1962414/092--dc23

Cover and book design: Euan Monaghan
Ebook formatting: Euan Monaghan

First Grand Mogul Books Edition: October 2025

Visit the author's website at johnrember.com

For Craig and Elizabeth Rember, my parents, whose love and good will and hard work taught me that life could be beautiful, even in grief.

Contents

Dr. Rieux resolved to complete this chronicle, so that he would not be one of those who hold their peace but should bear witness in favor of those plague-stricken people; so that some memorial of the injustice done them might endure; and to state quite simply what we learn in time of pestilence: that there are more things to admire in men than to despise.

—ALBERT CAMUS, *The Plague*

Prologue

March 22, 2020

MY BOOK, *A Hundred Little Pieces on the End of the World,* was released March 15, 2020. Subsequent events have made it more relevant than it was at its publication. The book was dedicated to a sensibility that could face deep civilizational disruption and still stay sane—through humor, through seeing things clearly, and through kindness to the people in our lives. That is mostly what I'm about these days.

I'm starting a new journal, to record our everyday lives in a world experiencing a new and often fatal virus. I'm hoping it will not become a Journal of the Plague Year, or even of the Plague Month, though I fear it will. Things could go back tomorrow to a disease-free state and we'd still be changed forever.

Regardless of what happens, Julie and I plan to witness these times, even if we're watching from an isolated valley in Central Idaho. Our lives are small, but our eyes are big.

Stay well,
John

On Having One's Book Tour Cancelled by the Coronavirus Outbreak

March 19, 2020

ON MARCH 15, 2020, the University of New Mexico Press released my *A Hundred Little Pieces on the End of the World*, a collection of essays contemplating the collapse of industrial civilization. In the introduction to the book, I state that no one can predict the future. "It is getting hard enough to predict the present," I write, before launching into meditations on an unsustainable status quo.

The UNM Press and I had planned a book tour in the American Southwest to introduce the book to independent bookstore owners, book clubs, and university philosophy and environmental science departments.

Then came coronavirus. A few days before the book tour was to begin, schools and colleges closed. Bookstores cancelled readings. The AWP convention in San Antonio, where advance reader copies of my book had occupied a table in the UNM Press booth, had gone ahead on schedule—at the price of halved attendance, cancelled presentations, and the resignation of one of its co-directors, who had wanted to call the whole thing off.

The world tour for my end-of-world book ended before it started, because of the end of a small and quite particular world, one inhabited by convivial book lovers, environmental seminar students, wine-fueled discussion groups, and ordinary people looking for an ethical alternative to fighting over toilet paper in Walmart.

My book was aimed at this disparate audience, although I hadn't anticipated the toilet paper fights, preferring instead to focus on cannibalism and arsenals in basements.

I live in the middle of Idaho, in a high and sometimes snow-covered valley, and although my spouse Julie and I hadn't spent the winter quarantined, it felt like we had. We were looking forward to cloudless skies, warm sunshine, and audiences prepared to laugh at doomsday jokes. I had written a funny-but-dark End Times book, which isn't a well-known genre, but it seemed to be appropriate for a world getting more and more absurd and risky. I had also dealt—more seriously—with the grief that would attend the end of civilization. When we realized the book tour wouldn't happen, we got a glimpse of that grief.

At least until we realized we were being stupidly self-indulgent, and that most people in the world had worse problems, some of them lethal, and that quarantine, at least for a month or two, would look quite a lot like business as usual for us. We are backcountry skiing in the days, reading by the woodstove once it gets dark, and keeping track of a pandemic from a distance—at least as much distance as a pandemic will allow. We've just received news of a Covid-19 victim in Sun Valley, fifty miles south of us, where daily flights from Seattle began early last December and continued through President's Day weekend.

So we're waiting, along with everyone else in the country, until this thing that has divided our lives into Before and After begins to reveal its nature. Thus far we've got enough food in the pantry to last us for a couple of weeks, and shelves and shelves of books, and a suddenly interesting CD collection that we haven't played through since the invention of internet streaming. We've assured the dog we're not going to eat her, at least just yet, although she hasn't made the same promise back to us.

I've realized, as well, that the audience for my book has increased, even if the word might take a while to get out. It's a book that explores the question of living well in tough times, behaving ethically in the face of deprivation and rage, and finding meaning in the small spaces of our lives. It's a kind of nano-survivalism manual. While it lacks the grim heft of an assault rifle and a crawl space packed with freeze-dried food, it delivers the promise that while there is life, there can be meaning, and it suggests ways to glean that meaning from a picked-over world.

*

You get a good idea of the value of your own advice when you have to apply it to your own existence. My coronavirus-aware-self understands that my recipes for the good life now have a life-and-death intensity to them, and that some of my jokes flirt dangerously with nihilism, which is hard on morale in any arena where theory becomes practice.

That's not to say my book and I have lost credibility. We've gained it. Not without a tradeoff.

My book was once able to guarantee my readers a conditional existence, cover to cover. I wrote it as a refugee from fragility rather than collapse, and that turned out to be a happy distinction. Now that distinction is in danger of disappearing. The scary stories I told around the campfire have a new audience, one made up of the aged, the immune-challenged, the diabetic, the asthmatic, the breathless.

A cancelled book tour creates a hole in time. Time itself, which once was divided into units of human agency, tends toward eternity, in which human agency is a dad joke at best.

You do what you can to fill the eternal spaces on the calendar. Cancelling hotel reservations becomes the occasion for sudden small friendships with the person who answers the phone, who tells you of other cancelled reservations, empty dining rooms and streets, and closed libraries. You promise to come back when this is over, realizing only after you've ended the call that you haven't been there yet.

You resort to ritual. In this neighborhood it takes the form of home maintenance.

You go outside, to check on the patches of lawn emerging from the snow, and decide you'll start raking up the pine needles early this year. The house needs stained. The lower branches of trees need trimmed prior to fire season. The deck, made uneven by frost heaves, needs you to crawl around under it and shorten some of its pilings with a battery-powered chainsaw, an activity you call deck yoga. You wonder how long batteries will last in a world that might not be producing them forever. You decide—trying to stand up straight after a session in the under-deck mud—that they'll last longer than you will.

The desk gets organized and cleaned. The scarred wall behind the wood box gets repainted. The emergency food in the crawl space gets inventoried, and you determine it will last at least as long as your book tour was supposed to. You spend a half-day fixing electrical issues in your old SUV with the help of your automotive partner, Mr. YouTube. You wish you'd fixed things two years earlier, when the rear window and locks had quit working in the first place. A friend calls and tells you his broadband has been out for three days.

You check on older friends. You have better conversations than you've had in years.

Books. There are a thousand or more in the house. It was a shock when you realized that you had more books than you could read in your life, a bigger shock when you realized coronavirus could shorten that life further.

You read articles in which authors recommend books that first awakened wonder and joy in their lives. They're going back to those books these days, finding comfort and strength in their vanished worlds.

It doesn't work that way with you. And yet, by looking at the titles that jump out at you from the bookcase, you come up with a classic reading list to fill those lost evenings when you would have read your own end-of-the-world passages to hopeful and good-willed young people.

Here it is—you don't list their authors because their book tours have been cancelled, too:

- *Ozymandias*
- *The Masque of the Red Death*
- *The Second Coming*
- *The Love Song of J. Alfred Prufrock* and *The Waste Land*
- *Moby-Dick*
- *The Sun Also Rises*
- *The Plague*
- *Lolita*
- *The Denial of Death*
- The Wikipedia entry on Nietzsche

These will keep your mind off your troubles for a while.

You hesitate about listing a Wikipedia entry as a classic. Understand that it's safer than reading Nietzsche in the flesh, in the same way that Nietzsche must have found it safer to talk about The Abyss as a metaphor rather than see it as a screaming horse being beaten to death in real time.

The coronavirus isn't a metaphor. It's a microbe, a literal one.

The first book I've started reading is *The Plague*. I've read it a half dozen times, because I used to teach it to undergraduates deeply infatuated with French postmodernists. I used to tell my students that the French writers who came after Camus were reduced to inarticulate, incomprehensible, untranslatable rage because they weren't Camus. It wasn't the Anxiety of Influence they were dealing with. When you come after Camus, you suffer from the Post Traumatic Stress of Influence.

The Plague is not just about the Nazis. It's not just about confronting evil. It's not even about getting the first sentence of your novel right. It's about being a doctor in a city where a communicable disease is killing the people around you. The deep hidden meaning of *The Plague* is not hidden.

Camus helps reassure me that the coronavirus is a literal thing. We live in an enormously screwed-up world because people seize on the literal and turn it into metaphor, and then turn around and start treating the metaphor as though it were literal. That's one of the reasons a horrible emptiness lurks on supermarket shelves where toilet paper used to be, or in your month-old portfolio statement from a few days before you were going to cash out but didn't. Stop turning those things into metaphor, and you'll find you probably have enough toilet paper and enough money to live long enough to die from lack of something else.

Economic systems are not giant sharks that die when they quit swimming. A virus is not a sentient being. Cigars are just cigars and the pharmaceutical-industrial complex is just a simple criminal enterprise, not Satan. Feckless government officials are not really the Deep State. The virus is not God's Wrath or evidence that we need to Vaccinate America Against Illegal Aliens.

As the pandemic widens, we will experience grief we didn't know we were capable of, but we will find strengths we didn't know we had. With luck these strengths will let us reject the metaphors that have transformed a communicable microbe into something that can destroy economies, abrogate treaties and contracts, move people to divide humanity into Them and Us, and cause people to wake up in the middle of the night in paralyzing fear.

Here's my nano-survival advice: Be nice to the people you're trapped indoors with. Read *The Plague* as a self-help manual. And don't get too upset if book tours are cancelled. We will, with luck and wisdom, carry on.

Getting to a Tribe of One

March 30, 2020

IN 1964, AS a freshman in high school, I sat in the Liberty Theater in Hailey, Idaho, to see Vincent Price in *The Last Man on Earth*, one of the first wave of living dead germ theory films. A plague turns the population into vampires except for Price, who's immune because he was long ago bitten by a vampire bat. Price goes around pounding stakes into sleeping vampire hearts by day. By night he hides from shuffling mobs of vampires in his mirror-and-garlic-festooned house.

At the climax of the movie, Price is mortally wounded by the mob. Dying, he stands up and screams, "You have killed the last man on Earth." The line, with all its drama, is met with indifference, which is about what you'd expect from an audience of the undead.

What I remember most from the film is not the death of the last living human, but an earlier scene where Price, wandering the empty daylit streets of Los Angeles, comes upon a Ford dealership. He goes in, sits in the new Thunderbird in the showroom, notices the keys in the ignition, and drives out through the floor-to-ceiling plate glass window and onto the wide and empty boulevard.

At that moment, a mix of 14-year-old insecurities and a yearning for freedom without limits made me envy the last man on Earth. I could have used a Thunderbird.

Still, by the time I walked out of the theater that evening, I had realized *The Last Man on Earth* was not about vampires or freedom, or even Thunderbirds. It was a film about loneliness. Vincent Price is a lonely man, especially once the female lead turns out to be dead.

*

The Liberty Theater is a much different place than it used to be. The actors Bruce Willis and Demi Moore bought it and refurbished and repurposed it. A troupe of actors performs plays there now, or would if the whole town wasn't under coronavirus lockdown.

Hailey itself has been repurposed and refurbished as a retirement home. The lower-middle-class town of my adolescence has been gentrified, and decent houses in the old part of town go for a million dollars. As a result, it's become a place full of rich, old, scared people.

Two Covid-19 deaths have already occurred in the local hospital, and Blaine County—Hailey is the county seat—has, at this moment, more cases per capita than any other place in the country. Enough staff at the local hospital have been infected that any new coronavirus cases are immediately sent to the cities of Boise or Twin Falls. Until enough people recover, the local hospital is mostly serving as a coronavirus clearinghouse.

The Hailey airport is full of the private jets of people with second and third and fourth homes in and around the Sun Valley resort 12 miles north. These people, sheltering in what they thought was a safer place than Seattle or Los Angeles or New York, have caused anger and resentment among the year-round locals. Empty shelves in the grocery stores and the fear of imported disease have caused people who used to be welcomed here for their money to be told to leave. Go Back To Wherever Your Learjet Brought You From is the gist of the social media messages I'm reading.

But ironies multiply when you start deciding who has a disease—or the right to a roll of local toilet paper—and who doesn't. Here in Sawtooth Valley, 60 miles north of Sun Valley, we have a population of Blaine County summer people, who disappear when the harsh weather hits in November and usually reappear when the snow melts in April. This year, these people are back early, fleeing the microbes brought by skier-packed jets that landed at the Hailey airport twice a day from early December on. Some of them, arriving in our valley as refugees, have been told to Go Back To Blaine County Where You Came From.

*

For half a million years or more, we lived in tribes, defined ourselves by our tribes, and submitted who we were to a tribal identity. People who thought of themselves as individuals were considered mentally ill.

Also, people in other tribes were Them, not Us, and if they threatened our tribe, they were expendable. As many tribes found out, it's not good to be a tribe when a bigger, more powerful tribe is next door.

The tribalism that has marked our politics since at least the Reagan administration has divided and redivided this country. Absent a strong impulse toward the universal, tribes have gotten smaller and more defensive. Race has been a reliable marker for division, as has nationality. Also education levels. Political parties. On college campuses, membership or not in fraternities and sororities.

Blaine County people. Year-round Sawtooth Valley residents.

I'm especially sensitive to this latter distinction because for the first 50 years I lived in Sawtooth Valley, I spent most winters in Blaine County, where there was a winter economy and an accompanying job. I was told to go back where I came from by people who had spent one winter here, even after I'd spent 10 years' worth of summers here.

But I've been full-time since 2004, and I'm now getting to the age where I'm one of the older full-timers. I have seniority, enough to tell anyone to go anywhere, at least with Sawtooth Valley as a point of departure.

But I'm hesitant to tell people to go back where they came from, even if they show up with bats perching on their shoulders, or a hunger for brains, or with Blaine County plates on their cars. I remember what happened to Vincent Price, who made me realize that real horror comes with the realization that you've become a tribe of one.

Coronavirus is not just a physical contagion. It's taken the self-image created by 40 years of libertarian thought in this country—an image of extreme individualism—and has mutated it into a deep solitary scream, where people you thought were in your tribe or even your family can be instantly and invisibly transmuted into The Other. An infection or lack of it can place you in front of a mob of people trying to kill you. You, The Last Human on Earth.

Of course, Julie and I—and Juno the dog—aren't going to succumb to that particular psychic infection. We'll confront the coronavirus as a tribe, but we'll be a peaceful and unobtrusive tribe. We'll try not to treat the people coming into the Valley with camping equipment or travel trailers as The Enemy. We used to call them tourists, and we welcomed their dollars spent in local restaurants and motels and sporting-goods stores. We still have a little trouble seeing them as enemies just because they might carry a virus.

Regardless of what happens, Julie and I will not leave each other. That's the promise I've made to Julie, and that's the promise she has made to me.

As for Juno, she knows something is up. If we're reading on the couch, she walks up and rests her chin on one of our thighs. She waits until one of us rests a hand on her head. Then the three of us look at each other, and I like to think that then some tribal melding happens. It's a tableau of constancy in an inconstant world, one still possible to imagine, at least for the moment.

Return of the Authentic

April 6, 2020

WE HAD AN earthquake last week, and at first it wasn't a metaphor. At 5:52 p.m. on March 31, a 6.5 Richter-scale earthquake hit about 20 miles north of us. I was sitting on the couch in Julie's office, holding a glass of wine and watching PBS News Hour pandemic coverage.

At first I thought it was snow falling off the house—it had been snowing all day and there was a foot of snow on what had been a bare metal roof—but after 10 seconds or so, I realized we didn't have enough snow or enough roof to account for the continuing roaring and shaking. A shelf of antique bottles above Julie's computer started wobbling, and four of them fell off, missing her computer screen and bouncing unbroken on the carpet.

That was the extent of our earthquake damage, at least until the next morning, when we noticed that our well water had turned orange. It cleared up a day later.

The next day, when the weather turned sunny, we could see dozens of slide-paths in the Sawtooths, and giant gouges in deep snow where huge boulders had tumbled down steep couloirs.

We skied new powder, and then, after the sun had done its damage, we skied new powder topped by serious breakable crust. Julie made it look easier than I did. I had one hard fall when my skis persisted in going one way while I went the other. Afterward, it was evidence that the body has its own tectonics, as my joints are a bit more flexible than they had been, albeit prone to painful aftershocks.

Today we'll ski up a local canyon, where we can climb for an hour and then shoot down our tracks to the car in 10 minutes, or even faster if we don't wait for the dog. We always wait for the dog.

In a warm week, our foot of new powder will have melted to an inch of skiable corn snow. If it remains cold, we'll continue with breakable crust. It was minus 5 last night, minus 9 the night before. The calendar indicates April, but April has yet to arrive.

The cold weather and a statewide lockdown have discouraged visits from our neighbors in Blaine County. They're having a tough time down there, with 400+ coronavirus cases, more than any other county in Idaho—more per capita than any place in the country—and 25 hospital beds and one ventilator.

The Sun Valley Resort is closed, its ski lifts stilled. Bars and restaurants in Hailey and Ketchum are empty and dark. The lockdown urges everyone indoors. If people need to go out for groceries, recreation, or virus-free air, they are told not to cross county lines to get them.

These are harsh measures in what was, until March, a winter playground full of athletic, road-tripping, bar hopping, highly social people who usually prefer hugs or more to handshakes.

We still see cars with Blaine County plates, but leaving one closed-down tourist town for another—whose tourist season hasn't even begun yet—probably isn't going to help damp down the pandemic or even improve a mood. Our bars are closed. Cashiers at the grocery stores ask people where they're from.

Walking back from skiing, we look at license plates, and then at drivers. We wave, but they don't wave back.

We're seeing the occasional pickup or SUV parked on melted-out turnouts above fishing holes in the Salmon River. Spring steelhead season is here. Cabela's-costumed people wade through drifts to the riverbank, keeping social distance between themselves and their guides.

It's early in the season for steelhead. Even on partly sunny days, snow squalls whirl over the water and riverbanks.

Past fishing expeditions included going to a warm bar after a day of frost-stung cheeks and eyes, lost fish, and missteps into too-deep-for-your-waders water. Once there, you told fish stories to people who told fish stories of their own. But now the bar isn't warm, and the bartender wouldn't let you in even if it were.

The pandemic has brought with it an uncomfortable truth about tourist economies—that without a narrative to accompany your experience, there isn't much cause to become a tourist. A bike tour, a road trip, a hike with crusty retired professors through the Lake District, a mule ride into the Grand Canyon, a celebrity sighting at a hot-spring spa—these are all story first and experience second.

You booked a trip, you saw, you returned to tell the tale. The tale is what you retain of your lost time, effort, and money. Now all you need is an audience.

For most of my life I've been a student of the tourist industry. My father was a fishing guide on the Salmon River, back when it still had salmon in it. As a child, I would wake up to my father and his clients arranging fresh-caught chinook salmon on our lawn for photo opportunities. I would listen to some of those clients tell my father they would trade their lives for his in a minute, even though they were important people, presidential aides and CEOs of giant companies and pioneering heart surgeons and book-writing New York psychoanalysts.

As I grew older, I realized my father was not selling fish—those could be had, for considerably less money, at any supermarket. Instead, he was selling a story about living with his family in a small house in backcountry Idaho, fishing and hunting and trapping for groceries, and getting up each day prepared for a complete change of plans.

He was an avatar of thinking-on-his-feet authenticity. That's what he intuitively knew his clients wanted. I've wondered if his clients who were psychoanalysts shared his intuition, and if their experience on the river consisted of fleeing their own dogmatic self-control for an unscripted half-hour of having a big fish on the line.

That's what most of my father's clients were seeking—a moment of authentic action, something to take home when all was said and done, something to distinguish a life from a profession, something that would take up the best sentence in the obituary.

I forgot myself for a moment, says the psychoanalyst, and I will value that moment forever. The CEO and presidential aide and surgeon say the same thing.

What happens in a tourist economy when the stories can no longer be told, when *social intimacy* can no longer be practiced? When the money isn't there for hotels and restaurants even if they were open? We're getting a hint from the ads on the Boise TV stations, which are flogging recreational vehicles and SUVs. Family units—Mom, Dad, and the kids—are seen hanging up the game consoles in their living rooms and escaping to the wilderness in their trailers and campers and tents. The RV dealerships are "Stacking Them Deep and Selling Them Cheap," a phrase that makes me think of an overcrowded cemetery.

I fear that we will see a lot of family units here in Sawtooth Valley this summer. There won't be a lot of places to park them, because Idaho is a state where the flat spots add up to an area the size of Delaware, and a lot of that has "No Trespassing" signs on it. Other families will be competing for parking spaces and warning their kids not to play with other kids. Meals and drinks once purchased in bars and restaurants will be prepared in wheeled aluminum boxes scaled up from solar ovens. Some of those boxes, by the end of the trip, will seem too small and hot for the family.

Sawtooth Valley is planning for business as usual this summer. Restaurants will be open. So will bars. Guide services will be guiding. Whitewater river companies will be rafting. Campgrounds will be camping. I can say this with confidence because most local income depends on tourists coming to our valley. Mortgages and business loans must be paid. If we had had social distancing when my father was guiding, our family would have gone broke, and I wouldn't be sitting here in Sawtooth Valley today.

When you have to make all your money in four months, you're not going to let a little pandemic get in the way.

*

By 2019, tourism in Sawtooth Valley had become far less authentic than when my father was a fishing guide. Experience had become standardized. The salmon in the river were a domesticated species. The mountains and streams and lakes people came to see were obscured by tour groups, dusty trail rides, interpretive signs, planted fish, and lakeshores pounded into dust by too many hiking boots.

We were accustomed to experiences that had been forcibly groomed to millimeter tolerances, mainly because clients retained attorneys for any surprises. We knew what to expect. Our summers were becoming as standardized as a Caribbean cruise, or Disneyland, or Yellowstone. Our Chamber of Commerce brochures were evidence that somebody had gone to a lot of trouble to ensure the predictability of the tourist experience.

In 2020, authenticity is threatening to return.

I am dreading the approach of tourist season, and not because last year a million tourists visited our valley from June through September. It's because we have no idea how many of them will return this year, and what their expectations will be. Will they assume they're coming to a place where they can forget coronavirus happened? Will they still queue in long lines outside the Stanley Bakery, waiting patiently for a place at the crowded tables? Will they shun each other, or us, or just Blaine County people? Will they leave telling stories that say at this moment, this thing happened, and even though people died, it was real?

I'm afraid there will be lots of chances for thinking on your feet this summer, not all of them worth paying a guide for.

This summer, people will not always be seeking authenticity. Inauthenticity will have value because it promises a safe refuge from the ground that's shaking under your feet, or a story that's too lonely to tell.

People will lie to themselves, I think. They will make up stories about coming here before they're here, and then they will try to live those stories when they are here. They will pretend that the Sawtooth Valley they visited in 2019 is the one they're visiting in 2020.

Their stories, like all lies, will get messier with each telling. Telling it will be the easy part. Finding an audience willing to believe it will be harder.

Skiing Downhill

April 13, 2020

YESTERDAY JULIE AND I and our neighbor Liesl took advantage of the spring freeze-thaw cycle, put skins on the bottoms of our skis, and hiked up the north side of Gold Creek. We parked our vehicles a mile downriver from the house, crossed a half-mile of snowy flat to the base of a sagebrush ridge, and began climbing its north-facing side. It's a vertical climb of 2,500 feet to the top, and it took us a leisurely two-and-a-half hours to get there.

From the top you can see the ice of Redfish Lake, and, to the east, the White Cloud range, covered with deep drifted-in snow in its nooks and hollows. High winds have scoured ridges down to the rock, but the drifts will likely last into July this year.

We've talked about skiing in July, because it's an activity that goes with social distancing, and we're worried we'll still be social distancing in July no matter what all-clear signal has been sounded by the CDC. We might need something to do in July, we think, although we may not, the bounds of certainty having been unfenced by the pandemic.

In the past I have said that one of these years I'm going to ski the local mountains at least once in every month of the year—it would be possible to do it, even in September and October, if you hiked to a deep north-facing canyon in the Sawtooths, where a shaded couloir melts down to clear ice that looks black from a distance. It would be a short run, and a fast one, on rock skis. But it could be done.

It's the sort of pointless stupid young male thing that you do for the sake of telling other stupid young males about it later. I've stopped doing that sort of thing for the most part, due to age more than wisdom. But lately—it's true: if the pandemic means you can't do one thing, you can do another. Even if you haven't thought about it for years. Even if it's stupid.

Lest you think we skied yesterday just for the sake of recounting it later, let me tell you that once we started down, we were on an inch of corn snow on a bulletproof base. The sky was blue, the air was warm, the turns were effortless and safe, and we skied down through the skeletons of whitebark pine, the local high-altitude tree that has been wiped out by blister rust in the last decade. They look like the clawed clutching trees in nasty fairy tale illustrations, but we slalomed around them in the sunlight, timing our turns with the rolling drifts on the ridge top.

Between the three of us and the dog we tracked up lots of terrain, grinning all the way. Carving a series of tight turns down a steep slope covered in an inch of slush is a good recipe for feeling like you're 18 again, except this time you're in better control. You do have to stop and rest now and then.

We hit the flats still able to stay on top of the crust, which was getting soft on slopes with direct sun, and reached our cars. There we found that Liesl's old Chevy Suburban had been vandalized. Someone had deeply scratched the paint on the hood, in four or five places. Those scratches, which spelled out "Go Home," had not been there when she had parked a few hours before.

Liesl is originally from Ketchum, and the Suburban—once her mother's—still has Blaine County plates, even though Liesl has lived next to us in the valley for almost a decade. She's a good friend, and a reliable and uncomplaining ski partner, and it's upsetting to find that the fear and anger of local Custer County people toward outsiders was directed toward one of our own. It's upsetting enough when it's directed toward outsiders, even outsiders who have been told to stay away.

Julie's and my vehicle, with its Custer County plates, was untouched. But the day itself was damaged. Our eternal spring ski day, with its sun, blue skies, and easy turns, suddenly collapsed into the dark thin edge of the present. Suddenly the world contained a shape-shifting pandemic, mortal fears, and evil of the most banal and human variety.

Scratching someone's car may not seem serious enough to deserve to be called evil. But it's the sort of thing that can turn into its own deadly pandemic. Some strains of trying to ruin someone else's day tend to become more lethal over time.

Julie and I got sick for about three weeks in January this year, along with lots of other people in the valley. We thought we had the flu even though we had gotten flu shots in October.

Symptoms: dry cough, shooting muscle pains, tight breathing, fatigue, a couple of nights of waking up drenched in sweat in a cold room. For a while I felt like I couldn't depend on my autonomic nervous system to breathe for me—that I'd have to consciously will every breath I took—so going to sleep was a matter of some anxiety.

But we got through it, and as soon as we could, we got back out skiing the backcountry. My lungs still feel a bit tight, but they work well enough, as evidenced by yesterday's climb.

It's likely we had something other than the flu, and we've thought that maybe, just maybe, Sawtooth Valley had Covid-19 before it was widespread in Blaine County, and maybe, just maybe, we gave it to them instead of them giving it to us. Maybe someone, vacationing at Sun Valley from Seattle, took a day off from skiing and drove up to see the mountains and have lunch. They left the virus to incubate in our community before going south again.

Many of us were miserable for a while, but we usually weren't sick enough that we couldn't go out to eat and drink a couple of times a week in the one place that stays open all winter.

We are all looking forward to taking an antibody test, once they've developed a cheap and reliable one. It would be nice to discern the nature of this virus better than we presently can.

Few people are comfortable with uncertainty, and the coronavirus has made almost everything—graduation plans, vacations, rent money, food, jobs, life itself—uncertain. I've made a habit of telling people they can't predict the future, and they shouldn't. Bad things happen to prophets. If they don't get crucified for being wrong, they get crucified for being right.

I'm trying not to predict what will happen to Sawtooth Valley this summer. Instead I'm confining myself to history.

History, in a month or so: closed bars, unemployed people, mistaken scapegoating and associated vandalism, a false impression that Sawtooth Valley hasn't had the virus yet and is still a safe place to go, people who social distance to 12 or 15 feet just to be safe, grocery stores that limit purchases to one of a kind, a tourist economy with no place to go for the tourists who drive up and down the highway, searching for an OPEN sign.

In a month or so, we'll see if that history has tailed into the present.

Here in the valley, it's taken the pandemic and resultant economic precarity to make us understand just how good our life has been. Tourists and their close kin, second-home owners, come every summer, bringing gifts and laughter, and then they go away, leaving us to enjoy our solitude.

All winter long, we dream of all the restaurants being open, and of getting lattes and mochas and huckleberry milkshakes from roadside stands, of having brunch any day of the week on open verandas. The anticipation of being there makes us happier than the actual being there, because tourists do bring problems of crowding, tacky staged experiences, and lack-of-common-sense accidents. But nobody starves. Almost everybody gets along.

It's been a golden age of tourism here in the Valley for the last fifty years or so, but golden ages never last forever. That's why they're called golden. The other ages are called silver, bronze, iron, and stone, if things go all the way to the bottom. We hope we don't have to experience even one of those lesser times, with their privation, their divisiveness, their shameless display of the dark aspects of human nature. No thank you, we say. Let's go back to what it was, when the paint on our cars was safe. At least for this summer, anyway. Please.

The Parable of Crow #1

April 20, 2020

UNUSUAL FOR THIS time of year: the garage swept, the workbench clean, the tools stored away in their proper bins, skis flat-filed and waxed. After sweeping up a half-gallon or so of mouse turds, I have remembered to keep the mouse traps baited and set, and as a result have caught eight mice, six in March and two thus far in April.

I place the mice I catch on the fence rail behind the garage, and the crows that frequent our compost pile in the winter watch from the trees along the highway. One of them—the alpha crow, Crow #1 for short—usually arrives within a minute. In a graceful dive-and-glide, Crow #1 comes in an inch above the rail, seizes the mouse in his talons, and heads for a rook nook in a nearby hillside cliff face. Once there, he swallows the mouse whole. It takes a little head-bobbing and gulping to get it down.

Over the years, I've concluded that Crow #1 hates to share. He doesn't waste time savoring a dead mouse bit by bit. He swallows it quickly, and then takes off again for the fence, where lesser crows are sometimes perching, looking for mice he might have missed. He drives them off by hovering over them, screaming insults, and threatening to violate social distance. Then he perches on the rail, supremely alone and proud, digesting, watching the other crows pick through the compost, malnourished vegetarians all of them.

My turd sweeping and mouse trapping and Crow #1's gulping and head-bobbing have occasioned a rereading of the hantavirus chapter in Laurie Garrett's thick 1994 book, *The Coming Plague.*

The parallels between hantavirus and the new coronavirus are striking. Both were previously unrecognized versions of known viruses. Both cause acute respiratory distress syndrome (ARDS), which drowns victims in lung fluid. Both cause kidney damage. Both have come from a wild-animal reservoir: bats in the case of coronavirus, rodents in the case of hantavirus.

But hantavirus causes death in an estimated 60 to 70 percent of its victims. Garrett points out that thousands of pneumonia deaths happen every year, but because most occur in the about-to-die-anyway cohort, few are tested to determine what kind of infection they have. As a result, we don't know how widespread and deadly hantavirus really is.

Rereading Garrett has caused me to wear a mask while sweeping out the garage, and gloves while I bait the traps and take mice from them. If I find Crow #1 beak-first in the snow below the fence rail, I'll spray the garage down with Clorox and try not to kill myself in the process.

It's occurred to me that if I die of hantavirus or Clorox-generated lung edema anytime in 2020, I'll likely be listed as a Covid-19 fatality. If Crow #1 dies of starvation, his death will be ascribed to the pandemic's economic collateral damage. There's a lot of uncertainty in this business.

The Coming Plague is on my bedside dresser. Laurie Garrett is a fine writer and it's comforting, during this pandemic, to find someone in solid control, even if it's only solid control of the language. I don't find the book morbid, but I do find it sobering in its insistence that only luck has kept us from another global pandemic as bad as the flu of 1918. In its index, there isn't an entry for a coronavirus of any kind.

In the bookcase, yet to be reread, are William McNeill's *Plagues and Peoples*, Richard Preston's *The Hot Zone* and *The Demon in the Freezer*, and Jared Diamond's *Guns, Germs, and Steel*. I've already reread Camus's *The Plague*.

After I listed *The Plague* as part of my cheer-up pandemic reading list, I had friends ask me if I was really serious about them reading anxious literature in already anxious circumstances.

Of course you should read it, I said. It's a story of human endurance against lurking evil. It tells how adversity, even as it brings out the worst in some people, brings out the best in others. It shows how doing what you can to be kind, when and where you can, is the highest and best use of your life. If those things don't cheer you up, I said, I don't know what will.

As for the other books, I find them cheering, too. They are evidence that Man Proposes, God Disposes, as long as you have a definition of God that encompasses lethal microbes, malignant intentions toward humanity, bullying crows, and Newtonian physics. It's nice not to have personal responsibility—much less guilt—for the mess we're in, to know that humanity is subject to forces so far beyond its control as to make even the idea of free will into the fakest of fake news.

It's easy to conclude there are no humans moving and shaking human events. All our names, not just the tubercular John Keats's, are written in water. Our works, no matter how much fuss and bother we caused when we were living, melt away in the same instant of geologic time as the rest of us. If you want to see who will be moving and shaking things long after you're gone, switch on your electron microscope.

The pandemic has been a proof-of-concept exercise for people who would effect worldwide change with a biolab. We now know that a pandemic can wreck economies, paralyze air, sea, and ground traffic, alter geopolitical balances, quell protests, and derail environmental movements. It can energize the kind of eat-its-own populism that emphasizes border security, germ-ridden immigrants, hatred of science and reason, and taking things back to where they were in an idealized and oddly empty past.

It doesn't matter if the pandemic started from bats or pangolins in the Wuhan wet market or in a military installation in any of a half dozen countries: the proof-of-concept is the same. Now that CRISPR gene-splicing technology is widely available, and vastly cheaper than a nuclear weapons program, it's easy to imagine that such technology will prove irresistible to the utopian thinkers and social tinkerers and military men among us.

I think of explaining this to Crow #1 when he drives the more craven crows off the fence rail, especially if I put more than one mouse on it at a time.

"Leave the other mice for the others," I say to him. "One mouse makes a meal. Two make gluttony. You'll cause resentment and anger among your fellows. They'll gang up on you when you're sleeping and peck your eyes out and tear off your feathers and eat you. And then somebody new will emerge as a new #1, and he'll be a worse tyrant than you were, having learned from your example. Haven't you heard what happened to the old Bolsheviks, after Stalin came to power?"

Crow #1 considers this. Despite limited spiritual ambitions, he's highly intelligent. But it's a kind of cold, reptilian intelligence that doesn't admit to mercy or error. He's heard of Stalin. He's learned from Stalin. He looks at me, and utters a guttural croak that I translate as, "More mice. Now."

"What about hantavirus? Maybe, for your safety, I should stop putting out mice altogether."

He's not worried by my words. Crow #1 can take care of his own safety. He's done it all his life. "More mice."

I used to believe that Crow #1 liked me and saw me as a kind and generous human being, not like the other human beings who poisoned or shot crows when they grew so numerous that they would eat crops in the field and break the branches of roosting trees and cover sidewalks with crow shit.

Instead, I fed him mice. Having watched him for years and never having spotted a sign of gratitude or empathy, I now know he doesn't just hate sharing, he hates the sharer.

"More mice. More."

"I may not always be here. There's a new virus going around. One day I may be carted out of this house dead, and nobody will put mice out for you."

Crow #1 thinks this over. He's wondering if my body will be draped over the fence rail for him. He's thinking contentedly of more bodies to come. He's lucky I never let my thoughts get away from me, else I'd get the shotgun and see how well crow under glass would serve as Sunday dinner.

"More mice," says Crow #1. I'm back in the house now, and he's just outside my window. He looks like he'd fly right in and peck me to pieces if he could. He's hard evidence that what you project onto the world can come right back at you.

Pandemic Tourism

April 27, 2020

WE HAVE SEEN the first 45-foot diesel pusher motorhome of the season. It was decades old, with sun-faded red paint—no big graphics or smoked glass—but it didn't look as if it had hit any deer or elk, and the giant windshield lacked the kind of crack network that indicates a third or fourth owner has forgone insurance.

We did hear exhaust gas escaping through gaps in the plumbing. No matter. It was going 85, maybe 90. The driver sat seven feet off the pavement, grinning like he was killing snakes. We calculated he could have stopped in a mile or two.

We ducked off the pavement into the barrow pit. He went by in a rush of wind, staring straight down the white line, charging the horizon.

We didn't see anyone in the passenger seat. In past Aprils, when the motorhomes of this size and condition hit the valley, they were invitations to rich fantasy.

…behind the flashing, speeding windshield, there's a one-hit rock band heading for the casino at Flathead Lake after a gig at Cactus Pete's in Jackpot. The lead guitarist is sitting on a queen bed in the back, strumming a new tune on a beat-up old acoustic. An aging girl singer is on the bed beside him, leaning close and humming along, which is bothering the driver big time. He plays bass and used to be married to her, but that was a tour ago, before she listened to that Cowboy Junkies CD and took up nose singing. Not exactly a no-fault divorce.

Sitting in the passenger seat is the band's sole roadie, who is also the drummer. They used to have a manager, but two gigs ago he took a job selling used cars. The lone backup singer—there used to be two—was asleep on the couch this morning in Twin Falls, but she's been in the motorhome's bathroom since Ketchum. They'd check on her but the door's locked. It might be time to grab the Narcan and break the door down.

The drummer is asking an existential question: "We'll hit Challis, Idaho in an hour. You want to stop or go on through?"

"Always a tough question in Challis," says the driver...

In April, it's easy to make up stories about the people in old motor-homes. Later in the season, when the shiny new Pace Arrows towing Lexus SUVs appear, the imagination has fewer options. It serves up retired Air Force generals/Boeing board members behind those expensive steering wheels, and their brittle-coiffed wives beside them, headed for Redfish Lake, where they'll get all 60+ feet of themselves stuck nose-first in the parking lot next to the Lodge. Someone who knows how to back a trailer will eventually get them out, but not before matrimonial courts-martial have issued sentences that indicate there are better ways to spend quarter-million-dollar travel budgets.

But not this year. This year, because of the pandemic, the Sawtooth Valley tourist economy will cater to different clients. There are no tired bands traveling between casinos these days.

And there's no guarantee that giant motorhomes will be purchased ever again. They require that two people, having made the discovery that even a 4,000-square-foot house gets cramped after a month of sheltering in place, will willingly pay a fortune to spend more weeks with each other in the landlocked equivalent of a Diamond Princess stateroom.

But alone? In a faded red, much depreciated but mostly well-maintained Class A motorhome, 30 easy years on it, fresh-bought from a broken-up rock band glad to be rid of it? The muffler is shot, but it's got a brand-new door on the bathroom.

To have your own defensible space, on wheels, with a roof-top solar panel, pantry shelves full of enough freeze-dried meals for a year? A half dozen extra bottles of propane, a chainsaw, cases of good wine, all the books you've been planning to read since college and before? To have a 400-square-foot world you can control, a door to it that you can lock, a flat streamside to park on a couple of miles up a grown-over logging road? You cleared deadfall to get to your campsite, and you felled trees behind you as you went. Also, you're armed.

What could possibly go wrong?

I'll leave that particular list to your own imagination, dear reader, but don't forget to include madness. It's going around.

In practical terms, we're facing a new migratory species in Sawtooth Valley this summer. The deer and the antelope and the sandhill cranes will be similar to previous years, but our tourists are changing from people seeking nature into people looking for a place with space, a nature free of infection and infected people.

They won't see themselves as happy consumers of natural beauty. They might not see the locals as happy purveyors of meals, lodging, and wilderness trips. They might not see their cash on hand as discretionary, and they may have come with their own supplies. They might see restrictions on where they can camp and fish and hunt as threats to their continued existence.

During the Great Depression of the 1930s, unemployed people walked the county roads of agricultural states, stopping at farmhouses and offering to work for food. There were lots of them, and most were turned away. In the cities, miles-long breadlines formed. It was a time of starvation and sickness, of formerly well-housed people becoming homeless.

It was not a time of violence, however. The homeless and starving and sick behaved themselves, mostly, except for the Bonus Army of out-of-work World War I veterans. They set up a protest tent city in front of Congress in 1932 and stayed there, demanding cash for bonus certificates that were set to pay off in an impossibly distant 1945.

The U.S. Army's General MacArthur tear-gassed them, burned their tents and hauled away their possessions. Young soldiers broke the bones of their demobbed comrades. Municipal police shot and killed two of the marchers. It was not our country's finest hour. If not for the Second World War, the name MacArthur would live in infamy.

Sawtooth Valley could see hungry people this summer. We do have tasty antelope and deer and elk in the meadows, waiting for the grass to green up. Fish will be in the rivers, judging from the number of hatchery tankers that have gone by the house recently.

But the fish won't last long. The deer and elk and antelope will graze on the valley floor until they hear the first rifle shot, and then they'll head into the mountains and get hard to find. Unless you know what you're doing, you can't live off the land here, and even if you do know what you're doing, you can't live for long without a trip to Costco.

It comes down to how benign Americans will remain in the face of 25 percent unemployment. The country held together during the Great Depression because the people who had jobs told the people who didn't that they deserved to be out of work, and the people out of work, for the most part, believed them. The government, fearing inflation, refused to print money and give it to anyone, veteran or not, and starving people accepted that refusal. They did vote out Herbert Hoover. He went peacefully.

None of that will happen this time. There will be free money from the government, and not just for big banks and corporations. Whether or not that will avert violence remains to be seen. Whether or not free money will retain any value remains to be seen. Whether or not we'll have an election remains to be seen.

When people with third or fourth houses in Sun Valley started hiding out from the coronavirus in them, local renters, laid off from their service jobs and facing eviction, started asking simple but awkward questions: Why do some people own three or four houses and some own none? How is it that you can afford a Learjet and I can't afford food for my kids? How can it be that interest rates have gone down on everything but my college loan?

Over time, awkward questions wear away the anesthesia of wealth. It makes for nasty people. A tremendous anger accompanies the lost complacency of the rich.

Over time, awkward questions inspire violence, either by the government or private security or by people with little left to lose. Over time—we really do not want to go there.

It's a matter of common sense, but it still needs to be said: most of the people we meet this summer, locals and tourists, will be in pain. It may be because of family members who have died or who have become incapacitated. It may be from the howling loneliness that comes when you haven't felt a human touch for weeks. It may result from unemployment, and bills due, and trips to the food bank that you used to contribute to. It may be the loss of a world, one that was predictable and secure and full of potlucks and Friday after-work drinks with friends, two-family camping vacations and sleepovers at the grandparents'.

We'll all be refugees from grief. The proper response is kindness, not fear. It's a safer way to treat angry and frightened people, for one thing. It's the way to a future where we can hold our heads up, for another.

Sheltering in Place

May 4, 2020

I HAVE FINISHED raking the driveway, clearing willow leaves and red pine needles off the gravel. For the moment, it's reminiscent of a Japanese garden, except it lacks boulders sticking up here and there, and maybe a bonsai or two. You don't want those in a driveway anyway.

Still, it looks good. I've cleaned up a small part of the world. There is order where yesterday there was only the random melted-out debris of spring.

We'll head for the post office later this afternoon, putting tire tracks over my rake marks. No matter. I still have the whole back yard to rake. Yardwork—if you imagine the grass you're raking contains the bug scene in the opening moments of *Blue Velvet*—can be a pretty intense experience.

I have gopher holes to fill before I can flood irrigate. I have a couple of fence posts to replace, and a rail.

The pump for the sprinkler system needs to be packed out of the garage, installed on its perch next to the sump in the back yard, and hooked up to its intake and to the underground pipes that supply the sprinklers. When I start it up, I'll find out if I successfully blew all the water out of the pipes last fall with the compressor. If I didn't, there will be a length of shattered PVC pipe that will create an artesian spring somewhere in the lawn. I'll have to dig down and replace a section. I've got the materials to do that, and the time.

Then I'll climb the ladder up to the roof and tighten the roof screws that have loosened since last May. While I'm up there, I'll sweep the chimney. I'll replace a plank in the deck, broken when the ice dam slid off the roof during the February warm spell.

I've already found a stronger plank in the just-thawed pile of wood

I've rescued from construction dumpsters over the last 10 years. It's on the deck in the sunlight. As soon as it dries, I'll cut it to fit. Once cut, I'll drop it in its place and screw it to the deck joists. Take that, Entropy, I'll say. Be Afraid, Arrow of Time.

Julie helps. Last week she was vacuuming the carpet when the vacuum quit. We got out the household tools, took the vacuum apart, carefully looked its bits and pieces over, found a broken wire and spliced it.

Julie took our other vacuum—the shop vacuum—and sucked all of the dog hair out of the house vacuum's nooks and crannies while it was apart, and then we put it back together. We turned it on. It worked better than it had in years. We had a shared moment of triumph that dwarfed any pleasure we might have gotten out of lifting a new Dyson from its Amazon packaging.

Even if we could have afforded a new Dyson in the first place.

Fixing broken appliances has been a rarely acquired taste in our culture, but it's about to become a survival skill. Supply chains are broken. Jobs and paychecks have disappeared, a good many of them forever. For the country's one-time middle class, money is no longer something to earn and spend. Instead, it's something you repay, and it won't always be there when you need to repay it.

Julie and I won't notice as much change as some people. We've been fixing things for 25 years. The last time either one of us bought something on credit was before we met each other.

We've traveled on tight budgets. We've avoided expensive restaurants like the plague. We've repaired cars rather than trading them in. Our clothes are out of style, and already were when we bought them at Sierra Trading Post. Our skiing hasn't required tickets for years. We've said that if most Americans had our spending habits, the economy would collapse in a month.

Not funny. Not anymore. Austerity is no longer a lifestyle choice for us, and we're aware that it never was for some people. Now, even when it's not life-or-death necessity, austerity is wisdom in a world where cause-and-effect has left the building. It will be a shock for those people who spent money as if the future would see a never-ending string of paychecks.

But household appliances and off-warranty cars are among the least important items on The List of Broken Things. They've been superseded by schools and colleges, medical systems, federal and state administrations, the hopes and dreams of recent college graduates, and a social contract that promised the Baby Boomers a secure old age. These things haven't been working for some time. Nothing in anybody's household toolbox has been able to fix them.

The pandemic has brought them out into the open, where everyone can see them. Their failures are generating consequences, and not just for the people they most immediately fail.

Broken systems have produced broken people. Paying interest on college loans has resulted in unbought houses, unapplied-for jobs, marriages that didn't happen, brilliant children who refused to even apply to college.

Uninsured falls off bicycles have resulted in trips to the emergency room and subsequent bankruptcies. Social Security checks don't dent food bills or rent, or even buy birthday presents for grandchildren. The human cost of these things never shows up on balance sheets. It gets written off, along with the people it represents.

The shutdown has highlighted breakpoints in the global economy. Stopping a just-in-time supply chain is easier than starting it back up again. Creating agoraphobics is easier than curing them. Videoconferencing is easier and cheaper than getting on a plane and showing up at a conference hall. A Caribbean cruise isn't an excuse to relax and forget you ever had a care in the world, because you've seen that getting on a boat can be easier than getting off one.

Depressing metaphors proliferate. Economies are compared to hearts that have quit beating for longer than 10 minutes, or motorcycles that have fallen over at a stoplight and are too heavy to lift back on their wheels. Civilization is compared to a game of Jenga: the tower you've built is four feet high, and tottering, and somebody's just pulled out the wrong block.

A friend who teaches says her students are asking what they'll tell their grandchildren about this time. I hope they won't be telling their grandchildren about the lost wonders of electricity, and gasoline.

When people talk about getting back to normal as soon as a vaccine is distributed and administered, they're assuming that a workable vaccine will be developed. They're assuming people will line up for injections, and not be scared away by rumors that it's part of a United Nations/Bill Gates mind-control conspiracy. They're assuming that habits of consumption and spending will return to what they were in the days before the pandemic, and that Julie and I will buy that Dyson after all, even if we have to borrow money to pay for it.

They're assuming that employment levels will rebound, and that we'll have a V-shaped recovery rather than an L-shaped one. They're assuming that the normal is a thing, and that recreating it is simply a matter of behaving like you remember behaving—which is true, as long as billions of people remember to behave along with you. It's likely some of them won't know what you're talking about. It's likely some of them won't want to behave at all.

By the way, the deck is fixed. I discovered the plank I had rescued from the construction dumpster was clear redwood. It cut easily and fit perfectly.

Six long deck screws are holding the new plank to the deck joists. It's not going anywhere.

I wish it were as easy to find the materials for a complete social and economic remodel, but we're a long way from plucking an FDR or an Eisenhower from the citizen salvage pile. I'm not sure who will be leading this country through the next few years of the pandemic, but it's a sure bet that he won't be the kind of carpenter that can do the job quickly, or well.

Keeping Public Employees Safe
from the Public and Vice Versa

May 11, 2020

IT'S MAY. FOREST Service trucks are making daily trips between the Stanley Ranger Station and the Sawtooth National Recreation Area (SNRA) Headquarters in Ketchum. Last summer there were a lot more, ten or twelve a day, usually with two or more passengers. Now, it's one person per vehicle, and only three or four go by from eight to five. We notice them when they pass. There's not much traffic since steelhead season closed.

Social distancing rules remain in place in Idaho. We are in Phase One of a four-phase plan to reopen Idaho's economy. Each phase is supposed to last two weeks, culminating in the opening of bars, theaters, and stadia, but Idaho's governor Brad Little has said that life won't return to normal until there's a cure or a vaccine, neither of which is guaranteed.

Phase One continues the closure of bars, restaurant dining rooms, hair salons and barbershops. Churches and business offices can open if they observe strict social distancing and require personal protection. Vulnerable people—the over 65s, the immunologically impaired, the obese, smokers, those with cardiovascular disease—are supposed to stay in their homes, if they have a home to stay in. People from outside Idaho have been told to isolate themselves for two weeks before coming out to enjoy the freedoms of Phase Two on May 15, which include wider access to sunlight, well-spaced restaurant dining, and haircuts.

Governor Little, in his first term, has become a right-wing governor under attack from his right wing. Outraged demonstrators have protested outside his office and home. One of our northern Idaho legislators has called him "Little Hitler" for his closure orders—but he has remained what he calls "data driven," which means he's listening to state health department epidemiologists, not Joseph Goebbels.

The reopening schedule depends on a continued decline in coronavirus cases. A super-spreading wedding reception, or a deliberate coronavirus party attended by people who want to get it over with, and we'll be back to bare-faced shouting people lining up on Idaho's statehouse steps, waving AR-15s.

Vulnerability is best understood from the point of view of the vulnerable, and it's safe to say that if you make your living in the tourist economy, you're feeling as vulnerable as any fat 75-year-old with a two-pack-a-day habit and a heart transplant. Sawtooth Valley depends on tourists to live, and if they don't show up, or if they do show up and don't spend their money, our local businesspeople will face the end of their worlds. About the only people who might be happy about these scenarios work for the Forest Service.

SNRA officials have closed Recreation Area campgrounds until June 5. The closure will not by itself cut deeply into our tourist season. Redfish Lake has had ice on it on June 5 within the last decade. Even in these days of global warming, it's not uncommon for a local June day to see frost, rain, sleet, hail, and high winds all before breakfast. That discourages tourists, who don't show up *en masse* until after the first day of summer. That's when we locals typically say to each other, "See you after Labor Day," knowing that those with tourist-industry jobs will be too busy to talk and too tired to come by for dinner or a gin-and-tonic on the deck.

The Forest Service has traditionally regulated tourist migration by means of parking tickets, road and trail closures, camping fees in developed campgrounds, and 16-day limits for dispersed camping, which refers to people parking their RVs or pitching tents in undeveloped areas without toilets or water. In recent years, some dispersed camping areas have been closed, forcing more low-rent campers into less low-rent real estate.

Dispersed campers are of particular concern to SNRA law enforcement, as summer workers—lacking housing—have camped in the gulches and vales around Stanley. In periods of high unemployment, people with makeshift campers and ramshackle tents have sought out isolated spots and set up housekeeping for the summer. They have tended to be less fastidious than their counterparts in pay-to-camp areas. The 16-day limit on camping within the SNRA has been enforced zealously, with methods that resemble those of the Border Patrol more than those of an agency created to make life easier for forest users.

Having lived in the valley since 1953, I've watched the Forest Service morph from a service agency into a regulatory agency. It's deteriorated in other ways, mostly due to budget cuts that have reduced its field employees to a fraction of what they were when the SNRA was established in 1972. As in any bureaucracy faced with declining funds, Forest Service administrators protected their own jobs first and adapted the agency's mission to fit.

The main thrust of their new mission is denying the public the use of public lands. A public agency doesn't need many seasonal workers if it can funnel the public into high-density areas where it obeys the regulations on entrance billboards and pays for its stay.

The three large lakes in the valley have become crowded profit centers. A few much-photographed Sawtooth destinations—Sawtooth, Saddleback, Goat, and Hell Roaring Lakes—serve as dusty daytrips for the majority of backcountry visitors.

Being a tourist in the SNRA has become an experience designed by a committee, on a winter afternoon, in an office, by people who view the tourist industry as a problem of moving people in, feeding them, taking care of their waste products, preventing stampedes, and moving them out so the next bunch can be moved in. Conceptually, the Forest Service is operating the SNRA as a feedlot.

At first, the pandemic seems to be an opportunity to further regulate Sawtooth Valley's tourist population. In the campgrounds, one can easily imagine every other campsite empty, fewer boats on the lakes, more road closures, and bans on the large family reunions we usually see in July and August. We could see masks on people floating the rivers, and mostly empty buses taking well-spaced passengers back upriver.

Those of us who grew up watching the Lone Ranger on after-school TV will do a double take if we see groups of masked horseback riders, expecting them to shoot up the first saloon they come to. Guest lists of weddings will be vetted to ensure that no one will fly in from a coronavirus hotspot. Old people will be permitted to watch at a safe distance, in groups of one.

You may find this picture disturbing and even horrifyingly totalitarian, but recognizable if you've been keeping up with the news. Similar measures have evolved as local economies across the country have dealt with coronavirus in their midst. In some cases, the virus has been more lethal to the economy than to human beings. Over time, a dead economy can result in more death than the virus itself.

The Forest Service does not depend on tourist dollars for its funds, so it faces few constraints on its high needs for control. If new cases spike, even in other states, we can expect closures to happen in high season. More roads will be blocked. Unofficial camping areas will be closed. If we have a bad fire season, you can expect check stations and pilot cars and campfire bans, as in past summers.

It may be that closures, restrictions, and self-quarantining will drastically reduce the number of our summer visitors. As painful as this might be for local businesses, it is probably the least-damaging outcome.

The armed demonstrators on our statehouse steps tend to fetishize camo clothing, and they pack weapons, sometimes in ways that have bystanders diving for cover. They tend to form public phalanxes in the face of official pleas to social distance. Appeals to their own safety or that of virus-vulnerable family members only convince them that the real life-and-death matter is maintaining their own world view. They actively disrespect any government, even a respectable cloth coat Republican state government like Idaho's.

The federal government is their biggest enemy, and they know a federal uniform when they see it.

It's possible we'll get swarms of these people escaping locked-down cities and heading for the designated wildernesses that surround Sawtooth Valley. Wilderness is strongly connected with freedom in the tourist mind, despite the fact that it's some of the most regulated real estate outside of downtown Manhattan. It's seen as a place where a bug-out bag and a rifle can allow you to live off the land for a year or two, despite another fact that if a few thousand like-minded people are out there with you, any wild game larger than a ground squirrel will be gone before winter.

Overwhelming unconscious forces can turn one person into a camo-wearing, open-carrying demonstrator waving a "Don't Tread on Me" banner. He'll sneeze in your face if you impinge on his personal freedom.

Equally overwhelming unconscious forces can turn another person into a uniform-wearing federal officer who takes seriously his duty to make people behave. Sneezing in his face will be a felony, and he doesn't like felons.

Self-awareness is not a big part of either process.

The pandemic has brought the deep impulse toward freedom and the equally deep impulse toward regulation to the surface of our lives. King Kong and Godzilla have emerged to do battle. Even if their avatars are limited and sometimes ridiculous human beings, those human beings are armed. If we're lucky, we locals will get to watch from a safe distance. Binoculars are recommended.

In the Meantime

May 18, 2020

JULIE VISITED HER parents, who are in their 70s, last week. She spent three nights at their house in Oregon. She helped them plant their garden.

Because both Oregon and Idaho were relaxing their pandemic advisories, it was a good time for her to visit, or at least a better time than later in the month, when more and more people would be grouping together in cafes, stores, homes, and parks. Lots of folks have reached the point where they yearn for a normal summer with normal restaurant dining, normal barstool conversations, normal riding around in pickup cabs listening to adult hits on the radio, and normal hugs instead of elbow-bumps. If there is another peak in coronavirus cases, we figure it will come a couple of weeks after things loosen up.

I didn't go. I stayed here and took care of Juno. I raked up the last of 31 wheelbarrow loads of lawn waste, dumped them in a low spot in our back yard, and covered them with a layer of topsoil. If I live long enough—four or five decades more should do it—we will have a lawn that is flat, mostly.

I spent a lot of time reading. I crushed all the wine bottles in the metal garbage can we use to crush wine bottles in. I buried the crushed glass in the anti-rodent trench I'm slowly extending around the back yard, where we'll have our own burrow-proof garden once global warming makes it possible to garden here. I swept the living room floor. I organized my toolbox. I discovered you don't need a mirror to practice elbow-bumping. You can elbow-bump your own elbows.

I didn't go with Julie because we are actively balancing risk and consequences these days. After sheltering in place for three or four weeks, visiting family who also have been sheltering in place is low risk. The consequences, however, are extreme if anything does go wrong. We do our best to minimize the things that could go wrong, and I was one of them.

Once you start playing it safe, a lot of things become either/or propositions. While Julie was gone, I had intended to drive to town each day and check the mail. Instead, I stayed home, to save on hand sanitizer. I was going to take Juno on a long hike. It rained, or looked like rain, so Juno and I stayed inside and played tug-of-war with her rope. On the last day of my solitude, I was planning to get out of my bathrobe before two in the afternoon, but I had to spend the early afternoon doing dishes before Julie got home.

I was going to cook myself dinners. I decided instead to make it through with a couple of giant bricks of Julie's lasagna I found in the freezer. Safer that way.

Julie told me that when she left her parents, she gave them hugs. "I couldn't help it," she said. "I didn't know when I'd be able to hug them again."

She gave me a hug, too, when she came in the door. That hug was probably more dangerous than the ones she gave her parents, because after leaving their house, she had visited the Os—Costco, Winco, Trader Joe's, Home Depot—and had loaded up the car with groceries and hardware and cleaning supplies. She had worn a mask and glasses and gloves, and religiously applied hand sanitizer every time she got back in the car, but she had still spent long exposed hours in the mercantile pest-pits of Idaho's Treasure Valley.

For Julie, shopping had been scary. People with no protection had been clustering in the store aisles, talking loudly and acting like there wasn't a lethal virus going around. There's a lot of misinformation out there, some of it indicating the virus is harmless, or is an engineered bioweapon designed to take down the world economy. Some people believe the pandemic is a fiction invented to make President Trump look ineffective in a crisis. These folks hug each other and trade arm-punches and pats on the back and yell rude things at people who are wearing masks.

At Costco, at least, they won't let you in the door if you're not wearing a mask, so you don't get yelled at until you get back to the parking lot, where angry men sit in cars while their wives shop. Coronavirus is gendering the shit out of things.

It took us an hour to unload the car and put everything away.

Uncertainty has become our watchword. When we speak with friends, especially ones who own businesses, we're careful not to ask them how they are doing. We don't want to hear bad news. But bad news is the risk you take when you make conversation. Usually it's about lost jobs or deferred trips to the doctor, or deepening loneliness, or a sudden realization that the future won't be what it was supposed to be. Your first impulse is to give advice.

Chances are that advice won't help. If it's about the economy or the pandemic, you won't know if your advice is any good, and neither will the person you give it to.

You can advise people to buckle their seatbelts. Quit smoking. Don't drive while texting or drunk. Be kind to other people. Be kind to yourself. Bring your mask when you go to Costco, because they've quit giving them out at the door.

That's about all the good solid advice I can think of at the moment.

Julie and I will have been married 24 years on August 17 of this year, and the time between that anniversary and our 25th was to be our grand jubilee—more of a grand potlatch, in our case, as it was going to burn through our discretionary income for the next decade. Between those two dates I will turn 70 and Julie will turn 50. As part of the festivities, I planned to continue to give readings from my March-published *A Hundred Little Pieces on the End of the World*, warning bookstore audiences and university environmental studies departments about the unsustainability of industrial civilization.

One of those readings was going to be in a gallery in London, and we had decided that once there, we would see a dozen West End plays and then travel through Wales and Scotland for a month before returning to Idaho. Later in the winter, we would visit Vietnam, where we had been for 10 weeks in 2010, and where we had been fascinated by a tourist industry that was new, and raw, and careening toward disaster. We wanted to go back and see what had happened. We wanted to look up the people we had met. We wanted to find out if their plans had worked out.

We suspect their plans have worked out like ours have, which is to say their plans are all gone.

For us, money earmarked for a celebratory year has been transferred back to savings. Instead of a parade of festivities, we're watching an endless series of days at home, which has given rise to routine, and routine has given rise to ritual, and ritual has concerned itself with balancing our lives on a low probability/extreme consequences risk axis.

We practice sympathetic magic, which means, in our case, we plan in the short term what we used to plan in the long term. The future has gotten shorter, but we still need to have one. Julie and I submit detailed policy proposals to each other for afternoon post office visits, breakfast take-out orders, the exact times and routes of afternoon walks. Sometimes, for a Zoom get-together with friends, we include a whole three tomorrows in our plans.

But three tomorrows is about the limit. We have no idea what will happen to us in a world where low risk is getting harder and harder to arrange. We have no idea about the future in a world where cause and effect have agreed to a no-fault divorce, at least in the minds of the people opening the Idaho economy.

Time has a macrocosm, which we know as geological time. It has a microcosm, which we're living in, day to day to day. It used to be that there was a middle range of time, which was where we placed our lives. We planned years of education for decades of careers. We signed up for mortgages that lasted 30 years and got married for life. (Julie and I are still married for life, in case you're worried. It's just that when you're almost 70 in a world with a pandemic that's selecting out old people, you don't know if *for life* is a long-term plan or a short one.)

But that middle range of time, if you believe Pleistocene actuarial estimates, is not something that a quarter-million-plus years of human evolution has prepared us for. Tribal life didn't design us for successful careers in the financial services industry, or to lead decades of slow and steady growth at a company. Only rarely do we find ourselves designed for quiet deepening wisdom as writers or artists. Maybe that's why we go for the Big Short, the quick bonanza of embezzlement, the deliberately blown housing bubble, the massive stock buyback that results in a hundred-million-dollar bonus, the best-seller, the triumph at Sotheby's. We're not built to live in that middle range of time, that cycle-breaking three score and ten, which is why when we do live in it, we get so anxious and crazy.

Maybe that's why Julie and I have adapted to our days. They are uncertain and temporary and terrifying and familiar and comfortable all at once. We are still mourning a long-term future that has disappeared, probably forever, but can look at that mourning as a needed part of our lives, a head start on the inevitable loss of the short term.

In the meantime—we're finding the meantime to be strangely consequential. We've put away ski equipment for the summer. The house is clean. The yard is raked, and a bumper crop of Russell Lupine is gracing the ditch bank in the back yard, getting ready to bloom after the first warm night. Our sole rhubarb plant has begun to unfurl dense leaves. A food order from Amazon has arrived on our front step, and Myla, the local UPS driver, left a Milk-Bone for Juno with it, a warm gesture that meant as much to us as it did to Juno. Julie's cooking has turned into a nightly jubilee. I have discovered a heretofore unsuspected ability to speed-load the dishwasher. Things around the house I should have fixed years ago are fixed.

I've been rereading Carl Sagan's *The Demon-Haunted World*, with its descriptions of witch-burnings and ignorance-inspired child abuse and all the other ceremonies of darkness with which humans propitiate the future. Sagan presents science as the only salvation for our consciousness—and given what we do to others in our scientific ignorance, the only salvation for our souls.

Something a lot like scientific ignorance is behind the events we watch each evening on the PBS News Hour. Terrible things are happening in this world, and we come away from each episode with another day's worth of survivor's guilt and survivor's knowledge. For us, the world is fragile, but for others—many, many others, who no longer have homes or jobs or money or mothers or fathers or children—it is irretrievably broken.

A Philosophic Interlude

May 25, 2020

A LOT OF pandemic narratives are competing for space in our heads. Some of them are outright assaults on reality, such as the idea that the coronavirus is no worse than a bad cold, or that it's a form of the flu, or that it's a booby-trap bioweapon designed in a Canadian lab and left out where Chinese spies could steal it and take it home to Wuhan, where it would explode.

The coronavirus isn't the flu. It has a higher fatality rate, for one thing, and spreads more easily, for another. It's not just a bad cold, unless that cold kills you or leaves you with organ damage. And I keep thinking Canadians are nice people and wouldn't do the sort of thing they're accused of.

Except for the bit about Canadians, you can trust me here. As a general rule, I try not to lie to anyone, except out of kindness, and lately even a kind lie looks cruel.

For example, evil Canadians will take advantage of people who have been told there's no such thing as an evil Canadian. If you think there are only good Canadians in your world, you're wide open to an evil Canadian sneaking up behind you, hiding a section of tar-sands oil pipeline behind his back, getting ready to bash you over the head with it. Or on the first day of your University of Wuhan North American internship you'll fall for the old *Bioweapon: Do Not Steal* Petri-Dish Trick.

So—following the example of our president's new press secretary—I won't lie to you, okay? At least not on purpose. At least not consciously on purpose. I'm not always on board with what my unconscious blurts out, and given how sleepy I am this morning, it's written most of what you've read so far.

But today it looks like my unconscious is looking out for you. It's warning you not to believe everything you are told, because there are liars in the world, and they will lie to you and then tell you their lies are the truth. You'll end up believing in a reality that doesn't exist. That's a workable definition of a psychosis. Or a prosperity gospel religion.

Here's a reality that does exist:

U.S. coronavirus deaths exceed a hundred thousand. More cars with out-of-state license plates are appearing in Sawtooth Valley. Our local inns and motels are open or opening. The first night Idaho's governor allowed indoor eating and drinking, the town of Stanley was full of bare-faced people touching each other, before and after dinner. We stopped opening the post office doors with coat sleeves.

In the grocery stores, people with bare faces look surprised and sometimes angry when they see people with masks. It's the age-old look of cognitive dissonance, a painful condition that occurs when what you see contradicts what you think you should see. It's endemic among humans.

People often ease the pain of cognitive dissonance by denying what they see, rather than changing their beliefs to fit whatever it is they're looking at. Over time they become as blind as cave fish.

Here are some relevant axioms:

1. Reality is not inside our heads. It exists apart from you or me, and it doesn't care whether you deny it or not.
2. A careful and honest examination of reality will yield facts you can use to conduct further examinations and find more facts.
3. Language can be used to communicate those facts to other people, who may, as a result, stop denying reality long enough to learn something that will save their lives, especially during a pandemic.
4. Even though language is a powerful witness to objective reality, it is always subordinate to it. Just because you can articulate something doesn't mean it's true.

These are demonstrably weak assertions, even if they do make the scientific method possible. They have been exposed as dubious by philosophers who are smarter than me and better with language than I am, although you wouldn't know it if you read their works in translation. (A lot is lost in translation from French to English, or so they tell me.)

Their arguments reduce the scientific method and objective reality to cultural artifacts, carrying unexamined notions of Anglo-European colonialism and the primacy of soulless scientific materialism. They've been helped out by quantum physicists, who have devised experiments that demonstrate reality *is* in our heads, at least if those heads are paying attention to cats in locked boxes.

No matter. In the past, when people have resisted Anglo-Europeans, they have been blown to smithereens by advanced weaponry. It wasn't philosophy, but it was a strong argument for soulless scientific materialism.

It's occurred to Julie and me that when we're still wearing our masks come mid-summer, angry people in the post office will tell us we're not supposed to be wearing them. If a person has driven for days to get to a green high mountain valley that once had a functional and welcoming tourist industry, they won't be happy when they find that a lethal virus has beaten them to it.

The Myth of the Frontier, which the Sawtooth Valley tourist industry has long capitalized on, is that high alpine valleys are pristine, untouched, there for the taking. What locals you meet are charming rustics, if not savages. Everybody gets to be a pioneer.

Tourists don't want to see personal protection gear on the locals, because it reminds them that they're refugees rather than explorers. It reminds them they're not even successful refugees, as the locals appear to think that they've brought the virus with them. Rustics in masks and goggles are not properly exuding the pioneer spirit.

The Salmon River Clinic has antibody tests now, but their positive or negative results are hard to interpret. We don't know that having the virus means you won't get it again. We have yet to understand the extent of residual damage once you've had it. We have a good idea that transmission of the virus requires both exposure and time, but we don't know how much time and we don't know what constitutes exposure.

Julie and I were going to get tested until we realized that if the test showed antibodies in our blood, we'd wonder about false positives. If it didn't, we'd worry about false negatives. In either case, we'd worry about touching anything in the post office just touched by a vacationer newly arrived from a South Dakota chicken-packing plant.

Scientists all over the country are working on these uncertainties, and they will eventually find answers. But the scientific method is slow. It takes years, and sometimes decades, to know something for certain. We have accumulated a lot of certainty because of science, but that's because we've been at it since the 16th century.

Even in the face of all we do know, uncertainty manages to stay ahead of certainty. Virologists know a lot about coronaviruses, but not enough to tell us how to end this pandemic, what a vaccine will look like, and how we can avoid second and third waves of the disease.

Most of us don't have the time for the scientific method, which is why many of us live in less scientific worlds, ones where things aren't so confusing and unpredictable.

More often than not, people prefer certainty to sanity. They'll tell you that there was no moon landing, that the destruction of the World Trade Center towers was an inside job, that JFK was killed by the CIA, that Donald Trump is our last best chance to defeat our reptilian alien overlords. They will tell you in one breath that the coronavirus is harmless and that it has been spread deliberately throughout the world by an elite that isn't satisfied with the 80 percent of the wealth that it already has. They will tell you that if we just burn down all the 5G towers, everything will be back to normal. (I'm not sure what we would have to do to get back to normal in Sawtooth Valley, because we don't yet have 5G towers.) They will mutter darkly about mind-control chips in vaccines, and longevity serum extracted from stolen babies.

That's not to say there aren't conspiracies. But the kinds of conspiracies we hear about during this pandemic depend on absence of proof, an abiding belief that all official accounts are cover-ups, and a cast of thousands that has obeyed conscience-shocking orders more or less simultaneously and perfectly.

These stories never include human incompetence as a factor in their outcome, which means they rest on a reality that doesn't exist.

Summer is coming to Sawtooth Valley, and with it, thousands of tourists from all over the world. We hope they're virus-free. We hope they're all sane, but we know sanity isn't easy to maintain when it requires a permanent state of anxious not-knowing. We hope that if things go wrong, our visitors don't go crazy and start looking for someone to blame.

We hope they believe in the scientific method, if only because it will slow them down. We really hope that they're not secretly all evil Canadians. We hope they wouldn't rather live through a worst-case scenario than face an ambiguous future. We hope they won't lie when they could tell the truth. We hope the same things for ourselves.

The Tourist as Other

June 1, 2020

IN 1953, MY father quit his job as a hard-rock miner and became a fishing and hunting guide in Sawtooth Valley. Our family moved from company housing to a 40-acre homestead nine miles up the Salmon River from the town of Stanley. My parents paid a hundred dollars an acre for the homestead. The purchase price included a working sawmill and a 20-by-20-foot lodgepole homestead cabin and eight sway-backed outbuildings. There were people in the valley who said my parents paid too much for the place.

From the standpoint of their finances, my parents had paid far too much. The 75-dollar monthly mortgage payment almost broke them. I remember my father chasing construction jobs in the winters, going from one layoff to another. In the winter of 1955, we moved five or six times. I remember the year because at a Thanksgiving promotional event in Buhl, Idaho, I was given movie tickets to *The Creature from the Black Lagoon* and my mother wouldn't let me go because she thought it would give me nightmares. She was right. It would have. I was a sensitive little kid. I still haven't seen that movie.

I digress.

Guiding was an unregulated industry in the early 1950s. Anyone could hang out a shingle and start taking people fishing, hunting, skiing, or floating the rivers. A lot of men, wanting to live a life that recalled the freedom of a vanished frontier, tried to make a living that way. Almost all of them failed.

My father made it work because he didn't want to go back underground—mining had a fatality rate, and he had packed dead men to daylight as part of his job. My mother, understandably, didn't want him to go back either. She was a registered nurse, and she could find employment wherever his winter job took us. The two of them worked and scrimped and saved through the winters until they could get back to Sawtooth Valley every summer.

They fixed up the biggest outbuilding so they could have a bigger house than the homestead cabin. My father told his clients to show up for breakfast there, at four a.m. He needed to get them fishing before daylight, because all the salmon holes would be claimed by other fishermen if he didn't. It helped that the river ran through our back yard, but it was elbow-to-elbow fishing in those days, with anger as a subtext. More than once, my father had people try to run him off his own land.

He charged his fishing clients 10 dollars a day. He guaranteed a chinook salmon on the line. Often that meant he would hook a fish and hand the pole to a sleepy client, and then coach the man (usually it was a man) through a half-hour of fighting the fish and maybe landing it. He guaranteed his hunting clients a good shot at a deer or an elk or a mountain goat.

His guiding business prospered. By 1960, he was able to charge his clients 20 dollars a day. Eventually he got a winter job driving ski bus at the Sun Valley Resort, while my mother worked in the Sun Valley Hospital. They were able to pay off their mortgage early. They bought a modest winter home in Hailey. My father had become a success in the tourist industry, supplying the same experience to his clients, over and over and over again.

My family did not call my father's clients clients. We called them dudes. We referred to the Idaho Rocky Mountain Ranch, a lodge and cabins just upriver from us, as The Dude Ranch. Dudes came to Sawtooth Valley every summer. They left when the snow came.

Dudes needed to have their fish hooked for them, their elk pointed out to them, their packs packed for them. They had to be shown the sights, and driven to trailheads, and told what lakes or mountains those trails led to. Often, they wanted to know the best places to eat or sleep, and the answer you gave depended on how well you got along with the owners of particular hotels or restaurants, and whether or not they had suggested their dudes spend time as your dudes.

Dude was not yet a term of endearment between adolescent males. You never called dudes dudes to their faces. Dudes were people, of course, but they were also a commodity. They didn't like to be referred to by a term that divided experience into the authentic and the staged, the autonomous and the herded.

Apologies to Tennessee Ernie Ford, but I owe my soul to the tourist industry, if the soul contains where you are in the world, your origin story, the sensibility you bring to the passage of time, tragedy, work, love, and your sense of what's real and what isn't. Without the tourist industry, I wouldn't be sitting here on the same 40 acres my father bought so he'd have a base of operations and a place to feed breakfast to his clients. I wouldn't have become a mountain manager for Sun Valley when I was 23, and I wouldn't have quit—no longer wanting to groom ski runs and herd people onto them—when I was 24. I wouldn't have become a writer of travel and wildlife and ski stories.

I wouldn't have skied a glacier in Greenland. I wouldn't have spent a week at Amanpuri, a boutique resort on the Thai island of Phuket. I wouldn't have bungee jumped off a 400-foot-high bridge in New Zealand. I wouldn't have gazed out the open window of a tundra buggy into the face of a Manitoba polar bear. I wouldn't have been wined and dined by the Andorran Chamber of Commerce. I wouldn't have used helicopters as ski lifts.

Bungee jumping is not a real experience. But it's hard to convince yourself of its unreality when you're 200 feet below the bridge you just jumped off, still accelerating.

If you're a travel writer, you look like a tourist and act like a tourist, but you're also a quality control officer for constructed experience. Whatever you're doing—skiing or boating or eating the national cuisine or watching a treed cougar killed by an arrow— you're also judging how your visit is staged, how well the sets are constructed, and how professional the actors are. You assess how much self-consciousness it will take before a façade crumbles, and then you check what's behind the façade in case it's another façade.

Then, if you can, you report back to all your readers that here's a situation they can safely pretend is real.

You don't have to worry that your occupation isn't real. There's plenty of reality in the low-grade anxiety of approaching deadlines, the luxury of rooms you could never afford on your own, your two-hour lunches with mountain managers and directors of operations. Your privileged look behind the scenes is real, as is your obligation to support the advertisers in the magazine you're reporting for. Mentioning rats in the shower or illegal payoffs to Olympic athletes or last winter's avalanche fatalities could be real, but it's a bad idea, and needs to be avoided if you ever want another assignment.

Two realities exist in every tourist economy. One is what the tourists see. The other is what the locals see. The more time and effort it takes for the locals to give tourists what they expect, the bigger the gulf between the two realities.

Local reality becomes more real as tourist reality becomes more unreal. As prices and expectations rise, what you see as a tourist becomes a tiny slice of what you see if you're guiding that tourist.

In the end, nobody wants to be a tourist just like nobody wanted to be a dude. In a spectacular display of counterproductivity, people start buying vanity plates and T-shirts that read *LOCAL*. Tourists start asking about secret spots where they won't meet other tourists.

Locals keep quiet about tourist-free ski runs, hidden lakes, picnic spots, and places where the elk hang out on opening day. They distinguish between good tourists and bad ones, and sometimes the dividing line becomes the size of a tip. They use acronyms like AFSV—which I won't spell out completely, but the SV stands for Sprinter Van.

There is a third reality in Sawtooth Valley, and that is the one occupied by retired persons who have been both tourists and tourist workers. Retirement has given us the time and the opportunity to reconcile what it means to be one or the other. We try to minimize the distasteful aspects of each. We try to forgive our own sins on either side of the divide.

Sins remain sins whether you forgive them or not, and the tourist industry itself has more to answer for than any of the humans in it.

It creates artificial experience and presents it as the real thing. It's terribly polluting. I'm not talking about jet exhaust, or the noise of a pack of eight or ten motorcycles as they go by on Highway 75. I'm not even talking about the smoking dark-windowed diesel buses that carry Allen & Company conferees to daytrips on the Salmon River.

I'm talking about spiritual pollution, which renders its victims unable to tell the real from the unreal, and unable to see why the distinction is important, even when their souls are in the balance.

Lately we retired people in the valley are being threatened by young visitors who won't wear masks, who won't social distance, who assume they'll just get the coronavirus and survive it and maybe even have a career if enough old people die. We worry about that attitude, but we can't do much about it, hunkered down in our houses as we are.

We note that the stores and restaurants in Stanley are opening. We hope the best for business owners. We fear the worst for ourselves and our weakened immune systems. We wear masks even if it upsets the tourists.

We worry that we're too sensitive for nightmares, even if they don't feature creatures from black lagoons. We fear the second wave, even as the unreal first wave of clients, dudes, tourists, and the past washes over us. God knows what else it's carrying with it.

House Arrest in the White Hotel

June 8, 2020

THE JOHNS HOPKINS Coronavirus Resource Center, as of this morning, lists U.S. Covid-19 deaths at 110,514. World deaths have reached 403,267.

It's not possible to grieve for every one of them—that would be beyond any human capacity—but you should not try to diminish them by comparing those deaths to bad flu years, or heart disease or cancer deaths, or auto accidents or overdoses. You should not say that we all will die of one thing or another. You should not quote Stalin and say that one death is a tragedy, a million deaths a statistic. You should not say Baby Boomers have lived their lives anyway, and they need to get out of the way. You especially should not say that to a Baby Boomer.

You should not say you don't know anyone who has had the virus. You should not divide 329 million into the number of U.S. deaths to show how low the death rate is, because not everyone has caught it yet. You're also ignoring the equivalent of 36.8 World Trade Center 9/11 deaths, which as we know can translate into 36.8 Iraq Wars. Keep it up and you'll be forced to rate some deaths as much more important than others. You should not do that either.

You should not hope that Donald Trump gets the virus, or Joe Biden or Nancy Pelosi or Mitch McConnell or your 90-year-old wealthy widowed aunt, who has promised you'll get all her money when she dies. You should not link death rates to race or economic class, because there are so many other factors involved that you'll be tripped up by one of the things you haven't thought of.

I'm not normally so generous with my should nots. But I've been rereading D. M. Thomas's *The White Hotel*, a 1981 novel that begins with a shamelessly erotic poem, describing lovers in an isolated mountainside hotel in pre-world-war Europe. It ends with the Nazis murdering a quarter-million people—one of them one of those lovers—in the ravine of Babi Yar, outside Kiev, in 1941. Thomas transforms his hotel—with its hundred whitened rooms, its thousands of guests and their tears and joys and erotic histories and tragic futures—into a metaphor for a single human psyche.

Each of us is a white hotel. Each of us contains chefs and waiters, maids and gardeners serving all those guests, whom we contain as well. Each of us features manicured gardens, dance floors, elegant restaurants, spas and sunrooms, endless doored corridors. Each of us is a life-packed structure of unimaginable variety and complex unrepeatable experience. Each human death is a loss beyond grief, and a million human deaths is the end of tens of billions of memories and moments, each of them the only one of their kind.

If you look closely, none of us qualifies as a statistic, whether we die in Babi Yar or intubated in an ICU.

You should not read *The White Hotel* during a time when death tolls are mounting, especially if you're sensitive to the darker notes of human nature. Things get too unpleasantly resonant, as the excess deaths climb from hundreds of thousands to millions, and their causes go from viruses to starvation to murder.

I'm not saying that the future will follow that tragic trajectory, but the past certainly did, in Ukraine, in the 27 years between 1918 and 1945. History doesn't always repeat itself, but it will tell you what to watch out for.

Last Wednesday, the house-bound weather prophets on Boise's KTVB news station, broadcasting from their living rooms, told us our mountains would be sunny and in the 60s. Julie and I decided to park at the backcountry trailhead at Redfish Lake and hike from there to the third Bench Lake. We had never been to it, despite having been to the first, second, fourth, and fifth Bench Lakes.

The third lake is smaller, and off to the side of the other four. You don't go by it when you're circumnavigating Mount Heyburn, which has been our usual reason for hiking through the area.

Wednesday was a day of reduced ambitions, because to hike all the way around Heyburn, you have to get an earlier start than we did. You have to take the first shuttle boat to the end of Redfish, climb up and over the snowy saddle between Heyburn and Braxon Peak, and drop down into Monolith Canyon. A mile down the canyon, you have to turn to your right and climb over the ridge above the fifth Bench Lake. You have to glissade down through car-sized talus and pick your way along the beaten paths that link the lakes until you reach the trail that descends the moraine on the northwest side of Redfish. You then have to trudge—because by that point in the trip you're trudging—five miles to Redfish Lake Lodge. When you get there, you will have climbed a vertical mile, what with all the ups and downs, and descended another. You will have gotten your ten thousand steps in, and then some.

Once at the Lodge, you get to order a margarita at the bar, secure in the knowledge that—to use the language of KTVB evening news ads for new gutters or remodeled bathrooms—you deserve one. You probably deserve two, if it's a nice evening and you're sitting in one of the Lodge's deep porch chairs, watching—with the amused and pallid voyeurism of the aged—young lovers acting out their own erotic poems on the beach.

Julie and I thought a hike to the third Bench Lake would be enough for us to deserve to split a single margarita. Also, although I don't seem to have suffered a loss of stamina, I've been feeling short of breath since February. We're postponing the big hikes for a couple more months until we know what that's all about.

We had to climb over and through a half-mile of downed trees to get to the lake, and posthole through the remnants of snowbanks. The lake itself is small and shallow. It sits in a dark hollow. It is surrounded by tall alpine firs. The skeletons of drowned trees point inward from the lake edge.

This time of year, the lake edge is flooded. Its beaches are made of last summer's yellowed swamp grass, floating bits of wood, and drifting moss.

The fish in it are only an inch or so long. We did see one that might have been six inches. It was chasing the others, having apparently grown big enough to eat its siblings. We tried not to judge.

We sat on a big rock at the edge of the water and started going through our supply of chocolate. We wanted to stay awhile, to get to know the place by sitting quietly, listening to the birds in the trees and watching the sun on motionless water. But the birds and the sun had disappeared. Dense clouds started coming over the peaks above us.

The water, made opaque by sudden winds, turned dark green. The trees began to shade toward black. We heard distant thunder. Then we heard closer thunder. Lightning flashed above us. Then really loud thunder. Then rain. Then hail.

We hunkered under one of the alpine firs, using its thick branches as an umbrella, trying not to think of it as a giant lightning rod. I began to curse myself for trusting the KTVB weather team. Then I began to curse the KTVB weather team for making shit up. Julie had brought a rain jacket, but I only had a sweatshirt to go over my T-shirt. The hail started coming down hard. The temperature dropped 30 degrees. The peaks disappeared behind banks of fog.

During breaks in the storm, we scuttled from alpine fir to lower-altitude alpine fir, hoping that we wouldn't pick the wrong one at the wrong time. We avoided the ones with lightning scars on their trunks.

It was an hour before we were back on the moraine trail, but the sun had come back out and steam was coming off wet trees, puddles in the trail, and us. By the time we reached the Lodge, we were mostly dry.

The Lodge bar, this season, has been relocated outside, into a trailer. Chairs on the porch have been spaced apart for social distancing. Tables in the restaurant are fewer than they used to be. There were lots of empty places. It's too early in the season for a full house, but it's become clear that even a full house won't contain as many guests as it used to.

A few people were sitting on benches between the lawn and the beach. The storm had cooled the air. No lovers were frolicking on the sand. After sitting in the shade of the porch for a while, we started getting cold again, and we decided against the margarita. We suddenly wanted to go home, where it's a quarter-mile to the nearest neighbor. An abundance of caution, as the phrase goes, settles over us at times we least expect it. We suddenly remember we're not sure the coronavirus will go away.

Other people are way ahead of us in this matter. They already know it's gone away. They're so carefree they make us nervous. We get anxious about total strangers giving us hugs, having improbably mistaken us for celebrities.

We made a pledge that if the virus ever goes away for good, we'll have those margaritas, and dinner in the Lodge dining room. We'll laugh and talk with Jeff and Audra, the incredibly nice people who are the owners and managers there, and we will all remember the summer of 2020 as a quick, intense storm of worry that was tough while it lasted but—thankfully—is over and done with.

The Salmon River Clinic has tested 40 or so Sawtooth Valley residents for coronavirus antibodies, and everyone has tested negative. For most of this spring, Julie and I thought we had had the virus in February. We haven't been tested, but everybody else's negative results argue that we haven't had it yet.

There is a problem. Some people who have had the virus show antibodies to it. Some don't.

It's a scientific mystery, and smart people are working on it. But it's not good news. A chance exists that once you've had the virus, you can get it again. It could be similar to the virus that causes dengue fever, in which first infections are occasionally mild enough to not be noticed, and subsequent ones painful and/or lethal. Different bodies react in different ways to the same infection, and we don't yet know what makes that difference.

We will know more by next summer. That's because this summer the country is conducting a massive experiment on our beaches, around our dining tables, in our restaurants and bars and grocery stores and hotels. Next summer, we'll have results on contagion factors and lingering symptoms and lethality. We'll know if we could have been carefree instead of worried, and whether or not worrying made the difference between life and death. We'll know if reopening the economy did or didn't cause a second or third spike in cases. We'll know the names of the dead, and the names of people who have survived. We'll probably know someone who claims not to have had it because it doesn't exist. We'll know a bunch of people, like ourselves, who will have no idea whether they've had it or not.

As always, everything we will know or think we know might not be completely true. It might be magical thinking. It might be flawed study parameters. It might be unusually persistent election-year misinformation.

But we live in an isolated mountainside tourist community, and we'll make do with what we can get. We'll continue to stream news and weather reports, and we'll try to keep up with the magazines we've subscribed to. Now and then we'll sit on a café veranda and catch the eye of a person a few tables away. We'll ask, because we've seen the out-of-state plates in the parking lots, "What's it really like out there, anyway?"

Everything/Nothing Has Changed

June 15, 2020

IN SEPTEMBER OF 1969, wearing a new $40 gold corduroy suit with a wide brown-and-white paisley tie, I boarded a turboprop in Boise and flew to Salt Lake. There I got on a Boeing 727 to Boston's Logan Airport. A few minutes after landing, I was standing in the aisle of a bus headed for the airport MTA station, holding onto my suitcases because I was afraid somebody would steal them.

The bus driver noticed me in his rear-view mirror. "Hey Harvard," he yelled. "Sit down before you fall down." His South Boston accent was thick and not the sort of thing decent people render phonetically.

Everybody on the bus looked at me. I faced a wall of smirks. "How do they know?" I wondered to myself.

I had been out of Idaho once before, on a train trip to Texas with my mother when I was five. I had flown before, but mostly in helicopters, fighting fire. I had never been on a Boeing 727 before, and if I had known then what I know now about the landing approach problems of 727s, I would have preferred crossing the country in an empty car of a freight train.

I figured out how to get my suitcases to Harvard Square on the MTA, but it was a traumatic experience. I had experienced trying to load five horses in a four-horse trailer, so I understood the concept of mass transportation. I just didn't think that humans would willingly put up with it.

I had transferred to Harvard from the College of Idaho, where I had spent my first undergraduate year discovering that big things were happening in the world, but not in my part of the world. I yearned to go someplace important.

Had I noticed, I would have realized that small things were important too, like learning to write, and reading history and psychology and philosophy. The College of Idaho had given me a strong start on all these things, and if I had been more patient and stayed there, I probably would have gotten a better undergraduate education than I ended up with.

But a Boise native named Fred Glimp had become a dean of admissions at Harvard after attending there on the GI Bill. Glimp made it his mission to recruit Idaho kids. With the help of a brilliant Twin Falls attorney named Lloyd Walker, he found a bunch of poor-but-reasonably-intelligent kids from Idaho Falls and Pocatello and Montpelier and Hailey and Fairfield.

I had an interview with Lloyd Walker. He told me I'd be accepted if I applied. I did, and I was. Harvard gave me a generous scholarship, which was likely Fred Glimp's doing as well.

I had been recruited into a good news/bad news joke. Leaving Sawtooth Valley for Caldwell had been culture shock enough. After a week in a barely-furnished dorm room in Dunster House, I experienced culture paralysis, culture carpet bombing, culture obliteration. Everyone I met seemed richer than me, smarter than me, better-looking than me, and had a Mercedes 230SL they had been given for high school graduation. The course catalog looked like a copy of *War and Peace*. The Dunster House senior tutor, with whom you were supposed to confer if you got into academic trouble, was the budding historian Doris Kearns. Kearns, if you believed the earnest dining hall gossip between political science majors, was the mistress of Lyndon Baines Johnson, the President of the United States. I decided that if I got into academic trouble, it would be safer to deal with it on my own.

The good news was that, thanks to the College of Idaho, I was a better writer than most of my new classmates. I had already learned how to study, and because I didn't have a social life, I studied—at least during that first semester.

I had been given a work-study job mopping floors in the dining hall, but when a position came open in Widener Library's circulation department, I applied for it and was hired.

Widener had three-and-a-half million books and closed stacks, and one of my jobs was to find and deliver books to the researchers who handed me a call number. I spent a lot of time finding mis-shelved books. I got good at it with time, and in the process learned how many books there could be on a single subject, and how many subjects there were. I reached the uneasy realization that it might be impossible to read all the books in Widener.

It was a miserable, lonely, anxious year. By mid-second semester I was behaving as though my grades and scholarship and pride in jobs done well didn't depend on studying, which is to say I had quit studying altogether. In early February I received a Valentine's card from my mother, who enclosed a five-dollar bill and told me to use it to find a nice girl and take her on a date.

Instead, on February 14 I went to the convenience store behind Dunster House and used my mother's gift to buy a four-pack of a carbonated catawba wine, a beverage (I'm being kind here) known as Ripple Pagan Pink. I put it under my coat and took it down to the River Charles, walked out to the Weeks footbridge (apocryphally famous as the spot where Al Gore proposed to Tipper), sat on its con-crete railing mid-river, stared moodily into the dirty water, and drank it all. I dropped empty bottles, one by one, between my dangling feet.

Occasionally I could see flashes of the goldfish schools the river was famous for. Each had been planted in the Charles when its owner, tired of tending to a pet store impulse buy, flushed it down the toilet. It was the worst Valentine's Day ever.

In April, the riots began. Antiwar protests were happening every week on campus and in the streets of Cambridge. People I knew had been injured by police and by fellow protestors. Tear gas seeped into the evening air.

Students living nearer to Harvard Square had it worse. Adams House, where bottles and bricks and floor lamps had been tossed from high windows onto police vehicles, was invaded by dozens of cops. People inside stacked couches and desks against their doors before a prudent police captain stopped the doors from being broken down and everybody inside being pulled out by their hair, beaten, and arrested. That had happened the year before, during the student occupation of a Harvard administration building.

Then the Kent State murders happened on May 4, 1970. National Guard troops shot into a crowd, and four students died. Fearing uncontrollable violence, Harvard cancelled the rest of the semester and gave everyone a pass in all their classes. We were told to come back in September. My academic ass had been saved by the deaths of four young people.

On May 15, two black students were killed by white Mississippi state troopers at Jackson State. By then, I was back at the College of Idaho, helping celebrate Spring Fling at Lake Lowell (whose carp were bigger and meaner than their flashy cousins in the Charles; they were rumored to eat ducks). Then I went back to Sawtooth Valley to work for the Forest Service, clearing trail until fire season started. It felt better to have a Pulaski in my hands instead of the gun I would have carried in Vietnam if I'd flunked out.

Partly because of that threat, my last two years at Harvard went better. I resumed studying. I picked classes where I could read good books and write about what I saw in them. My grammar skills added a grade point or two, gifts from grad students who valued literacy over content. I found a nice girlfriend, one I regretted not marrying for 25 years, until I met Julie.

I graduated with honors, but didn't attend Harvard's commencement ceremonies. I had invited my parents to my graduation, but they had seen too many scenes of violence between cops and protestors on their TV, and they were afraid to come to Boston and navigate the city—and spend all that money—just to see me walk across a stage. "We really didn't want you to go there in the first place," my mother told me. "We worried you would get killed."

My parents' decision not to come was the excuse I needed not to stick around. I was sick of feeling poor, sick of the guilt of leaving my girlfriend, sick of wanting a Mercedes 230SL, and sick of missing Idaho. I had a cabin in Stanley that I could live in and a job that paid enough to live on. I could be an adult, not a student. That was the rite of passage I was looking forward to. I told Harvard to mail my diploma to Idaho.

*

Fifty years on, the civil disturbances that marked my college years are recurring, not because of a foreign war but because of stomach-turning police murders of black people. Giant but mostly peaceful demonstrations have driven a president to his bunker in the basement of the White House. The American border fence has been shrunk to a two-mile long perimeter in Washington, D.C.

Campuses have been closed down again, but not because of the demonstrations. Students have been sent home due to the pandemic. This time even the College of Idaho has closed. Graduations across the country have been cancelled. Most graduates received their diplomas in the mail. They and their families have been deeply disappointed, but graduations are not considered essential rites of passage.

I'd go further and say that in some cases, they can be harmful rites of passage, if they give you the illusion that your diploma represents an education. For me, going to Harvard mostly taught me what I didn't know. That year of cancelled classes, the long educational searches in the dark stacks of Widener Library, watching cops knock down and beat protestors with nightsticks, not marrying, avoiding the hard classes, developing a taste for Ripple—all these conspired to make me feel a lot more ignorant and stupid at the end of college than at the beginning. I spent my 20s filling holes in my education, my 30s filling in the holes in the holes, and so on. I did get a graduate degree, an MFA that allowed me to return to the College of Idaho for a couple of decades as a professor of literature and journalism.

I didn't go to my MFA graduation, either. The last time I walked across the stage for a diploma was high school. I've been on the stage while other people walked, but I was there because I was the graduation speaker.

Commencement ceremonies may have been beside the point for me, but other ceremonies *were* the point. Getting married to a person I love transformed me into a different person, and a better one. I'd hate to have missed it.

Some other things that I can now identify as rites of passage:

Finding a teaching job and discovering I was good at teaching. Getting fired from it. Getting hired back. Getting fired a second time. Building a house. Leaving the house I had built. Getting hired to teach college.

Becoming a full professor didn't feel like a rite of passage, but quitting that tenured position did.

Also, a long-ago night in the Christiania Restaurant in Ketchum. I had been drinking Grand Marnier on the rocks, a beverage of considerably higher quality than Ripple Pagan Pink. I was sitting at the bar next to the wait station, having a pretty good time with an astonishingly beautiful cocktail waitress. I had hopes the pretty good time might get even better. She had just told me her boyfriend had moved in with another woman.

That was when Lloyd Walker, drunk and alone, still a lawyer but in an advanced state of senior partnership, walked up to the bar and recognized me from the decade-old interview that had gotten me on the plane to Harvard. He didn't like what he saw.

"You think you'll be young and beautiful forever," he growled. "You won't be."

He greeted the waitress by her first name, ordered another drink, and walked back to his table. Gloom descended on the Christiania bar. The pretty good time was over.

If I ever write another graduation speech, it will be hard to resist quoting Lloyd Walker.

These days I'm approaching my 70th birthday. It's generally considered a rite of passage, but I'm not sure it will be. You can really only recognize it after the fact.

Which sustains my hope that I'll wake up on the first day of my 71st year realizing how little I know, and how many holes in my education still need to be filled, and that nothing I've done thus far in life is complete. I'll know that 70 is just another number, and the real work is still ahead.

Life as a Russian Novel

June 22, 2020

I'VE NOW WRITTEN 13 weekly journal entries. This is the 14th. A quarter of a year has gone by, faster than if I hadn't been meeting Monday deadlines.

In a quick 39 Mondays, I'll have a record of mostly internal events from March 2020 to March 2021.

If the town of Stanley ever buries a time capsule, I'll include a copy. If the time capsule is exhumed after a thousand years, anyone who reads my words will say, "If only he had known what was coming, he would have relaxed and enjoyed himself."

People in the far future feel free to give you advice. They tell you not to worry, because whatever happens, good and bad, has already happened.

Easy for them to say. I'd pay more attention to them if they were more specific.

Last Wednesday, June 17, Julie and I awoke to find four inches of soggy snow on the deck. The previous afternoon, we had gone for a walk along the beach at Redfish and had watched as a shuttle boat full of backpackers had headed for the trailhead at the other end of the lake. It was raining, but snow was beginning to obscure the tops of Mount Heyburn and the Grand Mogul.

"At least they won't have to worry about mosquitos," I said.

We drove into Stanley from Redfish, checked the mail, then came home and started a fire. I packed in enough wood to last the night. We ate dinner and watched protest marches on the news. We watched worried public health officials talk about clusters of new coronavirus infections. We watched a story about the dismembered and burnt bodies of two children being dug up on their mother's new husband's eastern Idaho farm. We watched the weather, but not as intently as we would have if we were headed out for a few nights in the Sawtooths.

I awoke in the middle of the night, thinking that Julie had gotten up and was running the dishwasher, but it was rain hitting hard on the roof. Then the snowline descended to our level, the night became silent, and I went back to sleep.

It has been a wet and cold spring here. The few warm and sunny week-ends have seen lines of RVs, pickups, and bicyclists on the highway, but tourist season hasn't really taken off yet. We haven't had to wait five minutes to get out of our driveway.

Local music festivals and art fairs and foot races have been cancelled. Hiking has been hampered by mud and snow and wind. Restaurants have opened later in the season than usual, possibly because their outdoor diners would have had to wear winter coats and gloves.

Where it's not snow-covered, the land has turned beautiful and green, but people who have strayed off pavement have gotten soggy and cold.

On days when the snow clouds come blowing down the valley, activities are limited. It's like any other January. We read and write and watch the evening news to see what's happening in warmer places.

If you want your evening news calm and reassuring, it's best not to watch stories from eastern Idaho or interviews with economists. Economists do not seem to be able to relax and enjoy themselves. They worry that the current plague year might turn into two plague years, or a plague decade. They worry that a safe vaccine might never be developed. They worry that a lockdown-triggered economic depression could result in millions of permanently lost jobs and repossessed homes and uneducated kids.

The only economists who appear to be relaxing and having fun work for the Federal Reserve. Jerome Powell, its chairman, periodically makes an upbeat speech where he talks about the future as though it will continue to resemble the past. We've got things under control, he says. Let us do the worrying for you.

Non-Fed economists point out that if the Fed's Board of Governors keeps keystroking zeroes into existence, the dollar will lose its status as a reserve currency. We can look to Zimbabwe to see what will happen then, and it's hard not to worry about that.

Last year, before the pandemic was on anyone's worry list, the mother whose children have been exhumed from an eastern Idaho farmyard declared that the world would end this July. She also declared she was going to save humanity from becoming zombies. Salvation required the soul being freed from the body that had become zombified.

In addition to her children, three other people close to her or her husband died last fall and winter, a small cluster of death now in search of a superspreader.

She's in jail now, charged not with murder but with child abandonment. Her new husband is in jail, charged with withholding evidence by burying it in his farmyard. Bail has been set at a million dollars for both of them. If they're charged with murder, which seems in the realm of possibility, you can imagine a plea for both of them: not guilty, by reason of saving the human race.

If you find it hard to believe that a mother would kill her own children, even as the world is ending, you probably aren't a family therapist. People whose job it is to peer under the slick packaging of families discover murder and incest and deliberately stunted lives. Parents will bring a child to therapy, claiming they don't know what's wrong with the kid. What is wrong is that the family story needed a problem child, and the kid drew the short straw.

Problem children die by accident or suicide more often than murder. When they don't die, their lives are hollowed out by spiritual and physical poverty, or they're exiled from any experience of intimacy. If they disappear for any reason, a replacement is found. Therapists' shorthand for this phenomenon is, "The players change, but the play goes on."

When the title of the family story is If One of Us Isn't Dying, None of Us Are Living, it becomes the therapist's job to change it to something boring, like Live and Let Live. It's a challenge. Most families will refuse to perform such a dull script.

Idaho has made international news with the children-in-the-farmyard story. People have assumed that whoever buried them is an insane monster. But if you look at the story—which contains the end of the world and a person who leads humanity to salvation—you find that the monster is depressingly human and familiar. It's recognizable as Abraham's story, central to Islam, Christianity, and Judaism. It's the story of Lenin and Hitler and Mao, the story of Jim Jones ladling out purple Kool-Aid in Guyana, and the story of the United States of America right now. It's a story that makes killing possible the minute you believe in it.

Other lethal stories are out there. Cops who choke unarmed civilians to death believe an old tribal story called Us Against Them. Nazi youth believe a story called We Are the Surviving Remnant of a Warrior Race. Physicians who addict other people to opiates believe a story, originally spread by pharmaceutical companies, called This Won't Hurt a Bit. People who betray the people who vote for them believe a story called The Suckers Deserve What They Get.

All these stories are lies. They can destroy you. One of the ways they can destroy you is to convince you that you can destroy others.

*

It's a beautiful world this Monday morning, chill but getting warmer as the sun moves above the mountains. Last week's snow has melted. Julie and I will be working outside today. I'll mow the grass, which has gotten so tall I have to drag the lawnmower through it backwards or it gets clogged and quits. I'll also trim branches on the trees, and wheelbarrow a few more loads of dirt into the low spot in the yard.

Julie will continue staining the house. She's already finished the garage and is lobbying for a third five-gallon can of stain, which she will use on the deck. She loads podcasts on her phone and paints away, steadily, until she covers the wall of the day.

In a week or two, I'll have the lawn under control and ready for fire season—if it's possible to be ready for fire season. I'll have completed a course of Deck Yoga, which involves crawling under the deck with a shovel and my carpenter's tools, in order to replace a couple of pilings that have rotted off at ground level. It's cramped and dark and wet under there. You end up attempting positions that would take years to master. What would take 15 minutes in the open air will take an hour of painful effort, punctuated by profanity.

Our story, these days, is called Being Good to Each Other. It's not really a story. It's more like a heavy Russian novel, of the type used as doorstops and sleep aids, able only to be read on quiet mornings after a good night's rest. It doesn't promise to save anybody. None of its characters shakes the world. The plot has a tendency to repeat itself, and nobody dies—at least we hope they don't.

The characters have flaws, but those flaws are foolish rather than cruel. Their virtues are a bit plodding, but persistent. They believe in friendship, although getting together with friends has become difficult in a suddenly vast country. Internal events have become more numerous and more important than external ones.

The characters worry rather more than is necessary. They brood over things they wouldn't have done if they'd known then what they know now. They determine to make new mistakes rather than the same old ones.

They worry about the enormous quantity of pain in the world. They worry about the stories that drive people insane. They worry that the world really is ending but people still go about their lives, jobs, and routines, even as they develop a hunger for brains.

They worry about worrying too much.

Julie and I do solicit advice from people in the near future, a couple of whom look suspiciously like older and wiser versions of ourselves.

"Don't spend energy getting upset about things you can't do anything about," they say. "If you have to worry, worry about us. You think we want to look back and see that we could have had a good time but didn't? That we got tired of counting our blessings? That we got overwhelmed by the evil that stains the fabric of the world? Stop that, right now."

These senior versions of ourselves must have gotten through to us before. For 28 years now, when we've argued, one or the other of us has mostly cheerfully given way. I've learned to tell Julie she's right even when she's wrong. Julie has learned to tell me that I'm right even when she thinks I'm wrong. Someone from the future must have made it clear to both of us that in our marriage, any judgment about who was right and who was wrong was premature.

Deciding what this pandemic means is no doubt premature as well. It's tempting to blot out uncertainty with a blanket statement of fact, but facts are in short supply, and will be for a while.

Our older selves insist we can live with that. This too shall end, they say. We will rise from this interlude, and greet each other, and tell each other, with joy and gladness, all that has happened.

They're quoting from Dostoevsky, and that means they must have read his last big book again, and finished it, and been cheered by it. It's a sign that there are far more years in the future than it sometimes seems, and more good in this world. That's the good news, for the moment.

The Great Unmasking

June 29, 2020

TWO NEW PICKUPS, their human occupants, and a barking dog spent last night in the Sportsman's Access parking lot across our southern fence. It's not a good place to camp. There's no toilet and it's right next to the highway traffic. People have to shit in the bushes. They have to listen to giant motorhomes blasting by at three a.m. If they're in a tent, there's a problem with headlights lighting up the tent roof.

Sprinter vans go by every five minutes or so. They aren't inherently noisy, but they come festooned with bicycles and kayaks and rocket boxes. At 70 mph they turn into giant plastic whistles.

Our house is close to the highway too, due to winter driveway snow-removal considerations, but we're sheltered from the noise by trees and willows and an east wall with small windows. Six inches of fiberglass insulation will stop a lot of road noise. The house does shake a bit when a big semi goes by, but there aren't as many of them as usual this summer. Road construction has started between here and Sun Valley, making what was a shortcut for truckers into a potential delay. The FedEx and UPS vans go by every day, because of a sudden increase in local online shoppers. The loudest noise we hear from them is when they knock on the front door to signal a delivery.

At the moment, I can hear the campers in the parking lot getting ready to leave. They have Boise plates on their pickups but they're probably new residents of that city, part of the flood of Californians that has arrived in the last several years. They got here just at dark, not really knowing where they were, with little time to find a quieter campsite. They'll spend this morning looking for one.

It's a good decision for all concerned, especially if one of the reasons they're leaving is to find a campground with a toilet.

*

Their license plates remind me that driving to Boise used to be Julie's and my way of being tourists. Once there, we cut loose with long impulse-buying sessions in Costco. We stopped for buffet lunches at Indian restaurants. We bought super-sized cups of syrupy mocha from coffee shops. We purchased sprinkler-system upgrades and shovel handles at Home Depot. We made necessary stops at Trader Joe's for peanut butter cups and chocolate-covered espresso beans. We bought hard copies of the *Idaho Statesman*—coin-operated paper machines in Sawtooth Valley became derelict shortly after the Great Recession—for the crossword puzzles and the thick sheaf of weekend sale flyers. The sale flyers in particular made us feel addressed, wanted, and respected, part of something far bigger than ourselves.

No longer. The *Statesman* has thinned and shrunk and become almost ad-less, and its crosswords have become too quick and easy. It's indicative of our free time and increased patience that Julie has subscribed to the much more challenging *New York Times* crossword puzzle website. She downloads them and prints them out, 25 at a time. She's become quite adept, even with the Friday and Saturday versions—with occasional help from me on clues that demand memories of vicuña coats and Billie Sol Estes and 1964 Pontiac GTOs.

Now when it's time to go to Boise, only one of us goes, wearing a mask and armed with a carefully winnowed list and a sketch of Costco's product placement plan. Shopping is an exercise in efficiency. You get in. You get out. You go only to Costco because they require all customers to wear masks, and when you've purchased everything on your list you drive back to Sawtooth Valley instead of checking into a motel and having dinner in a nice restaurant and seeing a movie. It's no fun doing those things alone, anyway.

Coming out of the Costco parking lot, you notice the clogged traffic on Boise roads, the parks full of maskless young people in too-close phalanxes, the gas prices so low you look for free-china-with-a-fill-up signs. The city has an *On the Beach* recklessness about it. People flock to its bars and restaurants. Its housing prices are still going up and up.

The people who crowd the sidewalk tables celebrate a little too loudly and closely. It's an exercise in sympathetic magic, an attempt to bring back the same old world of 2019 by exaggerating the same old 2019 moves.

I suppose we're doing the same thing when we grab a giant cart and wave our card at the person guarding the door at Costco. But for us, at least, it no longer feels like 2019. It feels like 2020, and 2020 feels creepy.

No problem. UPS has begun delivering Costco.com orders to our door.

The campers have left. They've been replaced by a fly fisherman, lured in by the fish icon on the Sportsman's Access sign. The fish is false advertising, because the Idaho Fish and Game Department fish trucks haven't yet dumped in the season's first batch of farmed rainbow trout.

The only fish in the river are whitefish and suckers and pike minnows, bottom-feeders all. You can catch them on small wet flies that mimic gravel-dwelling insect larva, but not many tourists fish for them. They lack the cachet of trout, even city trout who never learned to feed in the wild and who will strike at any flies that resemble hatchery food pellets.

Later in the summer, when the location and amounts of fish dumps will be posted on the bulletin board in the Stanley Post Office, cars and pickups will crowd the Sportsman's Access. For a lot of our tourists, catching a hungry farmed fish is what passes for an encounter with nature.

The fly fisherman will leave after an hour of fruitless casting, and be replaced by another fisherman, and then another. Near dark, another camper might be lured in by the pup tent icon on the Sportsman's Access sign.

Stanley has begun its weekly summer street dances. Every Thursday evening, a band plays in front of the post office, and people dance on the closed-off Main Street.

At the first dance of the summer, crowds of people milled about the dusty dance area, some of them dancing but most of them standing around in tight groups, yelling to be heard over the band.

Almost none of them wore masks. They were not in our town to remind themselves that a pandemic was going on. They were here to stop worrying and have fun. Watching them from a distance, we also wanted to stop worrying and have fun, but that wasn't likely to happen until January, when the street would be safely empty and the dancing, if it worked, would bring a foot of powder snow.

In the Mountain Village Mercantile, where we get fresh produce on Tuesdays, the checkout clerks put on their masks if a customer is wearing one. They take them off when a customer is maskless. We assume they've been instructed to attend to their customers' emotional comfort.

Our emotional comfort depends on the Mountain Village's parking lot. If it's empty, one of us will go in, wearing a mask. But four or five cars will often show up while we're in there, and the store will become crowded with families with screaming kids and groups of laughing adolescents buying beer and Doritos. There's an unhappy return-of-the-repressed recognition when they see our masks.

We hasten to the checkout counter and get out. We hope we haven't made Stanley seem creepy to the other customers, even if they've made Stanley seem creepy to us.

Still, they should know they can't escape the virus by coming here, no matter how pristine the valley looks, no matter if our case numbers have remained low, no matter if they think the pandemic is a hoax concocted by the Deep State to make the Trump Administration look bad.

I've got my response all planned out when someone tells me that my mask indicates I've stupidly bought into the pandemic hoax.

"You don't want to get this thing," I'll say. "I've had it, but I'm not sure I'm over it. I'm trying to stay away from people because I don't want to give it to them. I know people who have died from it. John Prine died from it."

One problem with saying all this is that except for the part about John Prine, I won't know whether it's true or not. I know Idaho people who died, but it was early in the pandemic and they may have died of something else.

Another problem with saying this is it won't change anybody's mind. The people I say it to will keep telling me I've been duped by people who secretly run things from behind the scenes. When two human beings disagree to this extent about the fundamental nature of reality, it calls into question the sanity of one or the other, and maybe both.

Idaho's viral infection numbers have been following a rising exponential curve that began with the opening of bars and beaches. Epidemiologists point to indices of contagion and note that if each infected person infects more than one person, it won't be long until everyone alive, and a bunch of dead people, will have had the virus. There's anecdotal evidence that a youthful sub-population has assumed they'll get the virus and live through it. They've quit worrying about the health of parents and grandparents and are deciding whether to pay off college loans with their inheritance or just buy a new car.

If that sounds harsh to you, you're probably too old to remember what it's like to be young and narcissistic. You've probably forgotten what the young and narcissistic see when they look at anybody over 40: an old person who is going to die soon anyway.

Bleak. But it's become clear that the future will be bleaker than the past, here and in Boise and everywhere else.

I like the past. I remember large friendly chunks of it. It was pleasant to live there. If I could keep living there, I would, but it's dangerous to even try. The people who attempt it become grotesques who exude the unreality of an Alzheimer's ward.

This summer a similar unreality is in the air of Sawtooth Valley, as our tourists become refugees from uncertainty and terror, obsolete versions of themselves who look like they've never had to worry about disease or economic depression or paying the unpayable. Unable to face the present, they've decided to cancel it and replace it with the past. As a result, their lives become mere ritual, empty repetitions of events that once had meaning, once-fun things that are now more defiant than pleasurable. Maybe that's the fate of us all, but it's painful to watch it happening to people so young.

Race Demonstration

July 6, 2020

THE CITY OF Stanley witnessed weekly social justice demonstrations in June. People stood at an intersection and held signs protesting institutional racism in general and the murder of George Floyd in particular.

These were not massive protests. At the largest, there were 24 or 25 demonstrators, 22 or 23 of them white people.

That Sawtooth Valley is a white tourist enclave in the middle of a white state is not an accident. A good many of Idaho's early miners were ex-Confederate soldiers, and they brought their politics with them. Add ethnic cleansings like the Bear River Massacre and the Chinese expulsions from Blaine County in the 1880s, the 1950s signs in Caldwell cafes reading "No Mexicans or Dogs Allowed," and the Aryan Nation's 1983 call for the establishment of an all-white nation in north Idaho, and you have a nasty cultural substrate, one that discourages people of color from thinking about Sawtooth Valley as a place where they can relax and have a good time. You can forgive them if white people carrying Black Lives Matter signs don't change their minds.

No matter how beautiful the Sawtooths are, no matter how warm and sunny the beaches of Redfish, no matter how welcoming the hoteliers of Stanley, the surrounding territory acts as a minefield of bigotry.

White people in the valley get to go through life without having to come face-to-face with the human costs of racism. We do think about racism, but in the abstract way we think about Russian hypersonic weapons and Israel's annexation of the West Bank and police savagely suppressing Hong Kong demonstrations. It's evil but safely distant. When we protest racism, we aren't talking about *here*.

It's a bit like not having any positive cases of coronavirus in your hometown because nobody has agreed to be tested.

I didn't join the Stanley demonstrators, but I admired their bravery. Idaho still has pickups whose back windows display Confederate battle flags. Armed men, clad in camo, have shown up at Black Lives Matter demonstrations in Boise, claiming to be protecting the peace. Letters to the editor in Idaho newspapers warn of Antifa agitators coming to town to break windows, sell drugs, and turn teenagers into angry dinner-table orators who question their parents' values.

A pickup driver yelled that our Stanley demonstrators were Commies. Another pickup driver told them to go back where they came from. Lots of people looked at them and then looked away, as if what they were seeing and what they were thinking were in two separate universes.

But other people in cars, and a few in pickups, honked their horns and waved in support. Nobody was run over. Nobody showed up with a gun to protect anybody.

Stanley has not always been so pleasant. In the 1950s and 60s, some residents showed up in their KKK robes at the town's Halloween parties. These were real robes, and real KKK members, and their costumes weren't a joke. There were bone-breaking fights between white people who had hired black people in their sawmills and other white people who wanted Sawtooth Valley to remain all-white. Black and Hispanic Forest Service seasonal workers were harassed, and few of them came back in subsequent seasons. Since Stanley had been founded, racial violence was always under the surface, and occasionally above it.

That was what I remembered when I heard of the demonstrations. Most of it was 50 years or more in the past. It seemed barely distant enough.

On the Fourth of July, the traffic on Highway 75 was a constant rumble, punctuated by horn-honks and brake screeches and squealing accelerations as people tried to pass in the face of oncoming vehicles.

That night, the City of Stanley put on its annual fireworks display, and after it was over, a line of cars left Stanley for the campgrounds upriver or for their homes in Blaine County. We couldn't have pulled onto the highway between ten and midnight if we'd wanted to.

Fortunately, we didn't want to. We went to sleep and when we got up at seven the next morning, the highway was empty. Because of the noise, no one was camped in the Sportsman's Access. The campgrounds downriver were silent. The sunrise slowly turned the whole sky shades of pink and orange. When the sun hit the meadow behind our house, its light backlit paintbrush and elephant's head and lupine. They lit up like unwavering torches in the still morning air. Looking toward the mountains, you could pretend that you were living in a quiet and beautiful world that hadn't changed much since the Pleistocene.

It was lovely to think that way, but the illusion vanished when the traffic began to pick up. We heard gunfire from the campgrounds. Someone was target shooting with a 9mm pistol. A pickup full of people unloaded at the Sportsman's Access, and we began to hear laughter and shouts from the river. Motorhomes went by, towing SUVs and boats.

Yesterday was the supposed end of the holiday weekend, but this year holidays have indefinite extensions. They may go on until winter, because jobs and school years have been the traditional reasons for having to end a camping trip. Now, our tourists don't have to get back to jobs. It looks as if their kids will not have to go back to school if they don't want to. Add in an extended weather forecast that has promised us warmth and blue skies for the next 90 days, and there's not much reason for them to head home unless the local stores run out of beer and tortilla chips or the money runs out or the forest fires get out of control.

Forest fires aren't a worry for the moment. Our wet spring and wetter June have left the valley green and damp and full of tall grass. It won't be dry enough to burn for another 10 days or so. In 10 days, we'll worry about tourists and their campfires, and the human costs of burnt forests, pandemic disease, and pooping in the woods. If they're still here after Labor Day, we'll have to ask them to leave. I worry that by then, their homes will be in foreclosure.

*

It's easy to understand what Ralph Ellison is getting at in his novel *Invisible Man*. He says that when nobody sees who you are, but instead sees what they've been culturally conditioned to see, parts of you disappear. You lose substance. Your life loses meaning. In the end you have to construct a room whose walls and ceiling are covered with high-intensity light bulbs, a place bright enough to see what remains of the self you once thought you had.

Julie and I have become invisible this summer. If we're seen lounging about on the beach at Redfish, people assume we're tourists. If they see us out on the river, they assume we've driven across three states to catch a six-inch rainbow, even when we've packed our going-to-the-symphony chairs out to the riverbank and are reading *New Yorker*s and dozing and occasionally taking the dog for a swim.

Yesterday two people in a raft floated by where we were sitting, passing within 10 feet of us. They might have seen us, but if they did their eyes moved on to other parts of the scenery. They didn't say hello, and neither did we. Even Juno sat silent. We all watched them until they disappeared around a bend a hundred yards downriver.

If we worked in the tourist industry, we'd have a different kind of invisibility. Waitpersons, cooks, housekeepers, horseback guides, and even the local Forest Service personnel all have roles and uniforms that make them extras in tourist industry dramas. Their duties demand that they follow a script, and as long as they follow it, nobody gets called out for breaking character.

Of course, tourists have their own struggle to remain visible. Our gaze takes a bite out of them.

For years, I taught *Invisible Man* to white college students in my literature classes, telling them to write essays about how its lessons about race might apply to their own lives. It's cultural appropriation, I told them. You're a white person taking on the forced empathy of a black person. Go ahead. Take as much as you want.

It was not a popular assignment. For the first time, my students saw that thinking about race could cause pain even when you were white, even if you were from Idaho, even if your religion said black people were the descendants of Cain. Many of them quit reading when they started realizing that everybody gets damaged when one group of people oppresses another.

The things you won't let yourself see end up devouring you in the darkness of your own heart. It's all there on every page of Ellison's book. The connections with your own white life are there, if you dare make them.

I don't know if my literature classes did any good, just like I don't know if our local demonstrations did any good. The lesson that some of my students took from *Invisible Man* was that everybody is white under the skin, which I don't for a moment imagine was Ellison's point.

But it nonetheless got young white people thinking critically about a system that destroyed some people and arbitrarily showered others with educations, jobs, and wealth. It may have been a small step toward justice.

I don't know what lesson the people who drove by our local demonstrations learned. I hope it was that white people, too, could be disgusted by the murder of a man in handcuffs, and by a police culture that allowed it. That seems an awfully small step toward justice—an awfully small step toward common human decency—but it's a step.

The Changed Context of Our Hopes

July 13, 2020

LAST WEEK IDAHO began to exceed 500 new cases of coronavirus a day, the apparent result of Boise's bars and restaurants opening, the start of tourist season in the mountains, and the declaration of almost everybody that they were tired of the pandemic and it was over. The beach at Redfish Lake was packed with more sunbathers than usual, and not just because of the relaxation of state restrictions. Some of them were geographical refugees, because the big beach at Stanley Lake had liquified and disappeared into deep water during the earthquake last March.

Despite an urgent but unenforceable mask recommendation by the city council, the streets of Stanley are filled with bare-faced pedestrians. Campgrounds echo with the gentle hum of dozens of RV generators, and in the undeveloped campgrounds west of town, the packed trailers look like FEMA staging areas before a hurricane. Customers crowd around the outside tables at restaurants. Trailhead parking lots are full. In what must be a record, 400 people left the Iron Creek Transfer Camp in a single day, on their way, presumably, to Goat and Alpine and Sawtooth Lakes.

It is a scrupulous ritualization of the normal at a never-again-normal time in our history.

In Boise, Ketchum, and Hailey, mask orders seem to be better enforced, so a lot of the tourists we see are fleeing municipal regulation. Our beaches and restaurants and bars—where no one is requested to put on a mask—now function as worry-free zones for people who don't want to contemplate the intricacies of viral infection.

For a few hours you can lie on a giant towel and doze. You can sit in a comfortable chair and be served dinner. You can get pleasantly hammered on gin-and-tonics while watching Game 6 of the 2003 World Series from a barstool. You can forget your mask because the people next to you have forgotten theirs.

You can forget about having to work from home. You can forget you can't work from home because you don't have a job. You can forget about concerts and classes being cancelled because of superspreading events. You can refuse to think about the possibility of having to share a house with a sullen 15-year-old digital-high-school student, 24/7. You can forget Boise State might not have a football season.

Forgetting. It's what vacations are for.

As Sawtooth Valley locals, Julie's and my normal is other people's vacations, so it would be logical for us to treat this crowded summer like any other. We could forget a few things ourselves and it's not like anybody—especially us—would notice.

Instead, we're scrupulously ritualizing the pandemic. We wear masks when we pick up our mail. We refuse to watch ancient sporting events, even when we know the Yankees are going to lose to the Florida Marlins. We haven't eaten in a restaurant since early March. (We have ordered take-out pizza, but Julie's been picking it up while I wait in the car, motor running for a quick getaway.)

We're not worry-free, even if our visitors are partying like it's 2019.

They seem more horde than herd this summer. It's not a positive transformation. These people scare me, and their status as young and gorgeous human beings (I'm referring to a select minority of beachgoers) doesn't help a bit. Their hearts are hardened against the Coronavirus God. Watching them act invulnerable and carefree brings to mind clouds of locusts, plagues of frogs, swarms of flies, and bats. Millions of bats.

Sawtooth Valley locals provide many services for summer visitors, but this summer we've added a new one: we do their worrying for them.

*

Another thing: my lawnmower quit. Mowing the lawn has been a comfort to me in these days of waning complacency. When I decided to attack the back yard last Monday, I trundled the mower out there and pulled on the starting cord. It refused to move. A bunch of small plastic parts had disintegrated in the pull-start module.

I spent the next afternoon working on an old and heavy Snapper self-propelled mower that had been in one of our outbuildings for 30 years. I got it running, but only when I poured gas directly in the carburetor, which meant it needed a new gas line and probably a carburetor rebuild. We managed to put it in the pickup, along with an even heavier antique snowblower that had caught on fire the last time I started it in December. I had replaced it with a new snowblower, but when something's built like a tank you don't just throw it away. You get it fixed if you can.

We drove the two machines over Galena Summit to a repair shop for small engines in the Wood River Valley. I had to argue with the owner to get him to work on them, saying they were family heirlooms with great sentimental value. He finally admitted he could probably get them running, but it would cost me.

I then went to a hardware store in Hailey and ordered a new lightweight push lawnmower, similar to the one I could no longer start. When we got home, I went to the Amazon website and found a new pull-start module to replace the one that had broken and stopped my lawn mowing in the first place.

If all goes well, in 10 days or so I'll have three functioning lawn mowers and two functioning snow blowers. The grass will grow and need to be cut. The snow will fall and need to be blown. I expect to be willing and ready to do these things. Barring extreme global warming, I will have comfort and distraction and freedom from existential dread all the days of my life.

The morning's news has made it clear that the country is losing the battle against the coronavirus. I can feel the familiar soulless cold shiver.

A few reasons to have a sudden urge to mow the grass, even if you don't have a lawn or a working lawnmower:

- Anecdotal evidence suggests having the virus doesn't confer immunity for long and you can get it a second time.
- Severe cases of the virus are associated with pathologies of the blood vessels, blood clots, and strokes.
- Symptomless spreaders. They're out there.
- Chronic fatigue and brain fog. They may have been out there all along.
- Exacerbating co-factors in coronavirus infections include diabetes, obesity, heart disease, COPD, emotional ill-health, type A blood, air pollution, pesticides, lead-soldered water systems, and the trillions of microbes in everyone's body that are harmless until they aren't.

Medical scientists are cautious when they describe any new data, because it's been difficult to control the parameters of a worldwide experiment with a virus that has a long incubation period, vastly different effects on different people, and antibody tests (and bodies) that don't always show antibodies when they should. Governments, including our own, withhold or make up death and hospitalization statistics. People lie on social media for political reasons, or just for the hell of it. Anecdotal evidence is useless but it makes headlines, and for most people, it's what passes for science.

Under these circumstances, the amount of data you collect and the amount of certainty you can claim are in inverse proportion.

I don't know how long New Guinean cargo-cults kept on painting radio dials on rocks after 1945, but they eventually recognized the changed context of their hopes. They gave up on the rituals they had once thought would cause planes laden with war supplies to appear on overgrown jungle airstrips.

At the moment, Idaho schools and colleges still plan to have teachers and students back in classrooms and on playing fields in

September. At the moment, infection numbers are following steeper and steeper curves.

Idaho's faith in sympathetic magic is strong. It has tried unrestricted openings of bars and restaurants. It hasn't gone well. But Idaho will try again, only this time with K-12 and college students. Come winter, they'll try it with skiers from Seattle. If this isn't an attempt to bring back pre-coronavirus times by doing pre-coronavirus things, it's close enough that cargo cultists would recognize the effort.

Even with my fleet of lawnmowers and snowblowers, I'm dubious about sympathetic magic. Our lawn might look pretty good by September, and our driveway might be clear in January, but I'm certain that neither will make it possible for Julie and me to look forward to a Friday night restaurant meal and bottle of wine like we used to. Would that they could.

Lonely at the Top

July 20, 2020

LAST TUESDAY JULIE and I climbed the Grand Mogul, the peak that rises from the far end of Redfish Lake. It's a loose pile of decomposing granite boulders that tops out at 9,733 feet. We won't climb it again.

At least that's what my 69-year-old knees and recently matured sense of caution are insisting at the moment.

We didn't take the shuttle across the lake because of coronavirus fears. Instead, we took mountain bikes up the Redfish Ridge Trail, and stashed them in the bushes when we reached the lake's south moraine. We followed the moraine into the steep valley at the base of the peak. Once there, we had less than a mile to go, but there were 2,000 vertical feet in that distance. It's steeper than it sounds.

Also, our March 31 earthquake had rearranged the big rocks we used to climb over and around and through to get to the top. Remembered safe passages ended in blank vertical walls of freshly-broken granite. We had the unsettling experience of seeing empty air where memory told us we had once walked.

I'm old enough to know memory can be unreliable, and, of course, old enough to have an unreliable memory. Even though I've spent most of my life climbing around the Sawtooths, they seldom have stayed the same mountains from one trip to another. Prior destinations have turned into unfamiliar territory, even when I'm returning to them for the third or fourth or fiftieth time. Either I've missed something during earlier visits, or I've become a different person placing importance on different things, or the rocks have softened and flowed into odd animal shapes that might or might not move when you're not looking.

Anyone who has spent time in the high mountains knows that

they become three-dimensional Rorschach tests, and what you see there reflects who you are more than what's physically in front of you. Not many people have ever climbed the same Grand Mogul twice, and that includes the person who climbed it last Tuesday and the person of the same name who climbed it years ago.

There isn't a lot of continuity between who we were, who we are, and who we will become. If names reflected our real identities, we'd all need a new one every morning.

There also isn't much continuity between one person's consciousness and another's. It takes years of effort and good will and many, many deep conversations just for two people to climb one mountain.

The last time Julie and I climbed the Grand Mogul, we were with Sarah, her youngest sister, Sarah's fiancé, and our dog Loki. It was 19 years ago, long enough that Sarah, then an undergraduate, now is a PhD voice therapist in Portland, Oregon. She and her fiancé have been married and divorced. Loki ended up with too many dog years and is buried under a tree in our back yard.

The Grand Mogul had been five different mountains on that long-ago day, but four of them were easier than the one Julie and I climbed last Tuesday. (Loki had acrophobia and had crept on his belly all the way up and all the way down. The trip had been his last session of exposure therapy.)

Nineteen years ago, there hadn't been a recent earthquake, and we hadn't had to climb up long slopes of shaky rocks, all of them covered with marble-sized bits of crumbling granite. Stable-looking footholds hadn't given way when we stepped on them, and our way up hadn't been repeatedly blocked by near-vertical headwalls. We hadn't spent much time feeling our mortality.

This time, mortality was a factor. We had to drop down and traverse several times, searching for a chute that looked familiar. Along the way, we crept below house-sized blocks of stone with claw marks on their undersides, carved there when the earthquake had moved their balance points six or eight feet toward open air. We followed the mountain around to a route we thought we remembered, but instead of finding it, we looked over a boulder's edge straight down at Redfish Creek, nearly 3,000 feet below.

Julie turned to me and said she was happy to stay where she was while I found a way to the top. If I really wanted to go, she said. If I thought I could make it, she said. If I thought I could make it back without dying, she said.

"We're only two hundred feet from the summit," I said.

"Two hundred?" she asked.

"Two hundred vertical," I said.

"I'll wait," she said, and stepped under a rock overhang that would protect her from anything loose I kicked down from above.

I had remembered the Grand Mogul as a walk-up. I was wearing running shoes because they're lighter and easier on my feet than my old leather hiking boots. They also fit into the pedals on my mountain bike. They don't grip as well, is the problem.

As I climbed, the terrain took on a new hint of lethality. Experienced climbers know that if one person in a group starts thinking about falling, little fear pheromones start moving back and forth between bodies, amplifying as they go. Julie and I had just given each other big doses of fear. I began to wonder how I'd made it to the summit before, and why I'd wanted to return. Several times on the way up, I stopped, dropped back down, and started up again, reaching for rocks that wouldn't move when I grabbed them.

In 15 minutes or so, I was on the top, which happily looked the same as I remembered it. A small flat area allows standing and looking around without feeling giddy. To one side, a short spire marks the real summit of the mountain. Its top is marked by a patch of red lichen.

I reached up and touched the lichen for luck. I had, as we say, summited. Then I turned and saw the lake, and the lodge at its other end, and cars in its parking lot. Boats were leaving wakes in the dark water. Everything looked a very long way off, as if I was watching the world through the wrong end of a telescope, and for the last time. It is possible to miss this world while you're still in it.

The afternoon was warm and windless. If Julie had come with

me, I would have stayed longer and taken some deep breaths and thought through all the steps I'd take on the way to safe ground. The day would have lost some of its intensity, and that would have been a good thing. But I was worried about taking too long.

I took too long. I got rimrocked twice. I had to sit down and breathe, mostly to rest but partly to calm down. Once, facing climbing back up and starting again, I crawled through the tight darkness under a boulder, not knowing if I could squeeze through to the light on the other side, or if there was any way down if I did.

I made it through, and finally found the handholds and footholds that allowed passage down a crucial 30-foot drop. When I got down to a place where I hoped Julie could hear me, I yelled as loud as I could. She yelled back. Fear and relief were in her voice.

"You miss me?" I asked when I finally stepped onto her perch under the overhang. It was an attempt to lighten the mood. It didn't go over well.

We arrived home 11 hours after we had started out. We were footsore and dehydrated, but happy. We were safe. We were alive. There was leftover curry in the refrigerator. I fell asleep on the couch while Julie showered. I assume she fell asleep while I showered. We heated the curry in the microwave, gobbled it down, slept for 10 hours, and didn't accomplish a whole lot the next day or the day after that.

The Grand Mogul looks solid and eternal when it's a dark silhouette against the sunset, especially if you're sitting in a soft chair on the porch at Redfish Lake Lodge, drinking a margarita and waiting to be ushered to a table in the restaurant. That was how our climbing day would have ended in a year that lacked a pandemic.

The Grand Mogul is not solid. It's not eternal. In fact, within a short stretch of geological time it will be shaken a few hundred feet shorter by a major shift in the Sawtooth Fault, which cuts loose every 6,000 years or so. Long term, the Mogul's boulders will be pried into sand by frost and carried by wind and rain into Redfish Lake, which will become a large grassy meadow, full of strange animals that have filled the vacant ecological niches left by the Anthropocene. We will be in some other geological era by then.

Only in comparison to a human lifetime is the Grand Mogul solid and eternal. The fact that it's rotting and falling apart is not good news for a 69-year-old human.

By yesterday, Julie and I had recovered enough from Tuesday that we hiked partway up the side of McGown Peak above Stanley Lake. There are some big slickrock mounds up there, and you can climb up on one of the bigger ones and have lunch while you look down at the lake. Stanley Lake isn't as big as Redfish, but it's a nice view. If you sit there thinking about geological time and mortality, they remain comfortably in the abstract. You can talk about mountains as if they don't want to kill you. You can talk about being scared without getting scared.

Julie: "Are you thinking terrible things about me because I chickened out and didn't make it all the way up the Grand Mogul?"

Me: "No. Of course not. I'm thinking that I shouldn't have climbed on up. Standing on top wasn't exactly a moment of triumph. I couldn't see myself as a brave mountain climber with the whole world beneath his running shoes. All I could see was a tired and frightened old man, worrying about you worrying that I'd slipped and fallen into Redfish Creek."

Julie: "It feels pretty helpless when you've been sitting in one place for too long, waiting for someone who's climbed on up. You yell, and they don't answer. You yell again, and they don't answer. I was just starting up to find you—what was left of you—when I finally heard you. The last thing I'll ever do is sit and wait like that again."

Me: "Good to know. Next time it won't be so lonely at the top."

Julie: "Unless it's the top of the Grand Mogul."

We really do talk like that. We talked like that for quite some time up above Stanley Lake, until it became clear to us that we were still alive, and even though living wasn't a safe thing to do in the mountains or anywhere else, we were still willing to give it a go, at least for the brief bit of geological time that we have goes to give.

Free Idaho

July 27, 2020

IN TWO OR three days, the pandemic death toll will reach 150,000 in the U.S. Here in Idaho, we have had 148 deaths as of yesterday evening, which doesn't seem like much in the big scheme of things (unless one of the 148 was your parent, spouse, child, friend, or coworker). Governor Little begins his press conferences by noting that two Idaho counties still lack any cases of the disease, which is his justification for assigning Idaho's public health decisions to cities and counties and state health districts. Different locales have different needs, he says, and apparently the need of the governor's locale is to foist responsibility off onto someone else.

The governor has good reason to look for someone else to make the tough decisions the pandemic requires. He's still under fire from the libertarian wing of Idaho's Republican Party for locking us down last March. Angry demonstrators, many of them carrying guns, have claimed that any government that requires masks or business closures violates their constitutional rights. They have forced their way into Health District meetings, shown up as threatening counter-demonstrators at Black Lives Matter gatherings, called the governor Little Hitler, and refused to wear masks in the face of polite requests from people at risk from the virus.

Refusing polite requests is another thing that might not seem like a big deal in the big scheme of things, but once again, if you're that person at risk, it illustrates how exercising one's own liberty can cause the injury or death of others.

We have gotten used to refusing polite requests in Idaho, where anti-vaccination memes and attacks on Planned Parenthood and guaranteed medical insurance have pushed health care out of reach of whole swaths of the population. It's the price of freedom.

It is tempting to place libertarians and viruses together under a moral spotlight and say that they both just want to exercise a little free will in their lives.

But viruses don't want freedom or anything else. They are little genetic machines without brains. They wouldn't know what to do with free will if you offered it to them on a nanoscale platter.

People who ascribe intelligence to the coronavirus cite its long symptomless incubation period, its airborne transmission between humans, and its rumored ability to reinfect its victims. These are all clever workarounds of human defenses against infection, but they don't indicate a malign intelligence on the part of the virus. Millions of viruses exist, and chance alone would dictate that these traits would come together in one or two or a half dozen of them. Roll the dice a million times, and you'll get something that looks like intelligence, walks and flies and quacks like intelligence, but has nothing whatsoever to do with intelligence.

Which brings me back to libertarians. You can look at libertarians as people committed to a moral philosophy that exalts individual choice over all else, but you can also look at them as little virus particles programmed to arm themselves, dress up in camo, and march down streets carrying thin blue line flags when someone or something tells them no. Free will is hard to discern among libertarians when you consider that most of their actions are reacting against the structures of culture, the social contract chief among them.

Morality doesn't enter into it. Intelligence doesn't either. Free thinking enters into it as camouflage for rigid cultural programming centered on private property, law and order, racial hierarchy, and tribal inbreeding. Libertarians, as far as I can tell, have little choice but to obey software installed in them by small-town culture in the American West.

When I was an advisor to college students, some of the smarter ones would, in the middle of their sophomore years, show up at my office door in crisis. Why, they would ask me, were they working so hard to get straight As if the only reason was to get into law or med school and then walk into marriages/careers/mortgages for 30 or 40 years and end up divorced and demented in a nursing home, alienated from their children and mistaking their CNAs for old lovers? I'm paraphrasing, of course, but this scenario was at the heart of their questions.

It was impossible for me to answer their questions kindly. I tried. I told them that this was simply the cycle of life for white upper-middle-class Americans and there were less pleasant alternatives. I told them that they would be helping people to lead lives blessed by health and justice. I told them that the joy was in the journey, not in the destination.

These answers, it turns out, were cowardly misdirections at best. There aren't many worse lives than ones that end up alone and demented. If that's what a life of privilege gets you, it's not worth it.

Also, I was spending time in faculty meetings with people who had gone into academe to help young people see the richness and nuance of the examined life, but whose middle-aged obsessions were less about self-awareness and more about getting tenure or making sure that someone in their department didn't have it easier than they did. I was pretty sure idealistic young doctors and lawyers faced similar transformations as they matured.

Finally, the joy of the journey wasn't apparent in the faces of my former students when they showed up in my office 10 years after graduation. What I saw was exhaustion and bewilderment coupled with a dogged waiting-for-retirement endurance.

In the end, my students' questions bothered me more than they bothered them. They got over their crises, took their GREs and LSATs, and passed into a vast constructed reality where free will, if they had ever had it, was no longer something to be expected or even yearned for. They were running in the harness, some of them more easily than others, but someone or something else had hold of the reins.

After some years, I realized that the examined life was a mixed blessing, even for a literature and journalism professor in a small liberal-arts college. I resigned and went back to Sawtooth Valley. In the presence of our pandemic, that may look like an act of wisdom and free will, but it wasn't. I just didn't have the stomach to make it to retirement.

The Swiss psychologist Carl Jung addresses free will as a matter of consciousness. Humans can make choices within a clearly defined arena, but only if they are conscious of the game that is being played there. You have to know the rules and you have to play fair.

That arena is quite narrow when you are young, because children have to behave in severely prescribed ways (the Swiss model, as it were). When you are an adult, it's wider. You can choose from a limited range of actions: you can get married or not, have kids or not, become a doctor or lawyer or other professional (again, the Swiss model). If you don't like the choices at all, you can become psychotic or a psychologist.

After 30 or 40 years, your actions will again become constrained, this time by old age. Your children will begin to treat you like a child, your body and memory will start to betray you, and death, the ultimate constraint, will come jogging onto the field, a ringer from the opposing team.

Jung complicates this vision of free will with his theory of archetypes, which he defines as the deeply established patterns of behavior that humanity knows as gods and demons and heroes and villains. You can fall into one of these archetypes, or it can fall into you, and your consciousness and free will will go away.

The good news is that when an archetype takes control, it feels great. It feels like you have made the choice all by yourself to become far greater than you've ever been before. You don't question what it means to be human any longer, or if you do, you have the glory-filled answer every time you look in the mirror. Becoming what you have become is the ultimate expression of enlightened free will, even if it means that you lack free will from that point forward.

One of the rituals of fall in the city of Stanley is bow-hunting season, which comes at the end of August. You can tell opening day by the camo-clad face-painted bow hunters who show up in the Stanley Bakery for breakfast. If two people dressed and painted like that sit down next to you at the counter, you are in the presence of archetypes. Just don't ask them if they've gone to all that trouble with costumes just to sneak up on a latte.

It's a bad sign that the coronavirus is programmed to refuse all requests, polite or otherwise, that concern normal life, business as usual, the *status quo ante*, or whatever you want to call it. We're not getting a V-shaped recovery. Links will go missing from supply chains, and Amazon orders will fail to appear, even if your credit card still works. Universities will die. Foreclosures will crash housing markets. Infection rates won't fall off to insignificance. We'll lack hundreds of millions of vaccine doses well into 2021 and maybe 2022. Deaths will not stop at 150,000.

Demonstrations and counter-demonstrations will gain permanent residence in the centers of our cities. Costumes will proliferate as archetypes come pouring forth from long-repressed memories of *Mad Max* and *Batman* movies. If these villainous times require gods and heroes, gods and heroes will emerge, because the heroic and the demonic call each other into existence. They both find their meaning in the overwhelming drama of battle between Cops and Commies, Freedom Fighters and Fascists, Good and Evil.

There will be blood. One of Jung's axioms is that archetypes use up, crumple, and discard the human beings they use to become flesh. Then they reach for another. If it's you or me, we won't be the first or the last humans sacrificed to a god.

Our governor is not a hero. He's uncomfortable and awkward in a suit, and it's best not to imagine him in a cape and tights. He stumbles through his speeches and looks tired and old. He's probably wondering about the dumb luck of his predecessor, who didn't have to deal with a pandemic or a broken economy.

He's trying to muddle through. To the extent that his own party will let him, he relies on scientific data to make his decisions. This sort of thing encourages the would-be heroes who will run against him in the next Republican primary.

For the rest of his term, he'll have to choose between the human and the heroic. So far he's chosen the human, and that's the far better and more realistic choice. Let some other sucker try to guarantee human freedom in the face of pandemic and economic collapse.

I don't want the responsibility for your free will, he's saying. Take care of it your own self, he's saying. Plenty of people will feel compelled to do that, even if in their superhuman rage they destroy what they're fighting for.

When Your Inner Child Is Smarter Than You Are

August 3, 2020

ON SATURDAY OF last week Julie and I drove out to Redfish. Once we got to the roundabout, we began to pass cars parked on both sides of the road. The backpackers' parking lot was full. The Lodge parking lots were full. The Visitor Center parking lot was full. If we had wanted to sit on the beach, we would have had to park in the sagebrush behind the stables and walk a dangerous half mile on a road crowded with fast-moving giant pickups.

Fortunately, we didn't want to sit on the beach. We just wanted to check out the numbers and density of the tourists, which usually only takes a minute or so. You drive in the Redfish Road, turn left at the public toilets, check out the beach, take another left at the Lodge parking lot, and duck back onto the pavement by driving the wrong way up through the lot entrance. You can do this if you tell yourself that the ENTRANCE sign doesn't specify whether it's the entrance to the road or the entrance to the parking lot. Also, you have to make sure nobody's coming or you get into a right-of-way dispute. You can win these disputes by pointing at the sign and affecting an attitude of deliberate obtuseness, but in most heavy traffic situations it's easier to just proceed on through the parking lot to the EXIT sign. At some point deliberate obtuseness becomes plain old garden-variety obtuseness. It's good to know where one starts and the other ends.

We drove into a traffic jam. Giant pickups were cruising for parking spaces in both directions, and stopping and waiting for people to move their cars when they had only gone back to the parking lot for sunscreen and ice. When we got to where we usually could see the beach, we couldn't see it for the bodies. Sun shelters marked out hundred-square-foot homesteads. The new Lodge lawn still had ropes around it and signs asking people to stay off, but people had stretched out beach towels and were sunbathing on the grass.

I don't think I've ever seen more people at Redfish. Nobody—*nobody*—was wearing a mask. I rolled up the car windows and put the air conditioning on recirculate, and slowly maneuvered through the traffic until we could head for home. "Pray for September," I said. Julie looked at the lines of parked cars on both sides of us. "Pray for January," she said.

You can argue that checking out the tourists is a form of cruel amusement, but Julie and I were doing what locals do all around the world when their homes are flooded with people buying commodified experience. Maybe it is cruel, because it's the amusement of the freak show, heightened by a little frisson of horror at the sudden realization that what's grotesque for you is normal for those people.

I'm not being deliberately obtuse here, even if the last thing the country needs right now is one more excuse for dehumanizing anyone. For that purpose, we already have race, religion, gender, political parties, age, education, physical disability, mental illness, and masks. I realize that each tourist who drives into Sawtooth Valley was once a child who had a vision of light and joy and green grass and white-sand beaches and clear water and bright blue skies. I realize that the twelfth armored motorcyclist in the group of fourteen that roars by my house on a Sunday morning still has that innocent little child inside, and he's trying to keep it alive in a way that works for him. The same is true of the humans who crowd the sand in front of Redfish Lake Lodge, or crumble the shores of the high lakes of the Sawtooths with their hiking boots, or cast flies for planted rainbow in the near-sterile riffles of the Salmon River.

But there are so, so many of them. They have become the human equivalent of the amoebae that illustrate the power of exponential functions in high-school math classes. Or the fermenting vat of brewer's yeast that poisons itself with its own alcoholic waste products. Or the overgrown flocks of passenger pigeons that darkened the skies and toppled the trees they roosted in, just prior to their extinction.

When tourists and the rest of us recreate, we really are involved in re-creation, and often enough, what we're re-creating is the world as we delighted in it when we were four or five years old. Julie and I have watched enough grandparents and grandkids on the Redfish beach to know that one can step into that joyous world at any age if one has a real child as a guide.

But our inner children are more delicate and less willing to smile upon everything they see. They can have a tantrum after too many minutes of looking for towel-sized patches of sand among the bodies and beach blankets. They can go into whining marathons when they've been cruising the parking lots for an hour, waiting for someone to pack up, back out, and give them their space. And unless our inner child is a Darwin-obsessed fertility specialist—we see them on TV occasionally, little short guys in orange jumpsuits—it will find little delight in sharing the beach with a thousand others just like itself.

My own inner child, I've realized, delights in a Sawtooth Valley that exists as it did in 1953, when I first wandered out onto the dirt of our new front yard and started playing in it. It was an untouched world, pristine and gorgeous, and I could see and take joy in every rock and stick and blade of grass. There weren't that many people in it, which is why my inner child now likes to go backcountry skiing in below-zero weather, or walk high empty ridges in the Sawtooths, or spend whole days climbing over logs, following trails that haven't been cut out in years. Lest you think I find no joy outside of extreme physical hardship, my inner child also delights in rib steaks coupled with well-made zinfandels (I acquired an inner fake ID for my inner child, years ago) and Julie's apple pies. There are worse ways to console oneself for the loss of a 1953-model world.

I'm sure that the tourists who crowded the valley this weekend have their own things to delight in, but I'm equally sure that they haven't found many of them. Once numbers have exceeded capacity, other people pose problems. You park a half mile away from where you want to be. You walk down the beach until unclaimed sand appears, and that puts you too far from the outdoor bar. You ignore the noise of boats, motorcycles, and diesel pickups, but at the price of constant subliminal irritation. Now and then you pick up your mask and put it on, however heavy its weight of implied mortality. The scenes you saw in the RV ads, the ones showing mountains silhouetted against sunsets, tumbling rivers, verdant stream banks, grazing elk and antelope? You put them out of your mind.

These are adult solutions to the disappointments, the unrealistic hopes, and the forcibly deferred satisfactions experienced by a child. There are no childhood solutions for those things.

You know the marshmallow test? If someone administers it to you as an adult, you'll pass it. You won't eat the single marshmallow, because you know you'll get two if you wait a little.

You won't even eat the two marshmallows after you pass the test. You'll save both of them for even later, and eventually find them hard and inedible in a forgotten pocket, in spite of an inner child who would have been really pleased to have just the one in the first place.

After a long weekend at Redfish, your inner child will need to have a serious talk with you. It would have been happy with a swim, a float in shallow water atop an old inner tube, a walk along the beach, an ice cream bar on a stick, and a sleepy ride back home. But instead you had to buy the boat and the motorhome, the 4-wheelers and the mountain bikes, reserve an expensive campsite for a week, make sure the satellite TV was working, and invite the neighbors along, who informed you, as they entered the motorhome with their luggage, that they didn't believe in masks because the coronavirus is a hoax.

It's hard and brutal duty, all of it. Sometimes adults have no idea what children really want, even when those children are inside them.

This Thursday Julie and I had guests. Ron and Michele are good friends who had been camping in Montana and were stopping by on their way home to Caldwell. Ron has retired from his job as ski coach at the College of Idaho, and he was relieved not to have to go back to an institution that has chosen—for the moment—to cancel fall semester sports but still hold in-person classes. Michele teaches at a Meridian alternative school, and the West Ada School District is trying to decide whether to hold virtual classes or put everyone back in the classrooms this fall.

Their Montana trip had been a vacation from an uncertain future. They had rented a small camp trailer and bought 10 days' worth of groceries and made reservations at a string of campgrounds from Bozeman to Whitefish, getting the hell out of Idaho until they had some idea of what would happen.

When they got here, they parked their trailer a quarter mile away, on the other end of our place. We ate dinner on the deck and had no trouble social distancing, even though we had missed them and wanted to hug them. We were adults and acted like it.

They told us that almost everyone in Montana was wearing a mask because of a statewide mask mandate. They said it was a shock to come over Lost Trail Pass into Idaho, because almost no one was wearing a mask on our side of the border.

It was apparent that Montana and Idaho are acting as a laboratory for the country as a whole. Studies involving millions of participants, ones that would have been prohibitively expensive for the NIH to set up and execute, are being done for free, simply because one governor mandated masks and another told his state's citizens to do what they felt like.

Ron and Michele also told us that they had talked to people in Montana who said the coronavirus would disappear on November 4, the implication being that the pandemic was a media creation designed to derail the economy and prevent a second term for Donald Trump. It was an interesting idea, but it had all the earmarks of a Russian intelligence disinformation operation.

We toasted the Russians, and said we hoped they were right, but they had been wrong before, and we'd reserve judgment until November 5.

We're reserving a lot of judgments until November 5, come to think of it. The next hundred days will be filled with more history than the calendar can hold.

*

Yesterday, looking around a house that was suddenly as confining as it had been all summer, Julie and I grabbed Juno and headed for the dog beach at Redfish. Since it was late on a Sunday afternoon, we were able to find a parking spot close to the Lodge. We walked to the trees at the top of the beach, put down our chairs in a shady spot, took off our masks and watched the tourists from a distance. They suddenly seemed to be worried human beings like ourselves, ones simply trying to enjoy themselves before other people's irrevocable decisions—and good or bad luck—sent their lives in one grotesque direction or another.

The Other Worries

JULIE AND I attended a lecture on climate change Friday evening, one of a series put on every summer by the Sawtooth Interpretive and Historical Association. We had already attended lectures on Nature and Community, Aboriginal Use of the Sawtooth Valley, and Central Idaho Earthquakes. This Friday's lecture was on Climate Change in the Idaho Mountains, and it reminded us that in spite of the pandemic and its command on our attention, there are other ways that our world might end.

The speaker was Alejandro Flores, an associate professor in the Department of Geosciences at Boise State. You may know Boise State as a football team, but it really does have a university attached to it, and some good, smart people teach there.

Dr. Flores is one of them. He began his lecture by describing methods of measuring climate change. He described how destructive such change could be to worldwide food production. He didn't come right out and say that people would starve because of climate change, but he did talk about climate induced migration, which is similar.

He also talked about the creep of the snow line up our mountains, and how snow serves as a diffuse reservoir for water. Mountains that are rained on hold far less water for far less time than mountains that are snowed on. The rivers that run off them are smaller and warmer than snow-fed rivers, and salmon and trout disappear, to be replaced by warm-water species such as carp and tilapia and snakeheads.

The audience contained people who have been lobbying for the removal of Idaho's Snake River dams, which were one of the factors in the destruction of the sockeye and chinook salmon runs that used to reach Sawtooth Valley. After the lecture, those people asked questions about how climate change would affect salmon restoration efforts.

It wouldn't do them any good, Dr. Flores said. He was being kind.

Idaho's salmon are a zombie species already, kept on life support by a hatchery-industrial complex. But even zombie salmon need snowmelt to live. No snow, no cold water, no salmon.

The SIHA lectures are held at the old Valley Creek Ranger Station, and due to anti-pandemic measures, the audience isn't crowded together under a large sunshade as in previous years. Instead, a well-spaced grid of flags marks the lawn between the building and the highway, and people place their chairs next to the flags. Social distance is maintained. Because the audience usually consists of people who respect science, almost everyone wears a mask.

It's hot on the lawn this time of year. Julie and I carry umbrellas as sunshades, and drink plenty of water, and try to arrive at the lectures having slept well the night before. I was worried that I might start nodding off while Dr. Flores was lecturing, because he was described on the SIHA brochure as "passionate about using advancing computational tools and techniques to understand integrated land systems where human activity is inextricably coupled to hydrologic, ecologic, and atmospheric processes across a range of spatiotemporal scales."

Fortunately, Dr. Flores didn't talk like that. He was, however, careful to disguise the tragic realities of climate change behind a bunch of numbers. It was up to his audience to think through what those numbers meant.

I needn't have worried about sleeping. Dr. Flores let slip a number predicted by the newest models for global warming, assuming that humanity continues to operate a fossil-fueled economy. He stated that we could expect the climate to warm by 4.3 degrees Celsius by 2100. That's 7.74 degrees Fahrenheit, which doesn't sound like much. On a lot of winter days in Sawtooth Valley, it sounds like an improvement, especially if you don't feel like snow-blowing the driveway.

But that sort of global temperature rise, amplified by local variations in geography, humidity, and seasonal weather patterns, will make large areas of the planet uninhabitable, either from heat or sea-level rise. We have only just begun to see climate induced migration.

Except for salmon. Dams or no dams, salmon won't migrate anywhere after a worldwide temperature rise of 4.3 Celsius, except maybe to Antarctica.

After sitting for an hour under an umbrella, with a mask on, in the hot sun, Julie and I might have considered migrating to Antarctica ourselves, but instead we went home, took off our masks, put our lawn chairs in the shade of the pines, poured a couple of glasses of iced sun tea, and watched the sunset. A cool breeze was coming down the valley. The year 2100 seemed comfortably distant. Barring sudden radical advances in life-extension science, we wouldn't live to see our world get too hot for us.

It might get too crowded, however. Peaks of tourist traffic in the valley indicate a direct connection to hundred-degree days in Boise and Twin Falls. Our neighborhood turns into a refugee camp, because even on our hottest days, our altitude of 6,500 feet means that the nights cool quickly. Instead of air conditioning, we open a few windows after dark and keep the blinds closed once the sun comes up.

Thousands of campers do the same, and don't roast in their mummy bags. The sleep-robbing heat that comes with high nighttime temperatures doesn't happen here. Yet.

Our winter temperatures, which used to hit 40 and sometimes 50 below in December and January, don't go there anymore. Last winter we saw one night of 25 below, but a warm front came in the next night and we had a warm, wet storm. We do get heavy snowfalls, but sometimes we get rain instead. The valley floor loses its snow in late March or April now, when it used to lose it in May. Every summer the patches of old snow in the Sawtooths get smaller. A tiny blue-ice glacier used to reside in the northern shadow of Williams Peak—the only one in the Sawtooths, as far as I know—but it's gone. It no longer frosts most summer nights. Some people are actually planting gardens and nurturing them intact all the way to harvest.

These changes have turned a valley that used to require a tolerance for cold and loneliness into a place where a lot of people want to live. If they can't afford to live here, they want to visit. As Idaho's snow cover shrinks, its deserts expand, and a place that used to require grit to live in now appeals to those who like their comfort.

Thus far, our population explosion is a local and seasonal phenomenon. But what happens when hundreds of millions of people start fleeing India and Pakistan and Bangladesh, Vietnam, sub-Saharan Africa, and the dust-covered ruins of Phoenix, Arizona? Where do you put people who no longer have a job or a place to live? How do you tell people to expect a few million new neighbors? How do you stop countries from going to war over shrinking supplies of food, water, and living space? How do you keep countries with nuclear weapons from using them the first summer their homeland becomes unlivable?

Of late, I've been giving readings from *A Hundred Little Pieces on the End of the World,* as part of a virtual book tour. We've set up a corner of Julie's office for PBS-style interviews, with good lighting and a chair and desk and a bookcase behind them. The bookcase contains a wide variety of novels—*Moby Dick, Lolita, The Bell Jar, Great Expectations, Fear and Loathing in Las Vegas,* among others more obscure—and they indicate that ours is a household that reads widely and occasionally deeply.

The readings have been set up by bookstores where I intended to read on my pandemic-cancelled book tour. Readings in Southwest bookstores and universities were to be followed by readings in Northwest colleges and libraries. I was expecting large audiences lured in by complimentary glasses of chardonnay. I was expecting dinner in nice restaurants after I read and answered questions. I was expecting difficult and occasionally hostile queries about my contention that industrial civilization won't maintain its rising trajectory much longer. I was expecting to sign a lot of books, because while *A Hundred Little Pieces* discusses many of the ways the world could end, it also finds love and community in the small moments we have left.

My Zoom audiences have been intense but friendly. Very few people have asked me end-of-the-world questions, probably because they've seen more than enough worlds end in the past six months. Their questions center on love and community, which is what you have left when everything else is gone. I didn't think that was the most important part of the book when I wrote it. Now it is.

You'll be happy to hear that I don't pretend to know the future. Having seen computer models fail in the past, I don't assume their predictions will come true. Dr. Flores's 4.3 degrees Celsius could be an exaggeration of what Earth's temperature rise will be in 80 years, or it may be an underestimate. As I put it in *A Hundred Little Pieces*, "In a world where cause and effect has abdicated, you can't predict the future. It's hard enough to predict the present."

But there *are* certainties in this world, and one of them is that the current pandemic is not the biggest problem humanity faces. Climate change is bigger. Nuclear weapons are bigger. (I write this on the 75th anniversary of the Hiroshima and Nagasaki detonations.) A brand-new pandemic with a 30 percent fatality rate would be bigger. Worldwide economic collapse would be bigger, especially if you've got children to feed.

I'm also certain that if the pandemic is a kind of practice catastrophe, we're in terrible trouble. We've flunked the preliminary test, sunk the ship on our shakedown cruise, and punctured the trial balloon. Our leaders have proven to be good at denial and lousy at everything else, including decent human behavior. We've dismantled public health institutions that might have given us public health and safety this summer. We'll never know for sure until we get the numbers, and they're not available on any spatiotemporal scale that I know of.

One of this summer's remaining SIHA lectures is again on Central Idaho earthquakes. It concerns the hazards of the Sawtooth Fault, a crack in the world that runs along the base of the Sawtooths. It goes through the middle of Redfish Lake, which means that if the fault cuts loose with a magnitude 7+ quake (it does this every few thousand years, and no one knows if it's overdue or not), we'll have a tsunami in the middle of Idaho. As it is, the tops of various Sawtooth peaks keep collapsing due to aftershocks from the March earthquake.

Julie and I will probably attend the lecture, even though it won't reinforce our faith in the stability or permanence of our world. Not much does these days, except our presence in each other's lives, and a delight in each other's presence. Most days, that's enough.

Good News/Bad News Joke

August 17, 2020

LAST WEEK JULIE and I visited her parents and raided their garden. We came home with fresh corn, tomatoes, cucumbers, chard, potatoes, peaches, blackberries, beets, and carrots—that's just what I can remember—and then, on the way home, we stopped and shopped at the consumerist holy trinity of Costco, WinCo, and Trader Joe's.

We spent our money in Ada County, which mandates masks, instead of Canyon County, which doesn't. That's the way we're using our constitutionally-guaranteed freedoms these days. We're choosing not to get sick and die if we can help it, and we choose not to do business in those counties that refuse to take scientific advice. We leave them instead to the tender mercies of Charles Darwin.

The shopping list was long, and neighbors had added to it. When we pulled out of Boise and headed up Horseshoe Bend hill, the car was riding low on its rear wheels. We made it home, a little more slowly than usual. We steered carefully around even small rocks in the road. If we'd blown a tire, we would have had to unload the trunk to be able to jack the wheel off the ground.

The good news is that we'll now be able to comply with extended stay-at-home orders if Idaho has an explosion of coronavirus cases once school starts.

The bad news is that out by the Bull Trout Lake turnoff, we passed a pickup and camp trailer that had run into the trees on the other side of the road. The state police were there, but no ambulance. It looked serious. Camp trailers don't have a lot of substance, and when they hit six-inch diameter lodgepoles at speed, as this one had, they turn into crumpled scraps of aluminum foil, bits of Styrofoam, broken

113

sheets of eighth-inch plywood, twisted steel trailer frames, and torn tires that move one way and then the other in the wind.

We felt the helplessness that comes when you witness someone's ruined day/vacation/life. It's the same helplessness we feel when law enforcement vehicles go by our house, lights flashing and sirens screaming, on their way to an accident in the upper valley. You'd like to help, but you can't, and anyway, if you showed up to help, someone in a uniform would tell you to stay out of the way.

Recreation in Sawtooth Valley has a casualty rate. Here and there, our roadsides are decorated with plastic flowers and crosses. They don't last for more than a season or two, except in memory, where they persist even when you don't want them to.

The coronavirus isn't the only reason we hunker at home in these days of heavy recreational traffic.

For seven years of my life I was a ski patrolman at Sun Valley, and I was one of those uniformed people who never acted helpless in the face of catastrophe. If someone broke a leg or sliced an artery with a ski edge, I could splint the leg or stop the bleeding, put them in a toboggan, and quickly slide them down to an ambulance at the bottom of the mountain. I rode with babbling shock victims to the hospital and did my best to reassure them that they would be all right.

I held an emergency medical technician card, which meant that in the summers I went on ambulance runs here in Sawtooth Valley. The accidents were more serious, but I noticed that if anyone was dead or dying, other EMTs jumped ahead of me on the roster. Death was a drug for some of them. They had an uncanny ability to show up early for motorcycle accidents or head-ons. I was more than willing to stand back and let them have at it.

The good news was that on the few occasions when I did deal with dead people, I reacted with an icy calm when loading their bodies into a toboggan or ambulance. I mentioned this to my supervisor, and she said that maybe I should become a surgeon. I later found out that she—having had wide experience as a nurse in big-city hospitals—didn't like surgeons.

I also applied for a job as a paramedic in Boise during a post-ski patrol year when a girlfriend had gotten a teaching job in Boise. At an interview with the head of a Boise ambulance service, I was asked about working with dead people. I said it didn't much bother me. I didn't get the job, didn't move to Boise, and didn't end up in a permanent relationship with that girlfriend. That seemed like bad news at the time.

It occurs to me now that although it was a good thing to go cold and do what needed to be done in a trauma scenario, it wasn't a good thing to articulate a distant relationship with the dead if you were being interviewed by someone who had been a paramedic for 20 years. It also occurs to me that bad news can eventually turn into good news, which is a source of real hope these days.

My EMT certification expired 40 years ago. I don't miss my ski patrol uniform.

I have a closer relationship with the dead now. Both my parents are gone, and the names of high school classmates appear with regularity in the obituary columns of the local papers. I cannot pass an accident without feeling grief for anyone who was hurt or killed. (That includes the folks who periodically immolate themselves on the altar of The Offensively Loud God on Two Wheels. There are people in the valley who cheer when one of them jumps a guardrail, but I'm content just to wish tinnitus upon them in their old age.)

It's good news when empathy enters your life gently. It's bad news when it comes with the brutal shock of grief for a dead child or parent or sibling or good friend you never had a chance to say goodbye to. Sometimes it comes with the patient whose eloquent last words destroy a surgeon's belief that bodies are simply machines on their way to the scrap heap, repairable until they aren't. It comes with the pictures in the wallet that belonged to the body a cop pulls from a wrecked car.

In my case, as a teacher, it came in the form of students who insisted on writing final papers when they were dying of cancer, or who gassed themselves in their parents' garage when a boyfriend had died.

A career can't take many instances of peering into other people's deepest moments of sorrow. Thirty years of my life were spent as a teacher. It was a good way to spend them, and a lucky one, considering that most of my students ended up happier and more skillful than I found them.

But it's not the successes you remember. It's the sudden flood-lit vision of the inconsolable that imprints itself onto your frontal lobes and recalls every feeling of helplessness you ever had.

You don't retire because of age or failing abilities. You simply experience the final hammer-blow of grief that makes each bright new class look like a spring-sown field of tragedy.

You try to leave them all laughing. That's good news for them, and you hope they will have more of it.

The school year is starting, which is usually good news in Sawtooth Valley. This year it's bad news, because for most of Idaho, students are not going back to the classroom or gridiron. School openings have been postponed so districts have time to acquire laptops and establish parking lot Wi-Fi hotspots in poor neighborhoods. In the meantime, there's no reason for parents to get the kids to practice or take them shopping for school clothes. They can keep dragging them to Sawtooth Valley instead.

It may be that our tourist season will extend into October. Already people are planning on living through the winter in the valley, in second homes or motorhomes or the vacation cabins of aunts or uncles, parents or grandparents. They're putting their kids in the Stanley School, where they think it's safer than in the cities.

Most of them won't last through the winter. November is the month when plans become subject to revision here. Worries about global warming disappear far up the exponential climate temperature curve. The shadows from the peaks, so cool and welcoming in July, become lethal.

Every fall we have people coming down from camps in the mountains, having discovered that snow makes life in the wilderness difficult and paralyzingly cold, especially in early season when you can't dig a snow cave. It takes a whole set of hard-to-imagine skills to stay warm, and you have to engage them more or less constantly. Walks through the woods become ice-glazed obstacle courses. Lakes freeze over, and you can listen to their cracking and booming every time a cloud obscures the sun. Waterfalls become staircases of stalactites.

The people who make it through the winter here get used to cold and solitude and worrying about staying warm. For the past few weeks we've been honoring November, cutting and stacking firewood. It's hot, hard work, in August. People have toppled from heatstroke while chopping firewood on 90-degree days, being ants when if they'd worried a bit less, they could have been grasshoppers. But that doesn't stop us.

This time of the summer, despite having been retired from teaching for 15 years, Julie and I start having teaching anxiety dreams. We dream of not being prepared for class. We dream that students are jumping up and down, screaming and yelling in our classrooms, using the light fixtures as trapezes, refusing to sit down and listen. We dream that nobody has signed up for our classes.

I have dreamed that I'm in finals week, and that for a semester I've taught my Monday-Wednesday-Friday classes, but have forgotten to teach my Tuesday-Thursday classes. I have to quickly come up with a final for a class I haven't taught. Students are taking their seats and opening their blue books.

I lack the presence of mind to remember they haven't been in the class either. I could say, "What? You haven't been to class all semester? What are you thinking, showing up for the final?" But I don't.

I've known colleagues who blame their students for their own shortcomings. Thankfully, my dream-self isn't one of them. Nonetheless, it's an awful feeling to have forgotten to teach a class you were supposed to teach.

During this coronavirus year, Julie and I toast the schools we left behind and wish the people who teach in them well, and then thank our stars that we're not teaching this year. We wouldn't know how to run a classroom as a Zoom session. We wouldn't know how to help students. We wouldn't be able to spot a failing student. We wouldn't know how to avert tragedy before it happens. We wouldn't be dreaming, but it would still be a nightmare.

Feelings of helplessness are being validated big time this August. The pandemic goes on and on. The November election seems sure to be stolen by people who have no qualms about giving aid and comfort to American narcissists, sociopaths, and magical thinkers. There are apparently enough of them in the country to have elected this president and this Senate once. In spite of their general refusal to wear masks, it looks as if enough of them remain on the rolls to do it again.

The stock market keeps going up and up in the face of a non-functional economy, indicating that it's been forcibly separated from reality. Manipulation of numbers—deaths, infections, unemployment rates, the Dow, votes—seems to be the reality-substitute of the day.

Julie and I are doing what we can to stay well. We are hunkering down and minimizing our contact with others. We're trying to keep friendships alive over the phone and in Zoom sessions. We're fine, hiding in the underbrush of this world, until we drive by a wreck, see a rise in positive-test percentages, or watch a motorhome look for a place to park for the winter. Then we think about the future, near and far, even though we won't—we can't—know what it will be until it gets here. That's good news, I guess, if the future is bad, and bad news if the future is good. Either way, it seems like a joke, although Julie and I are, this August, having a little trouble laughing.

Fire Season

August 24, 2020

THE AIR IS opaque between us and the mountains. A metallic haze
has turned the trees across the river into shadows. Lots of tourists
ended their weekends early. Nobody spent last night in the Sportsman's Access just south of us, and since Nobody spends winters there,
we welcomed him back as an old friend and neighbor gone too long.

Today, when tourists stopped at the Sportsman's Access to fish,
they didn't leave their pickups. Instead, they sat and contemplated
the gray and featureless horizons up and down the valley. Then they
started their engines, turned around, and drove off, despite the thick
hatches of midges that hovered in the air above the floodplain.

Not that the bugs would make anybody's fishing any better. Idaho
Fish and Game hasn't been dumping hatchery rainbow in the river
this year, at least not next to us, and last year's planters—the ones
that survived the winter—are educated enough to tell the difference
between a dry fly and a midge, especially if a tourist is using a big
flashy dry fly. That's what most of them use, judging from the ones
we find stuck high in the trees back—but not far enough back—from
the water.

In the weeks before the fires started, the Salmon River was low and
clear, burbling and beautiful behind our house. Julie and I got in the
habit of carrying our lawn chairs across its shallow riffles and unfolding
them on the shady, grassy slope above the far bank. Once seated, we
would flip through a short stack of *New Yorkers* and show each other
cartoons. We would doze. We would watch Juno swim after sticks.

Or we would just sit, quiet and happy, and drink cheap wine from scratch-clouded polycarbonate wine glasses.

We're easily amused, I know. But by the time we walked back to the house, most of what we had sought across the river had been supplied by an hour of shade and tumbling water. We didn't go home disappointed.

We haven't been across the river for a while. California and Oregon are on fire. The products of their combustion swirl in a giant eddy that stretches across Idaho from the Oregon border to Yellowstone Park. We're near the center of that eddy, and the fire-freed allergens of juniper, ponderosa, sagebrush, cheat grass, and crested wheat float in the valley's air. Walking out to the river would start us wheezing and sneezing, and that sort of internal distress would outweigh the small joys we would be seeking.

We stay inside, but we have to leave the windows open at night to cool the house. Mornings, smoke lingers in carpet and corners, and causes the occasional three- or four-sneeze sequence, along with dry and itchy eyes. Taking a deep breath, even inside, causes a reflexive cough. We take shallow breaths. We put antihistamine drops in our eyes. We sneeze into our elbows.

"It's the smoke," we say. "It's not Covid-19."

Of course, we don't know it's not Covid-19. Any sneeze, anytime, anywhere, by anyone, puts us on edge. Worldwide deaths from the pandemic have passed 800,000. Each one of those people had a different idea of what they'd be doing right now.

Going away from the river doesn't help the situation. This time of year the rabbit brush is blooming. If we were to climb the hill across the road, I would be sneezing constantly by the time we walked back into the house. Julie would look at me with alarm. "No sore throat," I would say. "No fever."

Which wouldn't necessarily be true. During fire season, I wake up with a sore throat more often than not, having breathed some seriously particulate-laden air during the night. My mouth is dry and so are my eyes. I stagger, sleep-drunk, to the bathroom, for eye drops, and then go to the kitchen for a glass of water. It helps.

Fevers are a different matter. Usually I experience overheating during the afternoons, when I've been sitting in a room where I too late remembered to lower the shades. The sun, hot and hazy, packs a wallop that it lacked in April, even though it's in the same place in the sky.

I start feeling feverish, even if I'm on the couch streaming the Boise TV station. Usually it's so much hotter in Boise that watching its TV weatherpersons complain can substitute for air conditioning, but this August the snow is gone from the Sawtooths. Our temperatures have reached the mid-90s. Schadenfreude doesn't provide the comfort it used to, anyway, because on the hottest weekends—at least when the smoke isn't making it hard to breathe—most of Boise is up here with us.

We have a digital medical thermometer in the house, but its battery is dead. Back when the battery was alive, I used the thermometer discreetly, worried that Julie would be worried if she caught me using it.

It might have been malfunctioning even then. Every time I used it after the pandemic had started, it read 97.2 F regardless of how I was feeling.

"It's not a fever," I would say, "97.2." I'd head for the ice cube tray in the freezer. I would fill a big glass full of ice cubes, cover them with the sun tea Julie's been keeping in the refrigerator, and would feel cooler and less contagious after drinking it. Then I would check with Dr. Google to see if a constant temperature of 97.2 F was a Covid-19 symptom. It wasn't.

So it's not a fever, so far. It's the heat. When I built this house three decades ago, I didn't give a thought to installing air conditioning. No one in the valley needed it then.

So far is a phrase we're using a lot these days. "How are you doing?" ask friends, calling from distant cities. Our answer is always, "Fine, so far. You?"

"So far, fine," say our friends.

It feels a little wrong talking like this, jumping into the conditional simply because a pandemic has brought uncertainty into our lives. Uncertainty has always been in our lives.

Julie and I took up year-round residence in Sawtooth Valley in 2004, hoping industrial civilization would last long enough for us to have a few more winters with gasoline and electricity. Industrial civilization has lasted far longer than we thought it would. We've done fine with a conditional life for 16 years now.

For longer than that, come to think of it. When Julie and I got married, a lot of people looked at my history and her lack of it, and said that we wouldn't last any longer than it took a couple of law-yers to unravel the knot. When people talked among themselves, they would say we were doing all right, *so far*. After some years, we began to realize that *so far* was a blessing. It was an expression of wonder, of rare happiness, of improbable durability in the face of an uncertain world.

The world really is uncertain. Tomorrow astronomers could discover the incoming comet that would collide with Earth and snuff out all life. A new coronavirus could show up, only this time it would have an Ebola-level fatality rate. The Russian military could have another false alarm like they did in 1983, but now they would take it seriously and launch a nuclear first strike against our cities. Global warming could continue to follow the rising curve that it's been following.

There's no need to get that dark about it. In five minutes or so, any evolutionary scientist can explain why it's a trillion-to-one chance that your genetic material somehow made it here from the Eocene, much less the Triassic. Any quantum physicist can say you're living in the (super)position of Schrödinger's Cat, sitting in your box in the dark, listening to someone fumbling with the lid.

We've been watching the news about California, and there are the usual August videos of burned houses, the hollow shells of cars and pickups in what once were their front yards. People tell news reporters everything they've worked for their whole lives is gone, and you know but for the grace of God, that person is you.

It's not a big jump from listening to those people to watching Judy Woodruff narrate the obituaries at the end of the PBS News Hour. We see pictures of coronavirus victims, pictures of their grieving families. It doesn't require a lot of empathy to know their grief could be ours.

But so far, those things have stayed safe within the boundaries of our TV screen. The few small fires in the valley have been contained. And if we've caught coronavirus, we've recovered, at least according to the Still Alive After 30 Days metric that the Idaho public health officials use. If the air is a dull gray, it still contains enough oxygen for us to take shallow breaths and keep going. We're surviving, and we're still able to face each day of this dismal year and what it brings with it.

So far.

One Fine Day

August 31, 2020

WE'LL GET VACCINATED. At least that's our hope. We also hope that the vaccine will be effective against coronaviruses and a bunch of other pathogens. One of the side effects of the Covid-19 pandemic has been an increased number of consultations with Dr. Google about the Zika, dengue, yellow fever, West Nile and Spondweni viruses.

You may never have heard of the Spondweni virus. It sounds terrible. Dr. Google tells you it can cause hematuria, hematospermia, and epistaxis. These are words for blood showing up in places it shouldn't, which can be scary but most often isn't fatal. Epistaxis, for example, translates from medicalese as a common nosebleed.

Spondweni virus itself is considered a mild pathogen. You get over it in two or three days in most cases, without lasting effects. It probably doesn't belong in the same paragraph as the others, even if Dr. Google put it there and caused all this anxiety in the first place.

Julie and I will get vaccinated next month, for the flu. Flu vaccine is not effective for much longer than six months, so we try not to get it too early in flu season. We also ignore rumors that it contains nanotechnology in the form of Bill Gates-supplied injectable mind-control chips, chips that will cause an overwhelming impulse to buy the newest version of Microsoft Office the minute it's available. Judging from the age of our version of Office, nanotechnology has a ways to go before it can control consumer behavior, at least *our* consumer behavior, which usually only responds to Costco sale flyers.

Also, we don't worry about thimerosal in our flu vaccine, because when it is used, each dose contains less mercury than a tuna melt, and the mercury it contains is *ethyl*mercury, not the far more destructive and long-lasting *methyl*mercury.

If you want to worry about mercury, an ahi steak marinated in honey and lime juice and put on a hot grill for a minute on a side and then devoured with wasabi is the sort of thing you should consider. Make that your dinner every evening for a month, and you will bioaccumulate enough methylmercury to cause enough brain damage to make you happily donate to Steve Bannon's Build the Wall charity.

We do worry the flu vaccine will miss its targets this year. Flu shots are readied well ahead of time, before anybody knows exactly which strains will be circulating. Last year the vaccine missed its target, mostly, and we caught something flu-like in December. Then we caught something else flu-like twice more, in January and February. We may have had a small relapse in March, or it may have been Spondweni Fever, picked up on that abnormally warm day when the mosquitos came out. It was a bad winter that way.

When and if a coronavirus vaccine becomes available, it will come with head-splitting ethical questions, not the least of which are—

- Do you wait until you have enough vaccine for everybody, so you don't have to prioritize one group of people over another?
- If your vaccine isn't properly tested, do you give it to military personnel under the guise of national defense? This isn't an idle speculative question. China has already gone ahead with such a plan, giving a theory-designed vaccine to real soldiers and hoping that theory has some relationship to reality. In our own country, we remember the Gulf War vaccinations, given to American soldiers on the assumption that as an invading force, they would be exposed to Saddam's chemical and biological weapons. Check out what Dr. Google has to say about Gulf War Syndrome if you want something to talk about in your Medical Ethics class in the coming semester.

- Do you give the vaccine first to high-risk groups? If so, do you define them by blood type, living arrangements, income, age, race, or political party?
- Do you force people to get vaccinated when they don't want to? Do you refuse to let unvaccinated children play sports or even go to school? Fines? Jail terms for child neglect? Squeeze chutes?
- You're the head of a family-owned pharmaceutical company, one that has just come up with a cheap, safe, and effective Covid-19 vaccine, arrived at with the help of extensive government-funded research. Do you: a) charge what the traffic will bear; b) make it available to everyone for free; or c) resign before you're fired for suggesting b)?

It would be nice to have a universal vaccine, one that would prevent any and all diseases for life. That sounds impossibly utopian until you consider that for a huge majority of children these days, the default position is health. Kids used to get sick all the time, and enough of them died that everybody knew what the term "replacement kid" meant.

Over the years, at least until Covid-19 came along, medical science developed enough vaccines for enough diseases that we had a *de facto* universal vaccine. People could finally worry about side effects. It's hard to overstate the improvement that represented over worrying about replacement kids.

Shortly after I was born in 1950, I had mumps, measles, and chicken pox, all of which I was lucky enough to survive without life-altering complications. Early on, I was vaccinated for smallpox and whooping cough, and received both the Salk and the Sabin vaccines for polio.

The Sabin vaccine contained domesticated live virus, but nobody worried about that as much as they worried about getting polio. Other vaccines had unpleasant side effects, but they were nothing as bad as what they prevented. I went to school with classmates who had been paralyzed, or who had heart conditions, or who couldn't hear because of infectious disease. My mother, a nurse, had dealt with the victims of these infections. I didn't like needles—besides the pain, I saw them as a monstrous violation of the boundary between my inside and my outside—but there was no chance of remaining unvaccinated in our household.

Tetanus was the one I remember, because it hurt, and the first inoculation wasn't the last. I got a booster shot whenever I stepped on a nail, which was about once a summer during my grade-school years.

In spite of the pain, as an adult I made sure I received a new vaccine whenever it was approved. When pneumonia vaccine was available, I got it. When meningitis vaccine came along, I got it. When I took a trip to Thailand in 1983, I received what appeared to be the entire 20th century's worth of vaccine research in one giant shot, courtesy of the Idaho South Central Health Department. It cost me ten dollars and left me with pain in my joints and muscles for a week. But I didn't get sick in Thailand.

Last winter I received, with some relief, my second Shingrix shot. I felt lousy for days, but not as lousy as I would have felt if I'd had a bout of shingles.

We are discovering that people can get Covid-19 more than once. It's not surprising, given that immune system responses to the virus are all over the map, and worldwide cases have surpassed 25 million. That's a lot of anecdotal evidence. If you have enough anecdotal evidence, you can prove anything you want.

It may be that for some people, getting the virus is a one-time thing. It may be that, within six months, everybody else loses the immunity acquired by vaccine or by having the disease. It's certain that as people who have survived the disease get older, lots of deaths will be blamed on a recurrence, or a mutated strain, or on a vaccine. It will be hard to design the study that will establish immunological certainty.

In spite of that, Julie and I will get a Covid-19 vaccine. We'll be worried about side effects, because the vaccine we get will have been rushed through FDA safety protocols. But there will be enough data to make a common-sense decision, one not dependent on anecdote or rumor, to be injected with one of the many vaccines that will be available by this time next year.

There's science out there if you take the time and trouble to look for it. Once you find it, you can reasonably have faith in it. Then you have to bet your life on that faith, which is the hard part. It's still easier than betting your life on the benign intentions of a virus.

There are fears within the scientific community that a Covid-19 vaccine won't produce herd immunity because too many people will refuse vaccination. The politicization of the pandemic has produced people who won't wear masks because they've been told masks cause or intensify disease or interfere with their freedom. It's doubtful the same folks will line up to be vaccinated.

Another factor in vaccine refusal is the eternal psychological problem of what's inside and what's outside. Judging from the number of people confused about it, figuring out where they end and where the world begins is not easy. Getting injected with anything is a violation of an uncomfortably permeable boundary. Because there are so many other, more nebulous violations of that boundary by powerful people and institutions who confuse their needs with your own, it's tempting to refuse whatever violations you can.

The conspiracy theories the anti-vaxxers have about Bill Gates or Big Pharma or population control stand in for what is really happening to them. That is, most people in this country really are being herded into a kind of squeeze chute, but what they're being injected with, as the chute holds them immobile, are social media memes, foods and medicines designed to be addictive, lifetime mortgages, unpayable college loans, and hours-long commutes to jobs that have no meaning.

Refusing to wear a mask and refusing to be vaccinated is a metaphoric response to the unrefusable assaults of day-to-day life. You maintain what boundaries you can, where you can, but they're never enough. Your small refusals, you hope, will compensate for all the big refusals you'd like to make but can't, the ones that remind you that you're being treated as a farm animal by the corporations and politicians of this country.

*

Julie and I had planned to go to Yellowstone and Chico Hot Springs for a week in October for my 70th birthday. Chico has a wonderful restaurant, nice rooms, and hot pools you can soak in until you get too warm. Then you can climb out, lie back on a chaise longue, and read murder mysteries until it's time to dress for dinner. There are worse ways to spend a birthday.

But it's not going to happen this year. We're not going anywhere without a vaccine, and even then we'll be cautious travelers. I doubt if we'll ever feel as safe as we did back in the days when there was a vaccine for everything, and we hadn't even heard of Spondweni.

If things go as we hope, this time next year we'll be planning a 71st birthday party. Even if it doesn't have the cachet associated with a 70th birthday, it will be a celebration of being alive. Even if we won't be heading for Chico next year, we will be thankful of our survival in the face of unknown odds, and of our ability to hunker down and wait out this plague.

If this plague is over. If it hasn't touched us with grief. If Dr. Google will let us out of the house.

Alpine Idyll

September 7, 2020

IT'S LABOR DAY weekend. I've just come home from Stanley, which was as crowded and unmasked as I've seen it all summer. I stopped at the post office and picked up this week's *New Yorker* and a couple of flyers from the Challis grocery stores, which I always look at to see how much cheaper their prices are than ours. They're cheaper, but not Costco cheaper, and they're 55 miles down the winding river road, and Challis folks sometimes get a little snarly at out-of-towners, especially if we're from the upper valley. Vicious rumors go around Challis about people with post office boxes in Stanley, mostly about key parties and drug use and people who believe in the virus and outrageous requests to the Challis School District for a second or even third teaching position at the Stanley School.

So we go to the Nampa Costco instead, even if it means we have to plan ahead.

In Stanley, it was 90 degrees at four p.m. Smoke was drifting over the peaks from California and Nevada. The sun had turned a deep dirty red. The shadowed sunlight didn't seem strong enough to make it as hot as it was. A line of people stretched from the takeout window of the ice cream shop into the middle of Ace of Diamonds, Stanley's main street.

Clusters of tourists were wandering back and forth between the Sawtooth Hotel, which hadn't opened for dinner yet, and the Stanley Bakery, which had been closed for two hours. The Kasino Club was open and busy and promised to get busier, with outdoor live music later in the evening. No one was in the post office when I went in, and no one came in while I was there. The wind gusted down the street, kicking up dust. The license plates on parked cars were from out of state, or from Boise, which these days is mostly the same thing. Town seemed busy but at the same time empty and alien. People's bodies seemed too tall or too short, their faces curiously bird-like, rat-like, dog-like.

If a plein air artist, with easels and paints and brushes, had set up in the cordoned-off post office parking lot, I would have checked twice to see if it was Hieronymus Bosch.

You may think I'm running out of big things to write about if I'm reduced to describing hallucinatory trips to town. Not true. Instead, the pandemic has made us into behavioral minimalists.

We don't do a lot, but what we do has meaning. Going to the post office has taken on the solemnity of religious ritual. The air there is heavy with the incense of disinfectant. Inside its double doors, masks are worn as sacraments. Each keyed mailbox acts as an altar of possibility, one that can answer or crush your prayers. One day you get a bill. The next day you get a stimulus check, one personally signed by Donald J. Trump.

If the post office is a church, even one dedicated to a savage and capricious god, it's still a sanctuary from the surreal streets outside. If Stanley is starting to look weird, it's because the tourist industry is poorly-rehearsed theater in the best of circumstances, and these times are not the best of circumstances. The local audience's willing suspension of disbelief is wearing thin.

Julie is not here. She's down at her parents' place in Vale, Oregon, helping again with her mother's garden, which becomes a cornucopia every August and September. She will return home tonight with garden-ripened tomatoes and fresh basil and four pounds or so of fresh mozzarella. We will have caprese salads for a month, for lunch, for dinner, and sometimes for breakfast.

It's what they eat in paradise.

January—the whole month—is the metaphorical dark evil twin of a September caprese salad. The only tomatoes available will be petroleum products cleverly crafted to look like the real thing. They'll be on cheerful display in supermarkets and now and then we'll fall for the ruse and buy one and take it home to eat it, which is a cruel trick to play upon one's own self, especially when the sun holds no heat, the woodpile is shrinking, and it's a day when the car, once you get it started, has to wait for a snowplow to even make it to the post office. Costco is out of the question. Summer, even as a concept, is out of the question. Gardens are glimpsed only in fever dreams.

I wasn't thinking about how hot it was last week, when I called up the office of our local energy co-op and ordered a new Blaze King wood-stove. Our old Blaze King woodstove, which I installed 32 years ago when I built this house, finally burned through the top of its firebox, so it no longer directed smoke through the catalytic converter. It lost efficiency, and last winter we woke up to a cold stove a couple of times. That's endurable but inconvenient, especially when it requires going out on a -10 morning and cutting kindling in pajamas and flip-flops. We got better, last winter, at cutting kindling before the fact, but we still decided to spend our stimulus check on a new stove.

Blaze King stoves are expensive. The old one had cost me $1,800 in 1988, which works out to $56.25 a winter. The new one is $2,900. It won't amortize out as well—unless it, and I, last another 51 years. The stove has a better chance at that than I do.

But the government wasn't giving me money to keep the economy going in 1988. Now it is. Even if it weren't, $2,900 is easier to come by than it was for me in 1988. In 1988, I was out of a job. I had just spent my last dime on a woodstove, after spending my other last dime on an MFA degree from the University of Montana. I had learned to write but I also learned that to make a living as a writer you had to hustle 24/7, be a voracious self-promoter, and be a prominent member of the Dumb Luck family. Buying a good woodstove was a way of putting some warmth and solidity into a fragile future. I might starve to death, but I'd die warm. Friends had reassured me that I wouldn't have to worry about staying warm after death.

But we won't discuss their reasoning in this journal of the plague year, which, after all, is about survival and not eschatology. Even though I've written an end-of-the-world book, I'm more interested in what happens while you're waiting for the end, not when it happens or what happens after it happens. I used to tell my students that if death is anything at all, it's a huge loss of perspective.

In that spirit, and in wanting to get up close to a stable substrate for reality, Julie and Juno and I went on a long early September hike last Tuesday. We got up early, packed a lunch, and headed for the parking lot at the end of Alturas Lake Road. The trail that starts there forks almost immediately, and the right fork goes up Alpine Creek, a huge and, for the Sawtooths, a wet drainage. It contains 30 or so lakes.

The Alpine Creek trail ends in a swamp after two miles. After that you're following broken and braided paths over logs and through bogs. The terrain steepens. Glaciated rock, some of it slick with moss, now and then obliterates all sign of any path. Finding one again takes some bushwhacking. When you do finally reach a lake, you find it has a headwall above it, one you have to climb up and over before you reach the next lake.

Up high, signs of other humans are reduced to thin beaten tracks through tundra. The climate changes. You start seeing spring flowers and square-toed mountain goat hoofprints. At the top lake, you're five or six miles away from your vehicle. You're also 2,000 feet above it. You have climbed and descended another thousand feet getting there. You look around for a place to pitch your tent, roll out your sleeping pad and go to sleep until it's time for dinner.

But you don't have a tent. You remember you're on a day hike, and what lunch remains in your pack is cracker crumbs, a couple of slices of weeping cheese and greasy salami, and a heat-softened granola bar, left over from a ski trip last winter. You've got a long way to go before you can sit on anything other than a rock or a log. It dawns on you that it will be a longer day than the one you started out with.

Julie and Juno and I went by 11 lakes in Alpine Basin. Each was surrounded by rock and meadow, and above them were rock spires.

Above the spires were peaks, and above the peaks, a cloudless and smokeless dark blue sky.

We walked through mossy sunlit meadows and through dry streambeds, their rocks smoothed into cobblestone paths by the action of frost and spring water. Going down, we had to pick our way through near-vertical rock bands, but we found routes through them and didn't get rimrocked. We walked by the tracks of baby goats in dry potholes. We walked under the clawlike branches of giant dead whitebark pines. We walked over lakes on rocks exposed by low water, grateful we didn't have to climb up and over the cliffs that formed the lakeshores in high water.

Every place we stopped, we would have liked to have stayed. We were deep in the midst of something solid, beautiful, and real. Once it must have been the whole world. Now it was confined to legislated wilderness. But we could experience it with all our senses, uninterrupted. After a summer of fighting through Sprinter vans to get to the post office, it was a relief. It was also a relief to see a bird head on a bird, a rodent head on a rodent, a dog head on a dog.

We saw gray jays and pikas and the occasional deer, which Juno has finally learned not to chase very far. No goats, but we knew they were watching us. On our way out, we finally saw other human beings when we caught up with another couple a mile from the parking lot. They frowned at us and only grudgingly let us pass, and when we did, they looked at us with the usual projected self-loathing of people who go to the mountains to get away from people.

Closer to the car, we met two people we knew, coming in. They had full packs and were going to stay out for two nights. It was late in the day, and we didn't think they'd make it much beyond the first lake by dark. We told them where we'd passed by a tent at that lake and wished them luck in making it up the canyon to a lake of their own. When we reached our car we were tired but happy, and grateful to be going home to a soft bed. Juno slept for a couple of days.

Our trip to the high country demonstrated that the real is only a big day hike away. But it's clear that humans can't live in the real for long.

Our new Blaze King's imaginative engineering is solid evidence of that, and so is our carefully cut and stacked woodpile, which needs a couple of pickup loads added to it before we'll make it through the winter.

Stanley and its post office and wandering tourists are all ideas made flesh—one doesn't become a tourist without ideas of who one is and where one goes—and by that standard, I suppose that Julie and I are ideas, too.

It's a good thing that ideas can come to life, and that a human being can have a decent time going through life as one. We just look a little scary when inspected up close, as Hieronymus Bosch, the old Dutch realist, knew. He painted people as he saw them, as creatures half-dream and half-flesh, running from demons. He could have spent all this summer in Sawtooth Valley, painting away, and his new work wouldn't be that much of a departure from his old, safe stuff.

Note to Self

September 14, 2020

THIS ENTRY IS my 26th posting. I am halfway through my journal of the plague year. I haven't missed a weekly entry, and I'm closing in on 50,000 words, which means if I continue apace, I'll have a reasonably hefty pile of pages by March 21, 2021. It's not often that Fate hands you the plot of a non-fiction novel, a writing schedule and word count, and the possibility of a happy ending.

Like a lot of paragraphs these days, the one above appears to have some integrity—and even a happy ending—until you inspect it closely. For one thing, I have no idea if we'll have a plague year or a bunch of plague years. I have no idea if I'll be alive on March 21, 2021. I'm planning to be, but a million other people were planning to be alive right now, and they're all in urns on the family mantel, or reduced to ashes floating down the Ganges, or lying under a headstone with one name on it or many. Fate can, and will, hand you a lot of things besides a plot for a book.

Also, Fate might just be handing you the plot for Volume I. Volumes II-X will come later. Fate might be handing someone else your manuscript, 50 years down the line. That's what happened to Daniel Defoe's uncle's diary. Defoe took what amounted to a family heirloom and used his novelist's skills to add drama and romance (and, it must be said, a lot of reputable research) to his uncle's 1665 work. He published it in 1722 as *A Journal of the Plague Year*.

These are tougher times for getting published than 1722 was. Even if you have a manuscript in hand, and even if it's reasonably well-written, even if you wrote it yourself, and even if all your friends tell you it's good reading, that doesn't mean anyone will publish it. So a likely fate for my own journal of the plague year(s) is that my entries will be printed on acid-free paper, which will be spiral bound between two sheets of durable plastic, and the whole package will end up buried in a university library or found in a box labeled Miscellany at an estate sale.

When I was an undergraduate at Harvard, I was a work-study student in the circulation department of Widener, the big research library on campus. It contained almost four million volumes at the time, shelved in eight stories, four of them above ground, four of them below. My usual job was to find books in the stacks, even mis-shelved ones, but on occasion I was detailed, with other work-study students, to open packages of books that had been willed to the library.

It was like Christmas morning. Sometimes the donated books were rare and valuable antiques, or first editions from the early Modernists, thrown in among forgotten best sellers from the first few decades of the 20th century. Sometimes books contained ten-dollar bills as bookmarks, which—as we operated under a monetary finders-keepers system—now and then brightened my cold gray Cambridge winters by paying for a date. Sometimes, stuck between the pages, there were notes to self, shopping lists, or love letters. We were under strict instructions to give any personal letters to our supervisor, who would scan them for financial importance and then consign them to the incinerator, whether they had historical value or not. He was a person who had respect for human privacy, even the privacy of dead lovers.

Sometimes we opened individually packaged manuscripts from the institutions we then knew as insane asylums, usually hand printed. Some of them were in manila folders and some of them were beautifully bound. It was hard to read the writing, and hard to understand the words even if you could read them. Reading them felt voyeurish—the people who had written them lacked the kind of filters most of us use to be regarded as sane. That lack had put them in a mental ward in the first place, and you couldn't read their words without feeling like a nosy and unwelcome intruder into a world best kept under wraps.

But our supervisor would take each manuscript, give it a file number (apparently there is a Dewey Decimal System category for the unsolicited and unpublished manuscripts of the insane), record it somewhere in Harvard's IBM 7000 mainframe, and give it its own punch card. It was then ready to be checked out. As far as I can remember, none of them ever were.

When our supervisor was asked why we didn't put these sad manuscripts in the burn pile, he said, "These are human lives we're handling. A lot of these people didn't start out crazy. They had hopes and dreams just like the rest of us, and these books are all that's left of them in this world."

I don't know how he reconciled his preservation of these journals with his almost religious passion for destroying letters full of affection. I suppose he thought that anyone who wills a manuscript to a library does want other people to consider it a book, one to be read, no matter how embarrassing or inarticulate.

I've been thinking about my old work-study supervisor in these waning days of summer. He had an inherent respect for most human beings, a quality that makes him stand out in memory. He made work-study jobs into tiny lessons in ethics, as when he would lecture us about what it meant to have closed stacks.

Because of book thefts by people who made a living selling library books to collectors, the stacks of Widener were not open to everybody. Faculty could go in, major donors could go in, administrators could go in, but teaching assistants, the people who really needed access to research their PhD theses, were barred. They were forced to hand call numbers to work-study students.

We would then go back into the stacks and search through the shelves until we found the requested book. If it was mis-shelved, we returned without it and said it wasn't where it should be. People who had waited patiently for an hour left empty-handed, sometimes in tears. One of my co-workers made the mistake of making fun of one of them, a young woman who, when she didn't get the book she had ordered, had screamed at him, called him an asshole, and stomped out of the building.

"These are people under terrible pressure," my supervisor told us.

"For less than minimum wage, they're teaching ignorant and arrogant little shits just like yourselves, and all the while trying to write a book that will someday get them a tenured position in a university. They're humiliated by the system, and broke, and living in tiny overpriced apartments in failing marriages, and their PhD committees are full of professors who hate them because those professors were once grad students too, and when they were, they hated themselves."

"How do you know all that?" one of my co-workers asked.

"Never mind," said our supervisor. "Just don't keep them waiting any longer than necessary. Be nice to them. If you can't find the book, look around. It will generally be within eight or ten feet."

Over time, I got good at finding mis-shelved books. And if I spent a couple of minutes talking to the grad students who had requested the books I would search for, I could generally find another book they also really wanted but didn't know it. They were appallingly grateful.

Only in my maturity have I realized that had I looked more carefully at those packages from the asylums, I might have found PhD theses that didn't pass their committees, ones that veered from astronomy to astrology mid-chapter, ones that revealed continental drift to be a Zionist Plot, ones that in the end exposed the New Testament and Shakespeare as commie conspiracies.

Come to think of it, some of those packages from the asylums probably contained PhD theses that did pass. You can have hopes and dreams on one hand, and you can have hopes and dreams and depart-ment meetings on the other. The last three are a tragic combination, and if you encounter them in the wrong sequence, you can end up checking yourself into an institution, if you can find one.

I don't know how my journal will be read in a few hundred or a few thousand years. Defoe seems a little dated, although he's not any-where near as dated as he was a year ago. The Great Plague and Fire of London aren't as far in the past as they were a year ago, either.

For some time, I've assumed that if an educated Roman, circa 410 C.E., had kept a journal of day-to-day life in Rome, that journal would be a valuable historical document now, mainly because Rome fell in

410 C.E. But as far as we know, educated Romans weren't thinking they were living in a period of any import. Rome was the Eternal City, and its destruction was inconceivable to them, no matter who was emperor.

The fall of industrial civilization isn't inconceivable to me, so I'm thinking if I can finish an additional 26 journal entries and somehow preserve them for 2,000 years, I will have written a valuable historical document. The only problem I can see is there may be no historians to read it, or the historians who have survived will have forgotten how to read and are instead chanting oral tradition sagas around coal fires in the cool-enough-to-live parts of Antarctica.

It's small comfort that I can write the paragraph above and not be sent packing to an insane asylum. Primarily because since the Reagan Administration, we don't have many insane asylums. But also, most Americans don't have the sort of faith in their culture that the late Romans had in theirs. It's pretty clear that divisive social movements, or climate change, or a new pandemic, or a crazed leader with a finger on the nuclear button will bring an end to the America we learned about in high school civics classes.

I'm sorry, but I have a gloomy sanity about all these things. If writing another six months of journal entries drives me a little crazy, I'll give even odds that I'll still be substantially more sane than the person who occupies the Oval Office next spring.

A confession: I have spent a great deal of my life in institutions full of insane people. I taught writing in colleges and universities to young people who were trying to make sense of their lives, alongside older people who had long before been driven over the edge by their PhD committees or by the ordeal of assembling exhaustive tenure applications.

I like to think that the skills I imparted to my students helped, and that having their thoughts down on paper, in black and white, helped them to see the real world more clearly—and for that matter, to believe there was such a thing as a real world, and that they shouldn't attempt a PhD if they wanted to stay in it.

Joan Didion said, "I write entirely to find out what I'm thinking." As near as I can tell, that's true of all of us who write. I hope some of my old students are still writing so they know what they're thinking. I hope what they're thinking is mostly in touch with the real.

What comes to mind now is an unfortunate routine we had at the circulation desk in Widener, back in the day. It may be the passage of time or just the headlines in the *New York Times* this morning, but that routine has somehow achieved the status of parable.

The circulation desk was three stories above ground on Three East, as I remember, and it was the only unalarmed entrance/exit from the stacks. People who could roam the stacks freely due to a trusted status were numbered in the thousands, and the vetting process had missed a few bad ones, or ones who had turned pure evil upon being awarded tenure. (It happens.)

The sector most distant from circulation was seven stories below us, the basement level of D West. Rumor had it that it was the home of the Cthulhu Collection, but it was also where obscure rare books were stored because it was temperature- and humidity-stable. We didn't go down there a lot, and when we did it was via the stairs because we didn't trust the elevator. It was lit by 25-watt bulbs, and usually one or two of them were burned out in each aisle between the ceiling-high shelves.

The bad people weren't book thieves. Instead, when some screaming assistant professor came running out of the stacks into the heat and light of the circulation department, it was because she had looked down one of those dark aisles in D West and had seen some guy standing there, giggling and mewing, wearing nothing but shoes and socks and a long trench coat spread wide.

We work-study students mobilized with sword-like newspaper holders, a blanket to wrap the guy in, flashlights and a book cart (you could turn the shelves into a prison with one of those parked against the mouth of an aisle). We'd charge into the stacks, run around to the West Wing, send the book cart down in the elevator, and rush down the stairs until we reached D Level.

If we found the guy—rarely, because most times he had disappeared into a nook or cranny we had only heard about and were never sure existed—we'd trap him with the book cart, wrap him in the blanket, escort him up and out of the building, and take away his library card. It was the happiest ending we could think of.

Satan's Carnival

September 21, 2020

DURING THIS EVER-DARKENING month of September, Ray Bradbury's 1962 novel, *Something Wicked This Way Comes,* has been much on my mind. It's about a small Midwestern community where nothing much happens until the day a demonic carnival comes to town. What looks like much needed entertainment—fortunetellers, clowns, freaks, a hall of mirrors, a merry-go-round—are really ways of stealing human souls.

Mr. Dark, the tattooed carnival owner, uses the shadowy desires of the townspeople to bring them under his control. He promises them what they most want—as much of it as they want, and then some—and their own desires make them monstrous. Then their souls slip from their bodies, and are quickly trapped in the tattooed illustrations that cover Mr. Dark's body. Those tattoos become portraits of agony.

Mr. Dark is not a nice guy, but in his defense, he's only trying to give people what they, in their hearts, really want. It's not his fault if they don't know when to stop.

What my heart wants right now is some clear blue sky. We have now had 10 straight days—at least—of haze and smoke. We can see the shape of Mt. Heyburn if we peer hard at it, but it shifts in and out of focus. Clouds of dark gray air move slowly through the trees across the river. It seems only a matter of time before the air itself grows brittle and falls to the ground as dust.

The sun has turned into a red dwarf. It's been below freezing in the mornings, which is a good thing, because not all the smoke in our valley is from out of state. A forest fire is burning 10 miles out Highway 21 from Stanley. Thus far it's burned about 500 acres. The prevailing wind has blown the flames away from town, and the smoke-lowered temperatures knock the fire down every night.

If the fire had started in the same place two weeks earlier, when the temperature was in the 90s and the wind was blowing from the northwest at 40 mph, Julie and I would have been packing suitcases and loading the pickup with photo albums, hard drives, and camping gear. We'd be getting ready to be homeless, which is still better than being dead.

The asterisk that comes with this statement is that to get to us, the fire would have had to come through Stanley Lake campgrounds, and the Iron Creek and Valley Creek subdivisions, and Stanley, and the Redfish Lake Lodge and campgrounds. If it had come that far, we would not just lack a home, we'd be overwhelmed by the tragedy of others. I don't know if I'm yet at the age where if I lost my home, I'd lose my mind to grief, but I'm definitely at the age where I might lose my mind to other people's grief.

I loaned out my copy of *Something Wicked* a decade ago, and probably told whomever I loaned it to not to give it back. I had realized I could never live long enough to read all the books left in my library, even the ones I needed to read for self-improvement.

I am aware of the implications of that statement. My capacity for self-improvement falls short of my need for self-improvement. I'll die a work in progress and be condemned to a few thousand less happy incarnations, a cautionary example to all good Buddhists.

Here, take this self-improvement book. It's an as-new copy of Thomas Mann's *Death in Venice,* published in 1911. Some of the pages haven't even been cut. It will tell you how to act your age and behave yourself in company. You might get further along in it than I did.

A small dark carnival came to our valley last week. Donald Trump Jr. and Kimberly Guilfoyle were at a Trump fundraising dinner at one of the new large houses in the upper valley. A place at the table cost $2,800, which isn't much for a Trump fundraiser, but I assume the invited guests found myriad ways to pad the bill.

The view wasn't good. Visibility was down to a mile, which meant the Sawtooths might just as well have been on Mars. Jr. and Kimberly flew by helicopter to the Smiley Creek Airport, so they didn't go by our house. They stopped long enough to get their photo taken with the folks waiting to meet them there. A few of them were willing to wear Trump masks and carry Trump 2020 signs and mug for the cameras. One woman asked if she could pray for a Trump victory. Then they got back in the helicopter and headed for dinner.

In the photo of the airport event that appeared in the Idaho Mountain Express, Ketchum's newspaper, Jr. is fist-bumping a toddler carrying an American flag. Kimberly is looking unhappy in a demure black dress, probably because she flew over Sun Valley but didn't get to stay in Sun Valley.

By the time the helicopter got to the fundraising dinner, a demonstration had formed on Highway 75. Twenty-five or thirty people were out on the road with Black Lives Matter and Biden signs. Passing drivers honked in support of the demonstrators. The dinner, I understand, wasn't as well attended as the demonstration, but a lot of times, these things succeed or fail depending on the weather.

In *Something Wicked This Way Comes*, Mr. Dark's carnival is welcomed to town. He offers respite from the boredom of everyday life. Once his victims have wandered through his hall of mirrors, they have a vision of what life would have been like had it turned out less tedious and exhausting. Two 14-year-old boys, the narrative characters of the novel, try to tell the town that it's all illusion, but nobody believes them. The adults would rather be told they're not trapped in their lives, they're not doomed to marinate in memories of old humiliations, and they don't have to live with their mistakes.

The Ur-lie that gives rise to all these lesser lies is that actions don't have consequences. All the middle-aged characters in the book have realized they have to live with their choices, and they don't want to. They regret marrying the people they married and regret not marrying the people they didn't. They've learned to hate the routines of their lives. They hate what they see in the bathroom mirror, and they hurry to inspect themselves in the funhouse, looking in its distortions for something better.

Mr. Dark has no power over happy people, or even sad people who take responsibility for their actions. He gathers in the souls of the finger-pointers, the stunted, the regretful, the lazy, the evasive, the vengeful, the cowardly. That's most of us, at the weak times in our lives. The problem is that Mr. Dark will try to weaken you further at these moments, so you'll never recover the soul you have lost.

I haven't had a lot of luck convincing people they have souls. We live in a secular age, one wedded to scientific materialism. If you tell people they'd better straighten up and start living right or their souls will get reincarnated as cockroaches, they'll just laugh at you. If you say their money will buy them a one-way ticket to hell, where their souls will scream for eternity in a lake of fire, they'll keep laughing. If you tell them their soul will end up as a grimacing tattoo on Mr. Dark's hide, they'll tell you they're not afraid of Mr. Dark or his hide. "Sometimes a tattoo is just a tattoo," they'll say.

But I believe people have souls, and that their souls urge a more or less constant progression toward a conscious existence. I think souls are the reason you buy all those self-improvement books and the ones about the dangerous shadow side of human nature.

I think souls are present in any moment of conscience. I think they're the reason you say, "There but for the grace of God go I," and then try to help the person you said it about.

Also, I think souls can get pissed off and just up and leave when people indulge in their worst impulses, such as when they line up for tickets for Satan's carnival.

That's why there are so many soulless people running around: they pissed off their souls, their souls left them, and they've been floundering around in unenlightened self-interest ever since.

The advantage to not having a soul is that you'll make more money. The disadvantage is that nothing you spend it on will satisfy you.

I don't believe these things because I read about them in the Bible. I read about them in books on theoretical physics, where I have learned that a reasonable facsimile of eternity exists, but time doesn't. Regular Matter doesn't really exist. Dark Matter does, and it may be the stuff of souls. Reality is looking more and more like a computer program with a perverse sensibility. New universes are created every time you open a take-out menu and choose an item you've never had before. Because you choose these universes into being, you are a dozen people, or a million, some with souls, some without.

We may be getting a little far into theology for an end-of-the-world blog, or too far into theoretical physics, but I don't think so. The end of the world brings up the question of what happens if people don't blink out like a turned-off lightbulb. That's not a question even theoretical physics can answer. I admit that even when I threaten people with reincarnation, I have little memory of having been there and done that.

I am certain it would be a better world if people believed they do have souls, and that those souls will spend eternity thinking about their little sins and their big ones—in other words, suffer the tortures that give rise to all of hell's metaphors.

You don't have to die to be tortured, either. Look at the British painter Francis Bacon's *Screaming Popes,* his series of soul portraits of the outwardly confident and autocratic and very much alive Pope Innocent X. The Pope occupies the psychological equivalent of a lake of fire, and he demonstrates how people can become inhuman while still appearing to be human.

Pope Innocent wouldn't have been happy had he seen any of Bacon's 20th century portraits of him, but the 17th century Church— the 17th century, period—would have been better for it.

If we could convince Donald Trump, and Bill Barr, and Mitch McConnell that they have souls, and that those souls will be agonizing over questions of conscience long after Washington, D.C. becomes seafloor, we would all be better for it.

*

In case you're wondering, I don't think Donald J. Trump or Don Jr. is Mr. Dark. I don't think Kimberly Guilfoyle is Lola from *Damn Yankees*, either, although she looks a lot like I imagine Lola looks.

I'm more or less certain that Mr. Dark is just a part of every human heart, one deeply opposed to our souls and capable of exiling or destroying them. If the Trump extended family comes across as a carnival of evil, that's because the family has disappeared all its souls, in an effort to disappear its pain.

Now they're all trying to pretend there's nothing missing in their lives. But something is missing, and the only thing they have to replace it with is money. But there's never enough. There never will be enough.

They're freaks in the worst kind of freak show, looking out at a world of people poorer and less powerful—but infinitely more human—than themselves.

No wonder they don't like us. No wonder they don't have any pity for anyone but themselves. No wonder they construct a social order that punishes poverty and powerlessness with death. No wonder they work tirelessly to increase the amount of grief in the world.

It makes the absence of their souls seem not quite so bad.

A Dark Wood

September 28, 2020

IT RAINED LAST night, big time. I woke up at three a.m. to the sound of water hitting our house's metal roof, pouring off the eaves and splashing onto the deck. It was a blissful awakening, even at that hour, because it meant the effective end of our 2020 fire season. We had made it through a risky summer of too many tourists and too many new campsites established in dry grass and brush.

The fire 10 miles out Highway 21 from Stanley is in the mop-up stages. Human-caused, it burned 2,300 acres over five days and turned both sides of the highway into vistas of bare black lodgepole trunks. Julie and I drove out to see the damage, in part because we had cut firewood there earlier in the summer.

We should have cut more. Everyone who was cutting firewood should have cut more, because all the dead and dry trees had burned up, and they had kept the fire expanding faster and further than it would have if they had earlier been carted off to a winter woodpile.

The Forest Service is in the awkward position of having to treat dead trees as forest resources when in fact they're sitting on thousands of acres of unexploded bombs. Decades of putting out fires means the fuel that's built up, when it does catch fire, burns so hot it sterilizes the soil. Cheat grass and other invasive species colonize the burned areas.

A climate that's getting warmer, precipitation that comes all at once on the rare occasions it does come, and policies that focus on managing increasing numbers of tourists rather than resources all mean the Sawtooth National Recreation Area will burn and keep burning as long as there are dense, deadwood-rich forests inside its perimeter. Once it does burn, it leaves viewsheds of rock and sand backgrounded by smoke-dimmed dry mountains.

The scar of a decade-old human-caused fire, across from where Fourth of July Creek hits the Salmon River, now exists as a barren heat island: 300 acres of black and white trunks occupying a bare landscape of granite and decomposed granite sand, one where new trees will not grow, and where the winter's snow leaves a month early. It's an ugly sight: barren, monochrome, and life-poor, compared to what it was before it burned.

This morning's air is cold and clear. Clouds remain in the sky from last night's storm, and the fogbank that forms over Redfish Lake on fall mornings has kept us from seeing Heyburn and Braxon Peaks. To the south, we can see mountains with snow on them. Now and then unfiltered sunlight hits us, and its warmth is unexpected and welcome.

The morning's news is about the nomination of the conservative Amy Coney Barrett to replace Ruth Bader Ginsburg, and about Donald Trump's insistence that if he loses the election, it will be because of Deep State fraud. The right-wing Proud Boys are demonstrating in Portland, along with left-wing counter-demonstrators. Brain-eating amoebas are in a Texas city's water supply.

Also, Idaho's Covid-19 one-day cases have hit 601, close to the record. Boise State's athletic department is focusing on mental health issues of its athletes due to "the uncertainty of sports during a pandemic." That uncertainty has increased this morning, with the news that BSU will have a football season after all, subject to the players in its league staying healthy, a couple of state quarantines being lifted, and no superspreading events resulting from tailgate parties.

Uncertainty in sports or anything else can't compete with the beauty of the world this morning and the joy that Julie and I find in being alive in it for one more day.

If beauty in the world is one of the things that keeps us sane, it occurs to me that we shouldn't keep setting our forests on fire.

*

Last Sunday we parked our car at the backcountry lot at Redfish Lake, hoisted our packs on our backs, and started walking up the Fishhook Creek Trail. The trail ends in a mass of deadfall at the wilderness boundary. The microclimate downwind from Thompson and Horstmann Peaks has produced a rainforest along the creek, an oasis in the Idaho desert.

We kept going, stepping over logs and wading through alders, avoiding the boggy spots where we could, all the way to where the canyon walls get vertical. It's only three or four miles on the map, but it's longer on the ground.

In places the deadfall was so thick we had to backtrack and try a different route. In other places we climbed up steep hillsides, only to find ourselves high above the game trail we were trying to follow. We ended up doing a couple of miles on steep and shifting talus slopes, side-hilling through dwarf aspen and avalanche debris. Fatigue became a factor. Knees and ankles became factors. We started thinking about things in our packs we probably could have left at home.

It was a six-hour slog to our destination, a lake with beaches of glacially-polished rock in a high hanging valley. We set up the tent in a place where the soil was deep enough to hold tent stakes, rolled out our pads and sleeping bags, and cooked a quick dinner. We were asleep by nine. Ten hours later it was light again. Julie got up and made coffee, and I, awakened by the smell of it, put on enough warm clothes that I could leave the tent, stumble over to our kitchen site, and beg a cup from her.

By the second cup, the sun was hitting our campsite, and the temperature was finally above freezing. Mist drifted across the lake. A meadow glowed red, green and orange on the far shore. Above the meadow, a jumble of glinting talus, and the high sunlit cliffs of the northern horizon. Above the cliffs, a cloudless dark blue sky.

Counting backtracks and circles, we covered the distance of a marathon on our trek, although it took us three days rather than three hours. Once we got beyond maintained trails, we saw no other people or evidence of people.

In spite of this summer's huge increase of visitors to the valley, the high backcountry has stayed mostly intact. The mountain meadows still held enough water to stay spring-like all summer long.

It's a delicate biosphere up there, but it's a biosphere that still looks much as it did a century ago.

That's not true of Sawtooth and Goat Lakes, or Alpine Lake above Redfish, or Hell Roaring Lake, or Cabin Creek Lakes. All these have become sacrifice areas, places so impacted by human presence that they've become human artifacts.

At Saddleback Lakes, an easy day hike from the shuttle boat dock at the end of Redfish, the lack of an official trail has resulted in a kind of stock driveway, a beaten path 50 feet wide. The same thing has happened on the way to Goat Lake above Stanley. At some point it becomes less damaging to the wild to construct a real trail, even if it means blasting one out of solid rock.

We passed by Alpine Lake on our way down to the Redfish Creek Trail and the shuttle dock. It was going to be our lunch spot, but the lakeside logs had been polished by too many butts, and the forest floor was a barren stretch of lifeless dirt all the way to the edge of the lake. A few years ago, the Forest Service attempted to get green things growing there again by fencing off overused campsites with crime-scene tape. Now the tape was gone, but despite fires being banned on the lakeshore, the crime scene remained.

We reached the shuttle dock at three p.m. Seventeen people were waiting before us, and when the Lodge pontoon boat arrived, we packed it to capacity. After three days on foot, it felt good to stand on a boat deck and watch the world go by, courtesy of an internal-combustion engine. But it also felt a little like living in an oxymoron, being packed on a boat with other masked nature-seekers, headed for a car in a wilderness parking lot, in a once-unspoiled valley now filled with giant houses, recreational vehicles, motels and hotels and a 300-person fire camp. Sawtooth Valley has become a great human swarm, mostly caused by people trying to escape the even greater human swarms of cities and suburbs.

Coming back into a human swarm of any size was a shock. I walked the quarter mile to the wilderness parking lot, got our car and drove it to the Lodge parking lot, and happily found a parking spot next to our backpacks. Julie had ordered margaritas from the bar.

We sat at one of the outdoor tables long enough to drink them, but it was hard to relax. Being out in the wild might have been good for our sanity, but when we looked at our fellow humans, it was hard to see them as benign creatures. They didn't look entirely stable to us, and they looked enough like us that the resemblance was disturbing.

These were people who were deeply damaging the natural world they depended on for food and oxygen and mental health. Julie and I, for all our low-impact camping, had arrived at the trailhead by means of our own internal combustion engine, pumping greenhouse gases into the biosphere. Besides, if you counted the environmental cost of our packs and sleeping pads and stove and freeze-dried food and down-filled bags, Kindle and phone and emergency first-aid supplies, our camping wasn't low-impact.

We were just as crazy as everybody else. At least we didn't have kids.

A few radical thinkers have suggested that civilization itself is a psychosis, and that if you're sane, you better not act that way or you'll end up in a locked ward supervised by Nurse Ratched. Listening to the election news on NPR on our way home from Redfish didn't do much to contradict that suggestion. Three days of wandering through terrain unmarked by humans had shown us that it's not easy to leave civilization or its mindset. It takes effort, and, at my age, pain, to get to a place where there's some kind of bedrock to reality, even if the human touch reduces it to—well—bedrock.

Season's End

THE SAWTOOTH NATIONAL RECREATION AREA held a volunteer cleanup event the last two weeks. Julie and I signed up to pick up trash left behind in the undeveloped campsites in the valley. These are places where people can park a trailer or pitch a tent on National Forest land and not have to pay. They can stay for a couple of weeks, and many of them stay even longer. All summer our landscape has been dotted with tents, trailers, campers, and motorhomes, some of them out in the middle of sagebrush flats, some of them tucked away up creeks and gulches.

It's safe to say the Forest Service has a growing problem (in addition to the problem of having to rely on volunteer labor for essential maintenance), as more and more people purchase RVs, and more and more people retire or become unemployed, and more and more people are untied from the school year due to the pandemic. For the poor, camping is a decent alternative to being homeless or sharing too small spaces with too many family members. For the construction workers on the new big houses in the valley, camping is a good way not to pay rent, assuming they could even find a rental to pay for. For the wealthy, whose motorhomes appear towing new Range Rovers—and behind the Range Rovers, boats or trailers full of 4-wheelers—the informal camping sites offer them space for their toys and arenas in which to use them.

So far this week, Julie and I have cleaned 34 campsites, if you count campsites by the number of fire rings we've taken apart and raked level. We've found fire rings built up against dry trees, in the middle of thick sagebrush, in thickets at the base of heavily timbered slopes. We've found broken lawn chairs, torn sleeping pads, stove tops, tent poles, tent flies, tent stakes, and tents. We've found new 4-wheeler trails up steep hillsides. We've picked up smashed beer cans, beer cans pushed down squirrel holes, beer cans with frost- and fire-swollen tops, beer cans full of bullet holes, and half-melted beer cans in the fire pits. We've found—and left undisturbed—mounds of unmistakably human shit.

We await the advent of cholera. We await the outbreak of shit-flinging class warfare between the tent-dwellers and the motor-home dwellers. We await the moment when the Forest Service finally lives up to its responsibilities and becomes the central Idaho distributor for Porta-Potties.

Last week's news, should you accept it as having some relationship, however oblique, to the truth: Donald and Melania Trump have Covid-19. Trump has had enough trouble with his oxygen levels that he's in Walter Reed.

Also, a recording has surfaced of Melania cursing Christmas and the donkey it rode in on.

Also, Donald Trump's decompensation in last Tuesday's debate has hurt him in the polls.

Also, David Brooks, for decades a reliable dispenser of Edmund Burke's conservative platitudes, has redefined conservatism to exclude Trumpism. Brooks's commentariat (which he claims not to read) takes him to task every week for being a smiling, deliberately obtuse brand of conservative that is willfully blind to the recessive line of descent that reaches from Ronald Reagan to Newt Gingrich to George W. Bush to Donald Trump.

Contrary to what you might think, our volunteer camp-cleaning exercise has not destroyed our faith in the human animal (although it has reinforced our faith that humans *are* animals). In most of the campsites we visited, people had made an attempt to clean up after themselves. Most of the firepits were not filled with melted beer cans and aluminum foil. Most of the campsite perimeters were not littered with garbage (although Julie found a rotting pound of bacon that caused her to hold her garbage bag out the window as we drove away from the Iron Creek Transfer Camp, looking for a dumpster). We found places where people had dug holes and buried their shit and toilet paper, which gave us hope that they would use Porta-Potties if Porta-Potties were available.

It suggests that humans can be educated to take care of their camping spots, and that most people will do the right thing if given the chance. So far the Forest Service has not put much effort into education, choosing instead to enforce regulations on where people can cut firewood, or harassing people who park along the No Parking signs on Redfish Lake Road, or waking up people at three a.m. in their tents, telling them to move on to another National Forest. These incidents have been part of the Forest Service's transformation from a service agency to an armed enforcement agency, and its change in management style from friendly requests to intimidation.

The worst incident of the week came when Julie and I passed by a camp that had been there a month, far in excess of the time limit. Whoever was there was also cutting firewood—there was a trailer containing a cord or so of cut and split blocks next to a pop-up tent and a fair amount of camp furniture. We could hear a boom box playing rap music.

We didn't go near it—we observe a strict don't-bother-the-tourists policy, figuring they don't come to Sawtooth Valley to be around the locals, especially if the locals have caught Covid-19 from last week's tourists. (This is not always the case. In past summers, lonely people have invited us into their RVs, showing us well-organized miniature kitchens, with miniature utensils and miniature pots and pans, every-thing in its place. These folks were widows and widowers mostly, and the RVs had been furnished with plans and dreams for two.)

When we started cleaning the empty campsites next to the long-occupied one, a woman came over and said hello. I asked her if they'd had any trouble from the Forest Service for staying too long or cutting firewood without a permit. "They're meaner than hell about those things," I told her.

She said she hadn't been camped there. She was just visiting a friend, who was leaving the next day. She grew visibly anxious, and I realized that she had seen us, with shovels, rakes, a wheelbarrow and a white pickup, as enforcers of government regulations. She immediately went back to her friend's camp, and they started packing up. That night they were gone. I hoped they hadn't been stopped and fined for cutting firewood without a permit.

It does not do your peace of mind much good to dwell upon what it's like to camp in Sawtooth Valley and then have someone threaten you with a police action, especially if you were the someone doing the threatening, however benign your intentions.

They left their camp a mess. I assume they thought we would clean it up for them, and we did. I've been feeling bad about the whole thing ever since.

Benign intentions almost always have unintended consequences. When my mother was in middle-stage Alzheimer's, she grew confused about what day it was. She had been a churchgoer, at least in the summers, when the Sawtooth Meditation Chapel held Sunday non-denominational services. Julie, because she could play piano, had been drafted to accompany the hymns, and she would stop at my mother's house and take her to church every Sunday.

A Baptist minister had come to town and was looking for parishioners for a church he was running in an abandoned motel. Someone had told him my mother lived alone and had a soul that needed saving. One Thursday afternoon we found my mother in her house, dressed in her Sunday best, waiting for her ride to church, frightened and confused. The minister had told her he'd be by to take her to his church—on Sunday, not Thursday. My mother wanted to know what had gone wrong to cause Julie not to take her any longer, and why church was no longer held in the morning.

We did our best to explain things, and both Julie and I were waiting when the minister and his wife showed up at my mother's door the next Sunday. We explained the situation to the minister and told him my mother had her own church to go to, and that it was a bad thing to further confuse an Alzheimer's victim, whether or not her soul was in the balance. "We're trying to keep her in her own house as long as possible," I said. "It scares her if you change what she's used to."

"We were just trying to help," said the minister.

"You weren't helping," I said.

(Since that time, whenever Julie or I do something that really annoys the other, we say, "*I was just trying to help*." Sometimes it works, sometimes it doesn't.)

The local clinic, which was between physician assistants at the time, owned a house for its employees. The minister and his family had rented the house. When a new PA was finally hired, the clinic board told the minister he'd have to leave.

The minister's wife went around Stanley telling everyone who would listen that the spiritual health of the town was far more important than its physical health, but the clinic board held firm to scientific materialism and got them out of the house. Due to Stanley's chronic housing shortage, the minister and his family had to relocate downriver to Challis, which always has outranked Stanley in the need-for-salvation department anyway.

Over the years I've come to think that all human beings have a Baptist minister in their makeup, and he comes out whenever any of us hits on an easy and simple solution to a complex and deadly problem. With the best of intentions, we decide somebody needs help, and we can help them. Instead, we make things worse. We reach beneath the surface of a life, and it's tragic down there. People end up more damaged than we found them, and unless we spend a lot of time trying to figure out why, our best intentions blind us to the harm we've done.

Every time I read a David Brooks column, I decide that's what he's up to. That's the way I look at every new Forest Service attempt to regulate the burgeoning numbers of tourists in Sawtooth Valley. I don't doubt that Donald Trump once really did want to make America great again. I don't doubt that Melania, as a small child, woke up to a beautiful world on Christmas morning, one where every choice was the right one.

*

Deer and elk seasons begin this month. The campgrounds at Redfish and Stanley and Alturas Lakes are mostly closed. It's been getting down to the low 20s in the mornings. Restaurants are getting ready to close for the winter. Traffic on the highway has slowed, mostly because of road hunters scanning the hillsides for targets. Once the shooting starts, the tourists without guns head for home if they've got a home to go back to.

Julie and I will continue our cleanups until the snow covers the campgrounds. Our garage is getting crowded with the broken camping gear and garbage we've picked up, so eventually we'll have to load it all back in the pickup and take it to a Forest Service dumpster. Our good deeds will be over for the year, unless we find someone who really needs our help.

Oh, Happy Ski Day!

October 12, 2020

IT HAS SNOWED. The lawn is white. In the high peaks, it looks like winter. The broad flat top of Braxon Peak has the start of a cornice on its north side. That cornice will grow enough to be there through next July if we have a normal snowy and windy November through March.

Yes, normal requires disclaimers these days.

NOAA's Mauna Loa Global Monitoring Laboratory notes that carbon dioxide levels in the atmosphere hit 417.1 parts per million in May of this year. That's a higher level than at any time in the last four million years, and it means Earth will become a solar oven. Of course, it's already a solar oven, but in its new form it will be much better at cooking.

Four million years ago, Greenland didn't have an ice cap. Indications are that it won't have one again, after another millennium or so. The Maldives and other island nations will likely have been centuries underwater by then, along with about half of Florida and nearly all the coastal cities in the world. Lots of people will have moved to Greenland, if they can move, and if there are people.

Closer to our own time, the Gulf Stream may stop warming Europe any day, and Europe might appreciate that, at least in the summers. Siberia hit 100 F this July, and will again next July, given that more and more of it has turned black due to tundra and taiga fires. Soggy storms, which used to drop snow in the California peaks, will create ashy mudslides this winter instead of 10-foot drifts. Winds reached 140 mph in an Iowa storm, and damaged or destroyed 10 million acres of corn and soybeans.

Not everybody thinks all these are due to changes in atmospheric composition. Climate science has been a contentious business since 1896, when the Swedish physicist Svante Arrhenius first postulated an atmospheric greenhouse effect. There have always been climate deniers, because climate science is full of apparent disconnects between cause and effect. It's hard to set parameters for a climate experiment, and anyway, when the experiment is called industrial civilization, every bit of data it yields is subject to interpretation by one interest group or another.

Computer models work well when you have a fixed amount of agreed-upon variables, not so well when you're arguing whether to include a bunch of them, and a bunch of others are going through phase changes, and there's a bunch yet of others you forgot to include in your last model, and a small bunch of unexpected interactions between phenomena you didn't expect to interact.

Carbon dioxide isn't the only thing warming the planet. Methane, nitrous oxide, chlorofluorocarbons, and water vapor are in the picture along with ocean heat absorption, water-column layering, and the explosive sublimation of giant methane clathrate deposits.

Add variations in solar output, El Niño/La Niña fluctuations, changes in cloud patterns, loss of seasonal snow cover, heat islands, volcanic eruptions, rooftop/blacktop deserts, and gamma rays generated by too-close supernovas (within a thousand light years or so), and it's hard to write the supercomputer program that will let you know if you'll be skiing this winter or next.

Still, in a few more weeks I'll be sharpening and waxing our skis, pulling our ski boots out of the crawl space and emptying my ski pack onto the kitchen table so I can throw it in the washer and go down a dog-eared checklist of its contents.

Every year our equipment gets a little more obsolete, but we haven't worn it out yet and, according to well-established muscle memory, it works just as well as the newer stuff.

The newer stuff is lighter. I have a friend who skis on new alpine touring equipment, and one of my telemark boots and one of my skis weighs the same as both of his boots and skis.

My ski pack is also heavy. It will contain a snow shovel, first aid kit, emergency mylar blankets, an extra pair of climbing skins, bungee cords, tools and headlights. Also candles and matches in case a fire is needed. Extra clothes. Extra energy bars. Extra chocolate-covered espresso beans. Sunscreen and water. A small piece of foam insulation to sit on. A radio and avalanche beacon.

Much of this equipment is on the list because it will allow a night out in below-zero weather if you get injured miles from a road, on steep and timbered slopes. Use it and you'll be uncomfortable, but you'll live long enough to see daylight, and possibly a helicopter. Possibly a snowmobile. If the slope isn't too steep or the timber too thick, you might get back to civilization in a heavy plastic sled, with a blanket and straps to keep you from falling out, and a tow rope to go forward and a tail-rope to keep your downhill speed from getting lethal. You will need friends at both ends.

You don't want to spend two nights out, not at below zero. That's one reason it's considered foolish to go skiing alone. Even when you've told someone where you're going, you can make a wrong turn and head down the wrong drainage. You can get caught in an avalanche or fall into a tree well or hit a tree with your head, and it might take more than a day to find you. You could die of the cold if you didn't die of those other things.

You don't want to be one of the people who die out there. People will say you died doing what you loved. That will not be true if you remain conscious all the way to the end.

Skiing is good exercise. When I've put on ski clothes, boots, skis, skins, poles, and the pack, I've gone from 180 to 225 pounds. On a good long ski day, I'll move those 225 pounds up and down 2,500 or 3,000 feet. It's cheaper than joining a gym.

Apparent disconnects are everywhere. There's a big one between the macrocosm—which includes droughts and hurricanes, uncontrollable fires, a pandemic, presidential politics, and climate refugees—and the microcosm, which this morning includes Julie and I and our ski equipment, the new snow on the lawn and our breakfast of sourdough pancakes, maple syrup, and bacon that she's just put on the table.

The microcosm includes a look at the top of Braxon Peak, which was bare yesterday and today looks skiable. There's a ski route down from the top, if I remember correctly, that starts down the bowl between the peak and the Rotten Monolith, continues down the steep slope above Monolith Lake, climbs back up to the ridge above the fifth Bench Lake, and continues from there down the Bench chain to the trail that leads to Redfish Lake Lodge. The last time I skied it was in April of 1975, alone. The nights of that long-ago month were still flirting with below-zero temperatures, but I wasn't of an age where caution was a factor in my thinking. It's a wonder I'm not still out there.

Caution has made the microcosm smaller since 1975. If the coming November brings snow deep enough to keep our skis off the rocks, Julie and I will put a track on an old logging road that winds up a nearby canyon. It's a climb of 500 vertical feet over a couple of miles, and you can get up to cruising speed coming back down if you stay in your tracks. Leave your tracks, and the slope is gentle enough that you'll slowly come to a stop in shin-high powder.

If and when we get a few good storms, we'll ski the hill across the road. It's steep. You have to watch the snow conditions. When there's avalanche danger, we ski the trees or stick close to the ridges coming down.

Usually we're skiing there by the middle of December, although I remember one year when it snowed 30 inches on dry ground over Thanksgiving weekend. The snowpack was stable. Just like that, we were skiing anywhere and everywhere we wanted.

The morning's news reveals that more people are dying from heat and drought. Wars are being fought over water. Refugees are massing on the borders of countries where it still rains. Thousands of homes in California have burned. Coastal communities in Louisiana have been wrecked by hurricanes. But the amount of misery that the climate is inflicting is small compared to the amount it will inflict in the next decade.

*

Over the last 25 years, Julie and I have tried to hunker down in a place where the catastrophes are survivable, and where misery can be balanced against joy. We've tried to live in a temporal microcosm—the present—which is way more survivable than the future.

We've done this more or less consciously, preferring to face problems that might yield to human will. When we need a winter's woodpile, I can sharpen the chainsaw and put it and a couple of axes in the pickup, and after a bunch of trips to the woods and a bunch of days chopping wood, we will have wood cut and stacked under the eaves. When our pantry starts looking like Mother Hubbard's, we can get in the car with our stimulus checks and come home with three months' worth of groceries.

When we get bored and start bouncing off the walls, we can walk out the door and ski for a day. But when we make plans, we make them for a day or two at the most. We know the greater universe—its climate, its politics, its megafires, its supernovas—could come crashing into our lives at any moment, and our lives of privilege and agency would be gone forever.

Are there ethical problems to living like this? Probably. Once you've decided that your civilization is on an irreversible path to self-destruction, you're not that far from nihilism. Attempts to find nihilism's shining moral core—Schopenhauer and Nietzsche come to mind—have not ended in greater happiness for humanity, or even for Schopenhauer and Nietzsche.

I do know that splitting firewood for an afternoon feels like a bigger accomplishment than writing a letter to one of Idaho's Republican congressmen explaining that the climate has passed tipping points that will make a return to normal temperatures and weather patterns impossible. I know that going skiing while we still have snow seems like the right thing to do, especially on mornings like this, when the peaks are shining white in the sunlight, the air is free of smoke, and the highway is empty of climate refugees.

Julie and I want our thoughts and our actions to matter, but the world where they do keeps getting smaller and more fragile.

*

I hope it's clear by now that I'm looking forward to skiing. If this year is like past years, I'll have the equipment in good shape for the first day when a foot or more of new powder covers the old logging road. We'll take turns breaking trail up to the end, where a big stand of moth-killed Doug firs stretches bare limbs out to criss-cross the sky. We'll pull the skins off our skis and start back down our track, making narrow little early-season turns whenever we get going too fast.

It will only be the first day of skiing, but it will be a good day, a harbinger of good days to follow, when the snow is deeper, the days are longer, and the turns are bigger, faster, and beyond counting.

Reality Check

October 19, 2020

REALITY HAS TAKEN a hit this October, and not just because of the presidential debate, the Supreme Court hearings, the counter-intuitive rise in the stock markets, the refusal of a substantial portion of Americans to wear masks, coronavirus miracle cures, and the revival of conspiracy theories about pedophilia and child sacrifice by a cabal of top officials in the Democratic Party. It's also because our local campgrounds are full of people with guns. We've been hearing rifle fire in the hills and, on the highway, the roar of diesel pickups pulling fifth wheel trailers. The unreality in which our newest visitors are living involves bloody theater, camo-flavored costumes, postures of dominance, and, if they're successful, some exceptionally expensive protein in their freezers this winter.

Also, I've again been reading R. D. Laing's *The Politics of Experience*, a 1967 collection of essays that details how our civilization—even the parts we see as useful, nice, or loving—inflicts a terrible violence on the people who live in it. By the time we've agreed to get out of bed in the morning, get dressed, go to jobs, get married, raise children and educate them, save money for retirement, buy extended care insurance, and write out wills and advanced care directives, we've pretty much bludgeoned to death the delighted toddlers we all once were, those small awed people who looked upon each sunrise with delight and joy.

Laing says that such violence makes us all crazy, because it forces us to believe in things that don't exist. Social hierarchies are like the Velveteen Rabbit from the Dark Side: they aren't real until they've been marinated in brutality. The same can be said of laws, armed forces, bureaucracies, political parties, industries, service organizations, universities, and even families. When you look at our politics, you see the barely suppressed anger and terror that we willingly live with, if only because we have been told there are bad people in the world, and they mean to hurt us, and everything would be better if they were dead. That's the real world for most people.

It isn't really real.

It wouldn't be so bad if there weren't a *real* real world, and if it didn't bear silent and sad witness to the unreal world we live in.

Laing is not considered a sane thinker at the moment. A number of biochemically oriented psychiatrists have diagnosed his neurotransmitters as seriously defective. He died in 1989, so he can't refute them. Crazy or not, he pointed out that culture constructs the unreal for its own purposes, and those purposes don't often concern themselves with the hopes and dreams of individual human beings.

That notion seemed reasonable enough when I was 18 and faced the prospect of being drafted to fight in Vietnam, and it seems reasonable enough a half-century later, when my life depends on a culturally-constructed Federal Reserve maintaining cultural faith in our culturally-constructed money so my culturally-constructed Social Security checks will buy me something real to eat. The system may have threatened to kill me then and may now be keeping me in groceries, but in either case my well-being or lack of it is beside the point. The point is that the culture can only continue to exist if enough people buy into its fictions rather than believing what they see.

Laing's gift to you and me is a perspective on our world that lets us stand apart from the real and unreal and discern the difference between the two. It may come as a shock, as an 18-year-old, that you're being sent off to die for the nebulous idea of freedom. But if you find yourself huddling in a foxhole because of that idea, it may save your life to know that the foxhole and the bullets whizzing above you possess considerably more reality. You'll keep your head down, for one thing.

*

When I found *The Politics of Experience* on the syllabus of a college writing course in 1969, it didn't change my perceptions all that much. Going from Idaho to the East Coast had been an object lesson in unreality anyway, and I was determined to go to my unreal classes, write my unreal papers, pass my unreal exams (the fact that I had to keep a C average or lose my draft deferment added incentive), get my unreal diploma, and get back to the real world of Idaho as soon as I could.

I kept my head down and behaved myself, but it took dumb luck to save me. On December 1, 1969, a draft lottery was held that superseded student deferments. My number was 117, which was high enough that I wasn't drafted, but it was a close thing. People whose number was 113 were drafted. (113 was Oliver Stone's number. He enlisted rather than being drafted, but anyone who's seen *Platoon* knows that Stone found a world where death and horror didn't exist in the abstract.)

I stayed in school, studying hard and keeping my grades up. I discovered if I stayed away from chemistry and calculus and took a full slate of writing and literature courses, I had no trouble getting As.

In spite of my success in academics, I had no desire to stay in that world. Before they even became possibilities, I rejected jobs and graduate programs that might have kept me in an urban and eastern environment. After my last class, I tried to drive from Boston to Idaho in two long stints, desperate to be home. I ended up exhausted and blind in a hospital in Rock Springs, Wyoming, having abraded my corneas by wearing contact lenses for 26 hours. My vision came back after a day of sleep, but it didn't improve the looks of Rock Springs.

That first summer out of college, I worked as a wilderness ranger in the Iron Creek drainage of the Sawtooths, cleaning campgrounds, clearing trails, and talking to hundreds of people on the trail to Sawtooth and Alpine Lakes. In those conversations, I realized that people in the mountains were following a script. The script was titled We Go Backpacking and Catch a Fish, or We Camp at a High Mountain Lake and Get Rained On, or We Didn't See a Bear but Thank God We Had the .357 Anyway. I tried to teach all of them a new script, titled

Leave the Place Cleaner Than You Found It, but they mostly didn't like it, or they didn't like it as well as We Spent All Night Shooting the .357 at Our Empty Beer Cans, which caused other campers to greet me when I walked into their campsites. In my uniform, I was seen as the manifestation of police power, and people who had been kept up all night by gunfire would enthusiastically act out the Arrest Those Bad People script.

Over time I began to see that the tourists I met in the wilderness were backpacking in stories that kept them from seeing the mountains and the lakes as the wondrous things they were. People saw my role as a guarantor of the Sawtooths as a stage set for pre-recorded material. Their slide shows, their climbing routes, their pack trips all had been previously reduced to the limits of their imaginations.

Who was I to tell anyone to forget their preconceptions and see things as they really were?

I resisted the role of cop, having seen plenty of cops behaving badly when I was a college student. I also didn't want to ruin anyone's day, no matter what they were doing. During my seven summers as a wilderness ranger, I issued warnings but no citations to people on motorcycles in the wilderness, people who were cutting switchbacks, people who had left plastic diapers in firepits, people who were rolling rocks down hillsides into lakes where people were fishing. I told people to cut it out—that was the legal phrase I used, and when they weren't completely devoted to the malformed narrative that had brought them to the mountains in the first place, they did.

I never did figure out what my own role was, beyond Keeping the Place Clean and Helping People When I Could and Trying Not To Piss Off Anyone With a Gun. It was just as well. If I had really gotten into it, I might have ended up as a Career Forest Service Person, which often enough is a drawn-out form of death.

Tourism is a noxious business, one that corrupts the realities of both buyer and seller. Once an experience costs money, effort is devoted to providing less experience at a higher price. Money is devoted to making some experiences more real than others. As crazy as it seems, a decked-out Sprinter van provides a more authentic wilderness experience than just a tent and a backpack, even when the Sprinter van spends a week parked in a wilderness parking lot. A peak that's been climbed a thousand times is less valuable than the peak that's never been climbed, and people spend their lives—literally—trying to find a real first ascent. The first photo taken of Mt. Regan from across Sawtooth Lake is more real—and valuable—than the ten thousandth, and every one of those ten thousand originals is more real than any Twittered or Facebooked copy. The tourist who takes a photo of Brett Wooley's old cabin on the hill below lower Stanley tries hard to find an angle that will miss all the junk Wooley piled around it to discourage the taking of kitschy photographs.

A photo of anything reduces its value. I say this having taken a lot of photos myself. I try not to take the photos a tourist would take, but sometimes the result is the same. What is intended to expand the universe shrinks it.

Gender theorists talk about the Male Gaze, the up and down look from an unselfconscious jerk that objectifies the people it lands on and makes them less real to themselves.

You can see something similar in the Tourist Gaze, and every time a tourist looks at a Sawtooth peak and takes a photo and puts that photo in a slide show, those peaks become a little less themselves and a little bit more someone's failure of imagination.

People see the slide show on the internet. They decide to come to Sawtooth Valley so they can put together a slide show of their own. The photo turns the real into kitsch. The cycle continues, downward, ever downward, until the whole world—if worlds can become self-aware—becomes resigned to its existence as a tawdry stage set.

It was hard for me to look at the tourists who crowded the valley this summer and not think they were fleeing catastrophe. Certainly, catastrophe was out there. The pandemic was beginning to tear at the flimsy fabric of consensus unreality. The president was telling lies about the virus. The economy was showing signs of collapse. Jobs were gone. Schools were closed. People were buying anything that seemed solid, including real estate and Sprinter vans, while their money was still worth something. Fear hung in the air like a wet sneeze.

R. D. Laing: "Only by the most outrageous violation of ourselves have we achieved our capacity to live in relative adjustment to a civilization apparently driven to its own destruction." That was a sentence I underlined 50 years ago, and while my understanding of how a civilization destroys itself has changed considerably since that time, the sentence itself still holds true.

We Don't Dance to *Wild Thing* Any More

October 26, 2020

ON THURSDAY EVENING of last week, Julie and I celebrated my 70th birthday. It was a quieter celebration than we had planned a year ago. It's hard to have a party when you're hunkering down and trying not to catch something.

Julie baked an apple pie, and created a couple of wedge salads, and we split a huge New York steak we had bought at Costco the day before. We tried to split a nice bottle of red, but we ended up full and sleepy before we finished it. Julie gave me a photo book of our many fall trips to Yellowstone. She also gave me a pair of suspenders, which, due to old-man-butt-shrinkage, have finally become necessary to keep my pants up.

We spent the evening (before we got too sleepy to talk) in a conversation that touched on how improbable it was that we were sitting across from each other. I was 38 years old when I taught my first college class as a new professor at the College of Idaho, and that class happened to be Julie's first one as a first-year student. Now we joke that we bonded at first sight. (Like baby ducks, we went for the first thing we saw when we broke out of the shell.)

It may have been more complicated than that. For one thing, at the time I was sure that professors with a modicum of decency didn't end up in romantic relationships with their students. These things do happen in colleges and universities, but they almost never end well, just like psychiatrist-patient romances almost never end well. Several years before, I had bartended in Ketchum in a bar where the only work rules had been to show up on time, do your job, share the cocaine, and don't sleep with your co-workers. The people who broke those rules gradually disappeared from the employee roster. (I didn't have cocaine to share—I had watched it turn too many people into incandescent assholes—but I had noticed that when the people who had it stopped sharing it with their co-workers, their co-workers wouldn't sleep with them anymore.)

Also, I was determined never to get married. At 38, I had pretty well used up my lifetime supply of good luck with women. I was about to give them up for a year or two and see how I did, and I was absolutely certain that I'd do better than I'd been doing.

Also, upon her arrival at college, Julie had joined Campus Crusade for Christ. She was attending hellfire sermons every Sunday and urging her fellow students to dedicate their lives to Christ or else. After spending most of my life as an agnostic, I had become a Christian Existentialist after the manner of Albert Camus, which meant that whatever joy Christianity offered came from hanging on the cross, and not from what, if anything, came after.

(Camus is improbably convincing about finding happiness in the midst of the unbearable, which is why he appeals to those who have finally decided to spend their lives alone.)

It took us a couple years of I-can't-believe-I'm-feeling-this-way craziness, but Julie and I finally confessed to loving each other the spring of her junior year. After a year of covert and anxiety-ridden liaisons, we decided to brazen things out, move in together and see how long we could make it work. That was 28 years ago. We'll celebrate our brazen 25th wedding anniversary in August of 2021. We hope to have more people at that celebration than we had at my birthday party, but if it's just the two of us, we'll still have a surplus of joy.

Spending 28 close years together means that you transform into a person you would have found unrecognizable before you met. Julie is no longer a fundamentalist Christian. I no longer have the lonely, harsh, and when-you're-dead-you're-dead outlook of Camus.

Instead, we have come to a cranky agnosticism, which stems from a series of unanswerable cosmic questions: Why is it, when you've lived long enough to make mistakes and learn from them, when you've become empathetic enough not to go around hurting other people through carelessness and judgment, when you've found somebody to love who loves you back, when life is good, and interesting, and full of things to do—why do you have to die? If you like this life, why do you have to leave it? Why do the people you love have to leave it?

We don't know, and won't know until we die, and I suspect not even then.

Camus, of course, would say worrying about the whys and where-fores of a temporary existence is the worst kind of wasting time. He didn't have a lot of patience with people given to navel-gazing, or who speculated about the motives of a god or gods, or who became so enamored of an idea they'd kill for it.

Life has no meaning, Camus would say, except the meaning you decide to bring to it. Your thoughts don't matter until they become actions. In fact, your actions are the only things that matter in your life, at least until you're dead. Then even they don't mean anything, at least not to you.

Camus called this scheme of things the absurd, and he asserted it is the wispy substance of our lives.

If Camus had an absolute, it was that we should all do our best to make life easier and more dignified for our fellow human beings. It would have been hard to derive that morality from his philosophy, which doesn't provide much distinction between good and evil.

Camus ultimately chose to deal with absurdity by following the Golden Rule, which was fortunate for the people around him, and probably for himself. It is, I'm certain, where the more thoughtful of us end up.

Treating others as you would like to be treated is a sort of moral Second Law of Thermodynamics. It's hard to escape it in the end, no matter your philosophical or religious pretentions, and it makes both treaters and treatees feel better. It certainly has made Julie and me feel better.

When I woke up Thursday, I made the mistake of checking the national headlines, which were all about the threat of a stolen election, the end of constitutional government, and the start of civil war. I then told myself that I would never see my 60s again, which engendered feelings of sadness and loss. I read the obituary columns in the local papers, and recognized some names, which added an acute sense of mortality to the festivities.

On the bright side, I got happy birthday phone calls from friends. I opened a stack of birthday cards, all of which assured me that I wasn't as old as I felt. Julie gave me a birthday kiss and told me I didn't look a bit over 69 and a half. We went for a walk to Goat Creek meadows and back. That afternoon, our friends Tom and Ellen, who are even older than I am and still kicking vigorously, came by for early pie, outside on the deck. It was barely warm enough to sit there. They gave me a T-shirt that announced to the world I was old enough to have heard all the good rock bands. I was also old enough to have heard some pretty lousy rock bands, but I decided there would be a better time to tell them that.

I ended the day feeling almost cheerful. The country and I were going to live, maybe for a year or two longer. I really had seen Jefferson Airplane in concert. I had danced to The Troggs (*Wild Thing*) and Tommy James and the Shondells (*My Baby Does the Hanky Panky*). Not many Millennials can claim those kinds of memories.

Seventy is impossibly old. That's what I've believed my whole life, and for most of that life I've also believed, following Epicurus, that where I was, 70 was not. Where 70 was, I was not. Therefore, I had nothing to fear from 70.

Now of course, 70 and I are occupying the same point in time and space, and I've had to admit that while 70 is old, it isn't impossible, and while it isn't the end of me, it's the end of something.

If my 70th birthday was the end of any chance for fame as a writer, it was always a longshot anyway. Olympic medals or Nobel Peace Prizes or being elected to a school board had disappeared from the radar long before 70 was even a threat. Children? Neither Julie nor I ever wanted any. A vast fortune? Not in this lifetime unless we win the lottery, and we don't buy lottery tickets.

What 70 ends is any lingering insistence that infinite possibilities are still out there. I'm lucky it took me as long as it did to get to that realization.

It's a paradox, but a tremendous freedom comes with your choices becoming fewer and narrower. You start noticing that if you worry about what will happen in 2050, you don't have the energy to properly worry about lunch. At this stage in life, lunch is the more important of the two. You won't be alive in 2050, so worrying about it becomes an exercise in the abstract.

It's amazing how much is in the abstract, once lunch is taken care of.

You resist lifetime memberships because they've suddenly become bad deals. Maintenance and refurbishment, in all arenas, become preferable to new construction. Time becomes like the generous bundles of cash in the campaign fund of a retiring congressperson. It's all yours.

The last few days have been cold in the valley. It was close to zero last night. The sky is a dark blue and the sun will be bright when it gets here, but it will be a while. For the moment, we're in shade and it's too cold to go outside. Julie's put four big pieces of wood in the stove and it's pumping out heat. It feels good. The size of the woodpile suggests we'll make it through the winter.

I've been dreaming a lot. I awaken with vivid and lucid images in my mind, mostly faces. I'm sure it's partly because I've been sleeping way longer than I should, but it's also because I seem to have had stowaways with me all my life, most of them since high school. They seem to have chosen this time of semi-quarantine to announce themselves. They are all 18, not 70, and I am beginning to wonder where they've been hiding. I worry they will eventually start speaking and reveal themselves to be nice people I should have looked up and dated in my 20s.

Maybe the mind releases the faces of your youth when you're strong enough to handle them looking back at you. Maybe the faces themselves are alive, and only when the mind relaxes enough to stop clutching at them do they escape and roam free. Maybe the memories of adolescence bring back an old certainty that anything is possible. It's when your possibilities start shrinking that your dreams, in merciful compensation, recast a wide-open future.

These are thoughts that will lead to grief and loss and regret if I keep worrying away at them. So many things could have been done better or not at all. I know that Albert Camus wouldn't approve of my spending time this way. Attend to the present, he'd say. You really want to make things better? Try not to do anything you'll regret 50 years from now. He'd grin. Little existentialist joke, he'd say.

Good advice, joke or not. Impossible to follow. I'm pretty sure this is what I will spend a good chunk of my 70s thinking about. In the meantime, Julie's face is in front of me. It's real, and it reminds me that I'm not alone, and for the moment, neither is she.

Eve of Destruction

November 2, 2020

ONE OF THE advantages of writing a journal of the plague year in 2020 is that you've got a lot of plagues to choose from. Besides Covid-19, there's the worldwide increase in authoritarians as heads of states, a malaise in our democratic institutions, climate hemorrhagic fever, a widening economic depression, a quick-spreading paranoia not just among conspiracy theorists, and, worst of all, an epidemic of human incompetence.

I haven't ranked them in order of importance. Any one of these plagues could, in a series of imaginable steps, result in human extinction before the end of the decade. If you can't imagine human extinction, I'm here to help you with that.

1. COVID-19

This morning's Johns Hopkins coronavirus map lists 9,220,933 U.S. cases of coronavirus and 231,077 deaths. World numbers tend to err on the low side, but they are listed as 46,688,370 cases and 1,202,605 deaths.

By itself, the coronavirus won't cause human extinction, but a number of its social side effects—job losses, homelessness, mental illness, inequalities of wealth, refugees, nuclear war—could make for a 2030 world without multicellular animals.

2. AUTHORITARIAN LEADERS

Off the top of my news feed, I can name a quick dozen: Erdogan in Turkey, Orbán in Hungary, Assad in Syria, Xi in China, Bolsonaro in Brazil, Duterte in the Philippines, Mohammed bin Salman in Saudi Arabia, Lukashenko in Belarus, El-Sisi in Egypt, Kim Jong Un in North Korea, Putin in Russia, Trump in the U.S. These are all people who have dismantled or are in the process of dismantling any constitutional obstructions to dictatorship. They have or are reaching for the power of life and death over the people they lead.

These people do not end well, because as Lord Acton observed, absolute power corrupts absolutely. A sad personal deterioration results from getting your way all the time. Authoritarians end up as emotional two-year-olds, surrounded by nursemaids who, out of fear of destructive tantrums, carefully control input to the leader's sensorium.

Normally, reality tempers our worst impulses, but in the case of successful authoritarians, reality isn't allowed to temper anything. Saying no to authoritarians becomes a capital offense. Disapproving of them becomes a capital offense. Being out from under their control becomes a capital offense. Being a rival country with aims of its own becomes a capital offense, especially when nuclear weapons are involved.

3. MORBID DEMOCRACY

A partisan U.S. Supreme Court, a politicized U.S. Justice Department, gerrymandered congressional districts, dark money in politics, ministries of propaganda disguised as network news organizations, a decline in voters who take voting seriously, the creation of shadow governments in finance and markets, crony capitalism, and terrorist organizations cross-breeding with law enforcement: any one of these threatens to kill democracy around the world. All of them represent might making right, in violation of honesty, truth, and fair play. While this sort of thing can work for a brutal minority in the short run, it eventually creates a war of all against all, the state of nature that Thomas Hobbes described in *Leviathan,* one that created lives that were "nasty, brutish, and short."

If you don't make it to 2030 because of the nasty part, the brutish part, or the short part of that description, you might be the victim of erosion of consensual government by raw power. If you do make it to 2030, you're probably a little nasty and brutish yourself.

4. CLIMATE HEMORRHAGIC FEVER

Having taught college classes in composition, I normally don't care for angry and sullen adolescents. But Greta Thunberg's shaming of governments and corporations and the climate scientists who aren't climbing on the back of the Merrill Lynch bull and setting themselves on fire in protest of global climate policy is probably appropriate. As she notes, lots of old white guys with rigid behavioral patterns who are creating a hellish future won't have to live in that future. (A lot of old white guys with rigid behavioral patterns don't believe her. They think they're going to live forever, mainly because they're in complete denial about their own mortality.)

But the climate scenario for 2030 looks like this: At where we are now—a degree or two Celsius above pre-industrial global temperatures—a number of feedback loops kick off. Methane clathrates are already subliming and rising toward the ocean surface in the shallows of the East Siberian continental shelf. That will add another 1.1 C to the global temp over the coming decade.

More industrial CO_2 emissions will add another half degree C. A lack of reflective snow and ice cover (early springs, late falls) will add 1.6 degrees C.

Extra water vapor in the atmosphere of our warming world will add 2.1 C. Other feedbacks, such as the greenhouse effect of chlorofluorocarbons, will add another 0.3 C.

Then, because the rising temperatures will have pretty much destroyed industrial civilization, all the sunlight-blocking dust and sulfur compounds and contrails and smoke that industrial civilization produces will go away. Non-polluted skies will add another 2.5 C.

It all adds up to 10.1 degrees Celsius of warming. That's 17.95 degrees Fahrenheit warmer than it was before humankind started burning coal. That might seem like a bearable change, but it's a worldwide average that includes Antarctica.

The folks who run the Arctic News blog, whose figures I'm using here, say that humans will go extinct with a 5.3 degree Fahrenheit rise, and most life on Earth will be gone with a 9 degree rise. They also say the deadly thresholds will be reached by 2026, which will shock and disappoint a lot of us old white guys who were looking forward to 2030.

Arctic News people are hard-core doomsters, but they practice the scientific method and that means they lie less than politicians. So even though they're predicting a future that will be populated by one-celled extremophiles, it's worth looking at, if only so you'll have an inkling of what Greta Thunberg is so pissed about.

5. CONTAGIOUS ECONOMIC DEPRESSION

Bob, who has been saving for a new Dodge 3500 dually with a Cummins turbodiesel, loses his job driving a potato truck when Farmer Jim can't sell his potato crop to China because of new retaliatory tariffs put on agricultural products, in response to U.S. tariffs put on the cheap Chinese tools sold at the local Harbor Freight outlet. Susan, who sells Dodge trucks at the local dealership, is thereby one short of her monthly quota, and she gets told to clean out her desk and go back to her job as a waitress in her family's breakfast restaurant. She would, except half the customers, who believe Covid-19 is a hoax and won't socially distance, have run off the other half, who believe it's real, and the restaurant is going out of business. Susan's also got two kids under five, and since she lost her job she's had to lay off Becca, her babysitter, who's been studying while taking care of Susan's kids and using her babysitting checks to help pay her tuition at the local community college. When Becca drops out of school, her literature class drops below the minimum and her adjunct instructor Paul loses one of the three classes he teaches at three different colleges. As a result, he defaults on the loan he took out to get his PhD. He also has a complete emotional breakdown, goes into a fugue state, and is found amnesiac and alcoholic, six months later, by his wife's brother, a reserve policeman, who has tracked him to a homeless encampment outside San Francisco.

In the meantime, Farmer Jim gets a relief check from the federal government, with which he buys a new Tesla, most of which is made in China but avoids tariffs by being assembled in the U.S. He wants to pay his good fortune forward, so he allows Bob, Susan, Susan's family, Becca, Paul's wife—newly a widow, due to Paul's suicide—and her brother to glean potatoes from his fields. Everything will be plowed under anyway next spring. Farmer Jim is glad to help those less fortunate than he is. If you ask him how the country's doing, he will tell you it's getting back on track and he's doing his part. If you tell him he should have kept Joe on the payroll, he'd say, "Are you crazy? I can't pay someone to drive truck when I'm having to give away potatoes."

Capitalism: It's all fun and games until there are no more potatoes.

6. THE PARANOIA OF CONSPIRACY THEORISTS

The Deep State is controlling your thoughts. The Bush Family is really a collection of lizards in human suits. Joe Biden is a pedophile. The Denver Airport is the ceiling of an underground city the size of New York. Cattle mutilations are the work of Satanists who can fly. The moon is a giant alien starship (we have photographic proof). The moon is a hologram hiding Heaven. Elvis is headlining at Cactus Pete's in Jackpot, Nevada. The Holocaust never happened (we have photographic proof).

Paranoia happens when psychic defense mechanisms get seriously out of whack. You're still sane when you pretend that it's really someone else who has something you hate in yourself, such as intolerance, a fantasy life that includes killing your enemies in slow and painful ways, a tendency toward lust, gluttony, greed, sloth, wrath, envy, and pride. It's normal, also, that as you get older and wiser, you begin to own the flaws you've previously pushed off onto other people. You come to understand that your vision of them is really a multifaceted mirror you've been looking into.

But paranoids double down on the idea that their problems are never internal. Reality goes out the window, and from there it's a short cognitive leap to a world where the laws of physics have workarounds, because what you see and hear and taste and feel are only cover-ups for what's really happening. Paranoids have, beneath their suspicion and hostility, a pathetic faith in any story that will allow them not to look inward.

The U.S. has become a paranoid country. If you see its projections onto the world and even onto its own citizens as a mirror image of itself, it's also a pretty ugly country, one willing to harm its weak and vulnerable in order to avoid any kind of self-knowledge.

7. HUMAN INCOMPETENCE

I am a fan of the Dunning-Kruger effect, which concerns people who tend to devalue genius/skill/wisdom and overestimate their own abilities. It doesn't matter if they're talking about quantum physics or a Tchaikovsky concerto, they see themselves as just as good as the other guy, even if the other guy has put in 10,000 hours of practice and they haven't. Dunning-Kruger considerably expands the Declaration of Independence's assertion that all men are created equal.

This would be fine, except that when you rely on the incompetent, things go wrong. Then the amateur piano players and walk-on theoretical physicists and hold-my-beer politicians (and almost every other human being who comes to a job long on confidence and short on expertise) start kicking the piano for producing the wrong chords, losing wrenches somewhere deep in the particle accelerator, and calling out the National Guard to control protestors. Often enough, they ruin beyond repair the things that needed fixing.

The current mistrust of experts and scientists in this country looks to me like a way for more and more people to pretend to be competent when they aren't. It results in a lot of people avoiding any situation where their skills would be tested, which means they foist jobs onto competent subordinates if they've got them. If they have already fired all the competent subordinates for insubordination, they don't do anything at all. Or they push the big red button just to see what it's connected to.

I've listed seven plagues here. If you check out the Book of Exodus, you'll find that Egypt, which had enslaved the Nation of Israel for 400 years, experienced 10 plagues before they decided to end their tyranny. (Just so you know: Blood, Frogs, Lice, Flies, Dead Cows, Boils, Hail, Locusts, Darkness, and the Deaths of All Firstborn Children.)

Those 400 years of slavery have some unpleasant resonances with our civilization's treatment of the world's poor, who do exist in a kind of slavery, even if it's the slavery of seven years of payments on a pickup truck.

Tomorrow is election day, and if this country re-elects the current hard-hearted Pharaoh, I'm pretty sure we're in for more plagues. The contemporary analogs of locusts, darkness, and the deaths of firstborns are out there if you want to match them up. They're going to be worse than what we've seen so far, and what we've seen so far looks like the end of us.

Ode to Joe

November 9, 2020

ON SATURDAY, THE Associated Press declared Joe Biden the winner of the 2020 presidential election in the United States. Full stop.

I didn't think this country would make it to a 46th president. For months I've been convinced that Trump would steal the election by any means possible, even mass arrests of Democratic officials. I thought recent spikes in Covid-19 would provide an excuse to strategically close polling stations. I thought Texas-style vote suppression would happen in Arizona and Georgia. I thought William Barr would make like Jehovah and smite Trump's enemies.

None of these things happened. While it is clear that we'll have recounts and ballot challenges, it's also clear that the Trump campaign will ask the courts to step into some slimy territory, and the courts, including the highest one, will not want to smite Trump's enemies if it's going to ruin their shoes.

There's been a dawning realization among the judiciary that credibility has become scarce and valuable. It's a thing to hold onto if you've got it, and that gives judges, no matter their partisan leanings, a handy excuse to rule based on facts and simple justice. Such rulings will not be friendly territory for the convoluted technical challenges contained in the Trump campaign's filings.

I still think we could have mass arrests of Democratic officials. The last century was full of arrests and massacres and civil wars when an authoritarian leader didn't like the outcome of an election. We all know it can happen.

And before it can happen here, a lot of people who have sworn to defend the Constitution will: a) have to violate their oath, or b) ignore the down-the-line consequences of far-out-on-a-limb rationalizations that they *are* defending the Constitution, or c) believe in the absolute Constitution-transcending goodness of Donald Trump and the corresponding evil of Joe Biden.

Sandra Day O'Connor is on record as regretting her vote, as a Supreme Court Justice, that put George W. Bush in the White House and enabled the endless and futile Afghan and Iraq Wars. At the moment, Chief Justice John Roberts is still dealing with Bush v. Gore, in the form of messy partisan expectations that the Supreme Court will decide the 2020 election. One hopes that he views O'Connor's regret as a cautionary example.

I think Roberts will oppose putting any Trump campaign litigation on the docket, no matter how hard Alito or Thomas lobby for it. Barrett, the newest Justice, may have the common sense and the sense of self-preservation to recuse herself from any decision having to do with Donald Trump.

(As an aside, if Stalin were alive today, he'd be saying things like, "How many divisions does the Supreme Court have?" Roberts may be smart enough to know the only power the Court will have in the future lies in the integrity of the justice it dispenses, and an intact country to dispense it in.)

I was sure Trump would get elected the first time. I was also sure he wouldn't last a year in office, because it wasn't hard to spot him as a serial liar and, after Nixon, I didn't think people—even Republicans—would tolerate a serial liar as President. I regret being right on the former, and wrong on the latter.

Republicans and the rest of the American people have a much higher tolerance for lies and the liars who tell them than I thought they did. Possibly that's because a lot of voters don't remember Nixon, just like voters of my generation had little memory of Warren Harding's administration trying to steal the country's strategic oil reserve. (If you want to know more, type "Teapot Dome Scandal" into your search engine. It will make you realize that executive branch lies didn't start with Nixon, something I naively believed in 1968.)

A low tolerance for lies and liars is not something I have in common with the average Trump voter, who might say lies are what politicians do in order to be politicians. I do believe some politicians tell the truth, or try to. I fervently hope Joe Biden, whatever lies he may have told in the past, has become one of them.

We need someone who won't lie, no matter how much it hurts, because to keep this country intact, we need a president we all can trust.

I've been using a simple litmus test for Trump for a long time, which comes not from my experience as a writer but from my years of building fence, digging ditch, and pouring concrete. It's this: You have two guys on your crew. One of them is honest and one of them is a bullshitter. You've got 50 feet of ditch to dig, a quarter mile of fence to build, and you have to set up forms for somebody's basement. Which guy do you want to work with?

I know a lot of fence builders and ditch diggers and cement workers voted for Trump. But if Trump had been hired on any construction job I've ever worked, he would have been gone after his first shift. The whole crew would have been happy about it.

Blue-collar Trump voters should recognize the obvious: the President of the United States *is* on their crew, and they have to depend on his skills every day. He has to see what needs to be done, and then he has to do it. If somebody's sick, he has to fill in. If something goes wrong, he has to know how to set things right. If somebody's reading the blueprints wrong, he has to spot the mistake before a whole week's work is lost. Believe me, this sort of thing can happen even when you're digging ditch.

We demand this sort of competence from blue-collar workers every day. Why don't we demand it of a president?

Almost nobody in this country sees themselves as working on a giant construction project. But on our good days, that's what we're all doing, and the good parts of our history were times when most Americans saw things that way.

I don't think many people, even in this election, viewed Donald Trump as someone helping them get their job done. I do think they saw him as someone who would punish the people on the other side, simply by his stinky presence in the Oval Office. It was important enough to own the liberals that half the country happily attempted the re-election of a bullshitter-in-chief. If Trump's policies threatened to make everybody miserable, at least the other side would be *more* miserable.

The trouble is, these same people are now fearing it's their turn to be the more miserable ones. They're angry and they're afraid to have Joe Biden as president, because since they were small, they've believed the one great purpose of life is to get even.

I try to tell the truth, but it's not easily told. Over years of teaching fiction workshops, I've told my students that the truth counts, even in fiction. "Don't tell bullshit stories," I've said. "Do the work. Invent the truth."

As you might expect, getting across the subtleties of that idea took up a semester or two. But there are ways of telling truths with fiction.

Here's a story: Jesus encounters a madman who is possessed by demons. Jesus casts the demons out of the man and into a herd of 2,000 Gadarene swine, who then run off a cliff into the sea, where they drown. The man is suddenly sane. He no longer has a problem with demons, and, since the story is set in pre-Catholic days, he's safe from relapsing while trying to understand the Trinity. The unfortunate Gadarene who owned the herd of swine does have a problem with demons, especially if he's mortgaged his farm to buy pigs.

I didn't make this story up. Jesus did, or Luke or Matthew or Mark. Even so, it is packed with truth:

a) Jesus is correct. He can cure your crazy by moving your demons elsewhere, like any good family therapist. b) Marx is correct. Jesus believed that private property is a crime. c) Ayn Rand is correct. Jesus, being Jesus, is the sole owner of all the swine in the universe, and he can do what he wants with his private property, even just to make a point about his divinity. d) Jehovah (remember Jehovah?) is correct. Swine are unclean. The demons were part of Jesus's cleanup crew. e) Satan is correct. Herd animals can be stampeded over cliffs if you get the big ones started in the right direction. Demons don't need to possess every swine, they just have to possess the head pig, his chief of staff, his attorney general, his majority leader in the Senate and maybe his personal lawyer. In a porcine hierarchy, a few demons can go a long way.

"There are contradictory truths in every story, even the story of your life," I would tell my students, were I still teaching workshops. "If all truths were consistent with each other, telling them would be a lot easier, and so would pig farming. So would living your life. But picking out the highest truth requires an acute critical intelligence. Some stories are truer than others."

Write that down.

Here's an undeniable truth: Donald Trump and Joseph Biden are both deeply damaged human beings. Biden has been repeatedly torn apart by personal grief. He's lost a wife and daughter and a son and has another son who is a recovering addict. Life has, on occasion, completely wrecked him. Parts of him, I am sure, will never recover. But enough of him has recovered to win the presidency and speak to the country about what it means to have deep unhealed wounds.

I've been thinking about Joe Biden's grief a lot lately, because I've long thought that grief causes Alzheimer's. The Trump campaign has claimed, since Biden became the Democratic nominee, that he's an Alzheimer's victim.

After listening to his speech Saturday evening, I don't think that's the case. There's still an intelligent, living, breathing person in Joe Biden. He has a long history of being flattened by grief, and a long history of picking himself up and dusting himself off and getting on with life. He may not always be articulate, but he's as skilled in the language of empathy and compassion as anyone I know. That's what Joe Biden has made of the tragedy life has handed him.

With that ability, I think he'll turn parts of this country into more emotionally intelligent places.

Trump's life is just as tragic, but long ago he chose to deny any grief or loss. It's what comes of being born into a family where a very hard game was being played. The slightest infraction was punishable by death, which was the fate of Trump's older brother Fred, whose only crime was not wanting to play the game. Early on, Trump learned he had to be a designated winner, because he had seen what happened to designated losers.

Biden was lucky he was an adult when tragedy struck. He was able to bring an adult stoicism to grief, put words to it and go on. One of the few gifts that grief leaves behind is empathy, and over time empathy makes you a stronger and more complete and less alone person.

Whatever chance Trump had for personhood was wrecked before he was born. That's what a toxic family will do to you. His grief hasn't gone away because he never allowed himself to feel it.

It's hollowed him from the inside. What's left in there is lonely and stunted, and from the looks of things, demented. Refusing to deal with grief doesn't mean it won't eventually deal with you.

Trump is equating losing with death these days. I don't think there's anything he wouldn't do to win this election, even now that he's lost it. That's why I won't be sure Biden is in the White House until Trump has gone into exile or has died or occupies Rush Limbaugh's soon-to-be-empty chair. Barring a judicial coup, those look like his February choices. What is not possible is that he'll have a long and honored career building houses for Habitat for Humanity.

Julie and I had a small celebration once the election was finally called for Biden. We opened a bottle of wine. We listened to Beethoven's Ninth Symphony, which we rechristened *Ode to Joe* for the occasion. We wished Joe Biden luck. He'll need a bunch of it.

We hope the next four years will see him begin to reconcile the two warring sides of America. Each half of the country wants to punish the other half. It's become more important for most people to have an enemy they can hate than to grieve for what they've lost. Biden might have the moral authority and the vocabulary to show us a better way.

It's an odd thing to wish for, but we hope Joe Biden will be able to teach us the language of grief. Awful things have happened to us in this century, and we need to know how to see them, name them, fully accept that they've happened, and get to work on fixing them. It's the only way we can forestall the greater griefs that will forever creep up on our blind sides.

Cheer

November 16, 2020

JULIE HAS INFORMED me that I need to write something cheery for this week's entry. I will try to fulfill her request, because fulfilling her requests is my default position in our marriage. She's an intelligent, reasonable, practical person, so most of the time what she wants is what I want, and she spares me the effort of having to write down a daily to-do list. A long time ago I came to the conclusion that almost anything Julie wants stems from her generous stock of good will, and unless she wants me to remodel the bathroom or something else that will cause me unbearable pain, I do it. You cannot believe the amount of argument this has saved us.

As an added benefit, Julie starts feeling guilty if she's been directing domestic traffic all day, and I can usually nurture her guilt from an embryonic abstract emotion into a full-grown literal apple pie steaming in glorious olfactory reality upon the kitchen table.

None of this would work if I didn't have absolute confidence in Julie's desire to make our marriage a place where we can both thrive, or if she didn't have the same confidence in me.

Over time, the confidence we have in each other has become the most precious commodity in our lives, something I wouldn't have believed when I was, say, 29, athletic, good-looking, bartending at Slavey's in Ketchum, and determined never to get married because being single was so much fun. (I had plenty of confidence in myself at 29. I didn't realize that it would vanish in the absence of love.)

Julie and I back up each other's confidence. And that's a seriously cheerful thing to write about.

*

Another cheerful thing is that 20 inches of snow have fallen in the past few days. We're still pulling winter clothes and ski boots out of the crawl space, and restocking packs with emergency-overnight-in-below-zero-weather supplies. (You tend to get careless about the cold and the dark when you're skiing through long sunny springtime afternoons. What is vital equipment in December gets removed in March to make room for brie, salami, cashews, chardonnay, sliced apples, chocolate-covered espresso beans, and sunscreen. April is a good month for lunch.)

Now we're refurbishing first aid kits and finding places in our packs for years-old granola bars. (January is a bad month for lunch.) I'll hot-wax our skis. I'll spray our bindings with WD-40, which stinks awfully, but once sprayed, the bindings don't get clogged with early-season snow and they don't make annoying squeaks when you walk uphill. I'll adjust our collapsible poles so they won't collapse in the middle of the season's first pole-plant.

When we've done all this, we'll start skiing the old logging road above the Idaho Rocky Mountain Ranch.

Over time, if there's a week or so of dry weather, the track will get nicely icy and it will be possible to hit dangerous speeds on the way out. Juno gets overworked at those velocities, so halfway back to the truck I usually pick her up and carry her. Since she's harder to carry than she was as a puppy, I ski as fast as I can for a half mile or so.

It helps if she's tired. If she's not, she gets nervous and squirmy ripping down a track on skis, with trees whizzing by on either side of us. I tell her she's an honored member of the 40-40 Club (40-pound dog doing 40 miles per hour), but even when she's tired, she growls at me when I take her in my arms. "Stop struggling," I tell her. "We haven't hit a tree yet." She's not convinced.

When she was a puppy, I'd put her in a backpack and cinch up the top with only her head sticking out, and she liked that better.

More cheer: Our new woodstove is more efficient than the old one, so we have achieved a functional increase in the size of our woodpile. We also blew a tire getting the new woodstove home from Idaho

Falls, and I realized that I couldn't depend on the other three because they were getting, like me, old and bald, so after a masked-up trip to Hailey, we have four new aggressive-tread tires on the pickup. Les Schwab gave me a deal, and the pickup looks 29 again.

Also, the snowblower started after a few pulls of the rope starter. I cleared the driveway, the path to the woodpile, and the deck. It's still snowing, and according to the weather report I'll have to snow blow again tomorrow and maybe the next day. No problem. Snow blowing is a cheerful exercise in November. It gets a bit tedious in January and thereafter. But it's still November.

I've been trying to find cheer in being 70, and it's not as much of a struggle this morning as usual. I'm still alive. I'm still able to pack a couple of armloads of wood into the house whenever the wood box is empty. I still have my wits about me. Also, I've finally accepted the fact that I'm no longer an athletic and good-looking 29-year-old, bartending at Slavey's in Ketchum.

Instead, it's come to this: for 70, I'm athletic. I'm no longer those other things. When Julie has to take a photo of me for publication, we have to get the light just right or I look a lot like Mark Shields on the PBS News Hour.

I'm happy to no longer be bartending at Slavey's or anywhere else. (Slavey's is now the Warfield Distillery and Brewery. Like a lot of other businesses in Ketchum these days, the Warfield looks mostly empty and dark when you drive by. But Christmas is coming. It remains to be seen if Ketchum in the winter of 2020-2021 will stay dark and empty, or if it will host a season-long festival of superspreading.)

But that's not really cheerful. Here's something that is: I'm not in the least envying my 29-year-old self. He was, as I remember, a difficult person to live with. He was playing fast and loose with his future (my present) and I'm lucky to be here today, with body and mind more or less intact.

He was not always nice to the people around him. As a bartender, he learned to be adequate. As a friend, he now and then fell down on the job. As a skier, he over-skied his abilities. He called himself a writer, but he wasn't. He was publishing short stories, and people seemed to like them, but he mistook good luck for skill and hard work.

That year, flush with tips and getting free employee meals and free employee drinks (one per shift), he bought a Sun Valley season pass and skied a hundred days. Over those hundred days he broke five pairs of skis. Once, he went down the Warm Springs side of the mountain without turning, trying to break two minutes top to bottom. He might have, except he hit a patch of ungroomed and icy bumps between the two Warm Springs lifts. He bounced through them at 70 miles an hour, stuck both ski tips into a steep mogul, broke one ski and ripped the bindings out of the other, and did five or six rag-doll somersaults through more bumps before sliding to a stop. He walked unhurt to the bottom of the mountain.

Not an isolated incident.

Now when I go skiing, I listen to a small still voice in my head. "When you have to choose between fast or slow?" it whispers, "choose slow, especially when you're skiing. Nice or nasty? Nice. Sad or angry? Sad. Sad or cheerful? Cheerful, unless you have to blind yourself to the world you live in."

The still small voice, encouraged by my silence, keeps going. "Cherish words that come easy, because there will be a time when they don't come easy. Don't break anyone's heart, and that includes your own. Always quit drinking an hour before closing time. Save some cash because the day will come when you can get five percent interest on a savings account."

I don't always obey the still small voice, to my sorrow.

A good friend—my age—says we have lived in the best possible time to be human. "Born in 1950 in America," he says. "Can't get much luckier than that."

I believe him. At least I believe the luck part. I didn't die in nuclear war or from Agent Orange or get AIDS or get on the wrong plane on 9/11. But beyond that, our luck needs to be qualified. If you were white, male, straight, middle-class, had parents who put your well-being ahead of theirs, graduated from college, enjoyed your work, saved enough money for retirement, had a circle of long-term friends, didn't get divorced, stayed away from foam-at-the-mouth politics—1950 was a great year to be born. It still doesn't let you escape being 70 and having to look back on all the things you would have done differently if you'd known then what you know now.

You also can't escape the enormous burden of not screwing up the life you have left.

Which makes it obvious, I suppose, that I'm not really giving up on my 29-year-old self. I need him and his mistakes and small cruelties for company, if nothing else.

I've known people who reached a certain point in their lives and cut off all contact with the people they once were, due to shame or embarrassment, mostly. It can be done, but it turns you into an emotional cripple, and emotional cripples are not cheerful. You die lonelier and more miserable than you would have if you'd welcomed your shameful past selves into your psyche. Those shameful past selves might be wonderfully impressed with what you've done to improve them, for one thing.

The person I was when I was 29 presents me with images and snatches of dialog that make me cringe. He still says things that are tactless and tasteless. He recalls, with unpleasant intensity, trusting people he shouldn't have trusted, and people who trusted him when they shouldn't have. He remembers letting good-hearted people believe he might improve if they worked hard enough to improve him (which is true, five decades too late). Overall, he was nasty when he could have been nice, promiscuous when he could have been faithful, stupid when he could have been smart, and went skiing when he could have read Dostoevsky. (I still go skiing when I could be reading Dostoevsky.)

My 29-year-old self must have had some instinct for self-preservation. Somewhere in the middle of that winter, he realized that bartending wasn't a recipe for conscious development over time. His job kept confronting him with overdoses, suicides, emotional breakdowns, bankruptcies, geriatric alcoholics—he had run out of fingers to count them on. At some point, a small still voice did get through: "If you keep this up, you're gonna die."

He eventually quit bartending and used his meager savings to go to grad school. There he read Dostoevsky and a bunch of French postmodernists, who all had the same lesson: once you're in a society or occupation or family, you don't have any free will to speak of. But you can leave those things if you find them toxic, and switch to better ones. That's where free will resides: in picking a collective to be a part of. You cannot, however, choose not to be a part of any collective at all without turning into a lonely, crazed old man.

After grad school I got a job teaching college, and that was the best stroke of luck of all.

It has been a happier-than-usual morning, thanks to Julie's request. I came up with more cheerful things than I thought I would, mostly by looking inward instead of outward, toward memory instead of toward a frightening future.

You can go blind, thinking and writing this way, especially considering what is happening outside this valley. But for today I'm content to focus on the collective Julie and I have chosen: ourselves, the friends with whom we have Zoom calls, the friends and family we email and call, the friends we see at a distance across parking lots or decks, the friends we sometimes even invite for well-distanced dinners. It's not a terribly cheery group, because we've all got our eyes open to what's going on in the world. But everybody tries to be kind. Everybody speaks the truth, and everybody tries to speak it gently. That's cause for cheer, and it gives me hope we'll all get through these dark pestilent months with laughter and good fellowship.

While We Wait

November 23, 2020

WE ARE FOLLOWING the news to see how Donald Trump fares as he attempts, by hook or by crook, to win the Electoral College vote on December 14.

I have no idea who will be inaugurated as POTUS on January 20. I do know if it's Donald Trump, he or his backers will have depended on the complicity of the Senate and Federal Judiciary. His second four years will rest on legal technicalities, never-before-used constitutional provisions, and the historical precedent (the Hayes-Tilden election of 1876) that brought this country Jim Crow, lynch mobs, the Tulsa Massacre, decades of virtual slavery, and the reconstitution, as a nation-within-a-nation, of the Confederate States of America. It's easy to imagine that a second Trump term will result in recognizably similar outcomes.

Here's something else I imagine: a second term will destroy Donald Trump. He is, as his every television appearance reminds us, a poorly aging mound of flesh, well along in a relentless process of corporal and cognitive decay. Big, angry, obese men don't get discounts on their life insurance policies. The future Donald Trump, through a combination of rage, age, and what looks like frontotemporal dementia, will be reduced to either a corpse or a nursing home resident.

That his nursing home might be the White House is not without historical precedent—Woodrow Wilson had a severe stroke in early October of 1919, and spent the remaining 17 months of his presidency unable to talk or walk, his condition kept secret by his wife, Edith, who acted as his proxy. One wonders how Melania would do.

The end of Trump will not mean the end of his policies. He's created a momentum toward cruelty that won't go away. Too many people have discovered the pleasure of humiliating their enemies. Far too many people have been taught to blame their poverty or misery or lack of education on people of different races or tribes.

Trump has accomplished a lot of division during his time as our leader, and it's impossible to think he did it all by himself. At the risk of sounding like a conspiracy theorist, it's unclear if he's in control of the forces that back him or if they're in control of him.

"Something there is that doesn't love a wall," Robert Frost once wrote. If he were alive today, Frost would be writing "Something there is that doesn't want these states united."

If there are indeed behind-the-scenes disintegrative entities powerful enough to swing the election for Trump, they'll be powerful enough to put down the meat ax and pick up the scalpel. If the Electoral College anoints Donald Trump, it will do so with the knowledge that it might be anointing President Mike Pence.

As long as I'm playing the prophet, let me say that the vaccines available by Inauguration Day will begin to diminish the pandemic and restart the economy, although for the poor and unemployed, it will be too late. The economic forces in play before the pandemic—financialization, inequity in wealth, automation, the increase in jobs with no apparent usefulness, misallocation of resources for housing and infrastructure— have all been strengthened by the past six months, and they won't go away because we all get vaccinated. Unfortunately for the people alive a generation from now, the pandemic distracted us from problems they will be facing. Instead, it let us concentrate our energies on ways to save the wealth, health, and comfort of Baby Boomers.

As a Boomer, I can appreciate that, but I also know when a civilization doesn't put the welfare of its young people first, it dies.

As a Boomer, I'm in one of the Covid-vulnerable groups, which means I'll probably get vaccinated before a bunch of other people. Young people can usually survive Covid without serious lasting effects, which is wonderful, but they cannot experience climate change without serious lasting effects. They cannot thrive in an industrial economy—because there won't be an industrial economy—when the amount of energy it takes to get a barrel of oil out of the ground and refined into its various products approaches the amount of energy in that barrel. They are already experiencing a financial system that rewards the few and impoverishes the many, and poverty has killed far more of them than the coronavirus has killed of their elders.

The vaccines are evidence that our civilization can throw money, intelligence, and accumulated knowledge at a disease, and within a short time make it go away. It sounds like a no-brainer, but we need to identify the more virulent diseases—economic, cultural, climatic—where young people are the vulnerable group, and we need to work just as hard for cures. The effort will require empathy, sacrifice, and good will. These qualities seem to have disappeared among the people who have the wealth and power in this country.

Our oligarchs suffer from a spiritual poverty, but it's just as lethal as the financial kind. We need a vaccine for it, and at-risk volunteers to test it on.

I'll admit that I'm worried by the prospect of an mRNA concoction rewiring the genetic material in my cells. That's what viruses do anyway, all the time, but still, it's a huge moment of trust in science and the good will of pharmaceutical companies when that needle slides into your arm. Every one of the many vaccines in development is years away from being declared fully safe, which makes me worry even more.

Still, Julie and I will get the vaccine when we can. At some point, trusting a civilization that has spent the last century lengthening the lives of its citizens seems reasonable, especially if you're like most people over 50 and are still alive because of it. It will be the end of the pandemic for us, one way or another.

I hope that shortly after my vaccination, Julie can get vaccinated as well and two weeks later, still kicking, we can finally go on a book tour for my end-of-the-world book. Our universe will expand considerably if we can get in the car and head for motels, bookstores, and real sit-down restaurants while they still exist.

*

If I keep away from the news, our winter of discontent turns into mere winter. A great white calm has descended upon Sawtooth Valley. A car or pickup goes by on Highway 75 every five or ten minutes, but the plows have been working, and snowbanks muffle the sounds of their passing. If I listen closely, I can hear the sounds of the woodstove fan and the hum of the refrigerator, but that's only when we're not listening to NPR or a podcast or music. During last week's storm, we had a couple of short power outages, and we realized how routinely noisy our household is, even in the quiet months.

The past three afternoons, we've been out skiing. The sky has been dark blue, clear and cold, and we've put tracks in new powder on a hard base. We had watched, with dismay, when a rainy day melted a foot and a half of powder down to four inches of slush, but then it got cold again. The slush froze to a hard, stable base layer that will be with us until April. Then it snowed another six inches.

A skiff of snow is in the forecast for today. I'd prefer something in excess of a foot. I don't care if I end up shoveling roofs this winter. I'm hoping for a giant snow year.

What's on the ground is fast, easy-turning snow, but we've taken it slow. It's easy to get tripped up, skiing in November—a half inch of frost on a high rock can ruin your day, and a ski sliding under a downed log can ruin your winter. Reports from Galena and Banner summits indicate that people are out there on their rock skis, pushing the season, but we'll wait until it snows another foot before venturing onto the steeper slopes.

It has been a thrill just to glide along in shallow snow, slaloming between sagebrush when we get going fast enough.

I had forgotten that I had sharpened and hot-waxed our skis last spring before putting them away for the summer. It was evidence that the past and some people in it are more generous and forward-thinking than I normally give them credit for.

It may be our informal quarantine, it may be the season, it may be my time of life, but lately I seem to have signed up for an elementary school memory-of-the-day. It's similar to the word-of-the-day you can get in your morning's email, except it appears in your mind's eye instead of on your computer screen. I have spent long moments thinking of things I haven't thought of for 60-odd years.

Once it was the face of a classmate, who inspired me to say to my parents, after my first week of first grade, that I had finally found a girlfriend. Once it was a leather ski boot attached to a wooden ski with a beartrap binding, sliding personless toward the rope-tow lift-line during afternoon ski lessons. Once it was our principal telling our fifth-grade class that the fourth-grade teacher had killed herself and we should be nice to the fourth graders that day. More than once it was our crazed third-grade teacher beating hell out of some little kid for singing the wrong verse in the right song, something third graders really can't help doing. Once it was our principal coming into class to tell us President Kennedy had been shot, and we should call our parents and go home if we could. Once it was simply an image of our principal with tears on his face, not because anyone had been murdered, but because he had helped move a giant freestanding coat closet in the school hallway, and where it had stood he had found 20 dollars or so in loose quarters, and had realized that over the years, bunches of little kids had lost their lunch money to the cracks in the closet's floor.

These memories are as real as yesterday's skiing through the sagebrush, with Juno running beside me, growling and barking as gravity started to widen the distance between us. They're considerably more real than starving children, contested elections, power-mad oligarchs, demented rulers, venal senators, and a civilization not expected to outlast the decade.

That makes me sound heartless, and maybe I am. Certainly I'm heartless compared to my grade school principal. Almost everyone is.

It's a bit frightening to have the past emerge bearing far more substance than the present. It may be that Donald Trump's troubled relationship with the truth is really a troubled relationship with his past, and his insistence on inventing the present has sucked the substance out of his days and ours.

It may be that when a country starts living a lie, sacred ceremony becomes empty ritual, laws become the clever tools of interest groups, history becomes a murderous fiction, and everyone you see on a television screen has been told what to say. As George Orwell discerned, memory has no place in a world where political power dictates the truth. Maybe what I'm experiencing is memory fighting back, demanding its due, presenting incontrovertible images instead of questionable narratives.

One thing's for certain: everyone, even Donald Trump, reaches a point in life where memories are all that's left, and if one has deliberately forgotten all memories, nothing's left. The same truth applies to countries, and it's being applied to this country as it selects a new president. We would do well, for the sake of the kids, to remember what's happened over the last five centuries on this continent, especially when we make decisions that will affect the next five centuries.

It's a way of getting back some of the reality that has been taken from us.

Living to Human Scale

November 30, 2020

DONALD TRUMP IS not, at this writing, conceding the election. He's demanding that Joe Biden prove he got 80 million votes, and is refusing to accept the election as evidence. He is demanding that millions of voters be exposed as cheats or dead people. He is demanding that election officials resign. He's challenging legitimate votes with baseless lawsuits that are thrown out as soon as they hit a courtroom. He has fired the federal official—his own appointee—in charge of keeping elections fair and honest.

Maybe he believes he lives in a country where a heretofore unknown street gang—the Deep State Democrats—has suddenly shown itself to be organized and committed and corrupt enough to destroy this country's democratic institutions.

That is some organization. That is some commitment. That is some corruption. I don't believe any of it. Having been a Democrat long enough to know they are unorganized, self-destructive, and attract more than their share of boy-scout types, I'm pretty sure the Democrats couldn't steal a middle-school student council election.

If there's a deep state, it exists in the laws, customs, and behavior of our nation's civil servants, who collect taxes, enforce zoning laws, run prosecutor's offices, and attempt to control pandemics. They're rule makers and rule enforcers. They often enough find a perverse joy in being obeyed to the letter, but they do keep the country running day to day. They are averse to making policy, and instead focus on making sure their own little bailiwick is a tidy and rigid place where it doesn't matter who's president. If a political appointee tries to change their agency from above, they will ignore, sabotage, or contravene orders. They are a force for inertia. Deep inertia.

I believe Donald Trump and his followers thought they had this election fixed. The right people were in place to manipulate votes, and enough doubt could be cast on mail-in ballots that they would be thrown out by friendly judges. Secretaries of state were in position to invalidate the votes of entire regions. Election officials had been bought, not with cash but with a wink and a nod that promised increasing power and higher positions in Republican politics if they did what was expected of them.

The outrage expressed by Trump, his base, and his supremely cynical enablers comes from having the kind of organization and commitment and corruption they accuse the Democrats of, but still coming up short. When the votes went for Biden, it must have looked to them like the Democrats had done everything they had done, but better. The alternative was to think that all their planning, all their fervor and sneakiness, all their elaborate propaganda, all their vote suppression and map sessions, all their last-minute phone calls to state legislators—all of these weren't good enough. It was less painful to suppose the Democrats had out-cheated them.

Is it hard to understand why Trump thinks Joe Biden must be part of an organization that requires absolute loyalty, absolute secrecy, and absolute dishonesty?

Let's not go there yet. Instead, let me remember a bunch of people who weren't bad, perverse, and ugly. They were all 18 years old, and in my first-year writing classes at the College of Idaho.

A thought experiment I asked them to perform: imagine our classroom as the center point of a sphere with a radius of a million miles. "Look how tiny this room is in relation to the size of that sphere," I told them. "Extend the radius out to Mars and Venus and Mercury, and we'd be that much smaller. If the sphere were to include Pluto, it would be so much bigger than we are that for all practical purposes, this classroom wouldn't exist. We'd be a misplaced zero in a vast computer program, a raindrop in a hurricane, a dollar in the federal deficit."

Then I asked them, "In this scheme of things, where is the center of the universe?" Silence.

"Include the galaxy," I said. "Include the Local Group, the clumps and threads that connect the Local Group to other galaxies. Extend the radius of our sphere all the way to the furthest quasar our radio telescopes can detect. Where is its center, still?"

Lots of frowns. A hand up, finally. "Here?"

"Bingo," I said. "Right here. But there are 25 people in this room. Not all of us can be the center of the universe. Which one of us is?"

Another hand up. "The professor?"

Big smile from me. "Six weeks into college, and you're finally learning something."

Then I spoiled it all. "When you start with your own point of view, of course you're going to be the center of things. But you're not. And no one in the universe will care where you think its center is anyway, especially if it's a sentient dung beetle a billion light years away with its own point of view."

A voice from the back of the room: "I thought this was a writing class."

"It's an exercise in right-sizing," I said. "If I could get you all to see how small you are in relation to the universe, and how impossibly far you are from its center if it has one, I might be able to teach you to look around and write down what you see, simply, honestly, and with humility."

I then tried to convince them that other people had their points of view, too, ones different from their own and worth thinking about. Later in the semester, I tried hard to persuade them that a human touch, a helping hand, a declaration of friendship or love or respect can turn indifference into something better. It wasn't really a writing class, in retrospect.

One of the things college students get for their tuition money is an understanding that the world is far less black and white than they thought it was in high school. That's why—I'm sorry to put it this way—people who have graduated from college vote far less frequently for demagogues than people who haven't. If they're lucky, they've been taught critical thinking, which means they have learned to recognize, time and time again, that reality is full of paradoxes and contradictions. Trump offers a simple world to live in, one where the Chinese are bad, immigrants are bad, NATO is ripping us off, liberals exist to be owned, the two types of people are winners and losers, and if you vote for him, you're a winner.

The world the educated live in is a lot more complicated, its issues far more gray than black and white, its joys more often of the cerebral cortex than of the limbic system. Those people getting their diplomas have, for four years, endured writing professors telling them to live, if they can, in a messy human world, one full of loose ends and frayed edges and dubious victories, one constantly demanding repair and forgiveness and, most of all, the hard work of seeing clearly.

"Sure you can be famous," I told my students. "In a few short years, you could be playing center field for the Yankees, filibustering in the U.S. Senate, arguing before the Supreme Court, doing brain surgery, accepting a Pulitzer, or running your own startup life-extension company. Maybe all at once. But there are better and more human-scale venues to excel in, better and more humane people to be."

I don't know whether I ended anyone's superhero dreams with these words. If I did, I hope their lives were kinder and gentler for it.

Once you decide you're the center of the universe, you can eliminate the evidence that you're not, simply by shrinking the universe to fit the limits of your perception. I joked with my students about being the center of the universe, but I had colleagues who took their universes and their central places in them far more seriously. It was an occupational hazard, one that resulted in some seriously tiny universes.

When you know more about your one thing than anybody else in your faculty meeting, you start seeing the world, including your colleagues, through the lens of your specialty. Fellow faculty appear as insects if you're an entomologist, delicate crystals if you teach geology, dubious business plans if you're in the Economics Department. If I walked into a faculty meeting after teaching a playwriting workshop, I could see flawed scripts taking their seats beside me. I could see happy endings or tragic ones, plot twists, flat spots in the action, full-length plays that had all the substance of one-acts.

Such distortions are harmless, mostly, unless you decide they're real instead of artifacts of perspective. Make that sad decision and you'll be stuck in character for a too-long run, with stupid lines and audiences loudly unwrapping the cellophane from hard candies. You'll never again be the person you were before you passed the audition.

When you look at Donald Trump as a victim of this process, it's obvious he wasn't in one of my so-called writing classes, at least the ones that focused on the pitfalls of unselfconscious points of view. These days he sees himself as occupying a bigger sphere than most people, and he's very much in the middle of it. He's found a lot of people willing to go along with that perception. The ones who won't are his enemies. The ones who will are his friends. Friends or enemies, they're all bit players and extras in his drama.

(If only that last rewrite hadn't added that subplot of the pandemic. It didn't add any lines for him, and he had to ad-lib, which he's not good at. Eventually, he just pretended that part of the script wasn't there, and that he could move the play forward on character alone.)

Pandemic or not, Donald Trump's superhero dreams stayed intact until he lost the election. That loss threatens more than just his dreams. The character he's playing has gotten bigger and louder to compensate for the disappearance of the human being he once was. He cannot let the final curtain come down without his role vanishing, and when it does, there won't be much left but an empty costume in the prop manager's laundry hamper, and orange greasepaint-stained tissues in the greenroom wastebasket. If he insists the play have an extra act, he'll keep lots of people up beyond their bedtime.

Toward the end of those long-ago writing classes, I began to read student essays that were full of researched facts rather than opinions.

They sometimes contained self-deprecatory humor, which always earned them a higher grade.

Also, instead of grand pronouncements on global communist conspiracies or illegal immigrants or the violent subtexts of Barbie dolls, I got heartfelt meditations on what it felt like to be the first in the family to go to college, or on the effects of a sister's corrective cosmetic surgery, or on the difficult relationships between two cousins, one a citizen and one with no possibility of citizenship. Students stopped playing it safe. They started sharing their joys and tragedies, and when I read their writing, I started seeing them as human beings. It made it hard to judge them, which was a problem when a big part of my job was to give them grades, but it made it easy to love working with them.

At the end of the semester, they were no longer stuck at the center of their respective universes. They were free to roam the one we all shared.

It takes years of practice to write to human scale, and years more to *live* to human scale. That's what I would have told Donald Trump if he had ever signed up for one of my writing classes. I don't think he would have paid much attention to me.

Even if, by a miracle, I could have shown up at his military academy as his new composition teacher, I don't think I would have been able to get through to him. He had already mistaken the shadow he cast for the person he was, and he liked that vast darkness for its size and its effect on others. If I had told him that being human is a kind of Goldilocks endeavor—not too big, not too small—he wouldn't have believed me.

"Being human is for losers," he would have said.

The Meanest 26 Days of the Year

December 7, 2020

6:30 A.M. MINUS 11.4 Fahrenheit. Dark, except for a distant waning moon. It's 13 days until the solstice, and it will be another 13 days after that until we've regained the same lack of daylight as we had this morning when I got up and started the coffee.

In another week, the moon won't even be visible. By the solstice, chances are good that nighttime temperatures will have hit 20 below. By the new year, if we haven't kept a sharp eye on the pantry, we will have run out of coffee and perished.

They will find us in the spring, our empty cups clutched in hands gloved by frost.

These worries occupy my mind these mornings, usually when I'm placing fresh wood atop the still-glowing coals in the woodstove. One look outside the ice-glazed windows and it's easy to imagine the days growing shorter right past December 21, getting even shorter into January and February, shorter yet in March and April. By June, the oceans will freeze.

Never mind that the house is warm and soon to be warmer. Never mind that Julie is up, and the kitchen will soon smell of bacon, sourdough, and high-caffeine coffee. Never mind that the size of the woodpile has been calculated to last the winter.

Something cold beyond reason starts gnawing at your awareness when you know you couldn't live through the night without the house, the woodstove, and Costco.com.

I am old enough to remember Sawtooth Valley before it had power lines and before Galena Summit was kept reliably open in the winters.

I can remember when the highway was a dirt road. I can remember when there were salmon in the river.

I remember our neighbors up the valley—Harry and Martine Fleming, Bill Sullivan, Stubb and Vella Merritt, Ted and Phyllis Williams, Morgan and Tiny Williams, Margie Shaw, Jim and Verna Decker, Sandy and Rosie Brooks. All of them are gone now, but for a while they formed a community of shared hardship every winter, one that helped cut firewood and shovel roofs and move cattle and pull vehicles out of snowdrifts. When Phyllis Williams played piano at the two-room Quonset Hut that was the Stanley School, the whole valley showed up to dance if the snow hadn't closed the roads. There was no TV. The phone was on a party line, and not everyone could afford to join the party. The people who kept animals through the winter couldn't let them out of the barns for weeks at a time. In deep snow years, they didn't leave their houses for months, except to keep their animals alive.

Our family was not part of that community—we left every fall for the Wood River Valley, where my parents had Sun Valley jobs that came with Sun Valley paychecks—but here, every summer, we were welcomed as the exotic summer people we were. My father was a fishing guide, and he visited the ranches up and down the valley, making sure he could take his clients along the Salmon River where it went through their pastures. I remember going with my father to a house-raising for Ted and Phyllis Williams—probably the last house-raising in the valley, because the Sawtooth social contract and its communitarian traditions were fraying even then—and afterward, I overheard my parents talking about Ted and Phyllis's daughter, Mitzi, who had left the valley and had been vocal about not ever coming back. My mother said it was because Mitzi had gotten a college education, which allowed her to live in a wider world, with ambitions to match.

Most of the people I've mentioned stayed too long in the valley. They finally left when their physical or financial health broke or was about to break under the weight of age, or long winters, or bad beef and hay prices. The kids had escaped as soon as they could. If they ever changed their minds and wanted to come back, the ranches had all been sold.

My parents retired here and eventually became the oldest year-round residents in the valley. But old age makes for hard winters. My parents also stayed too long, and our memory of their last difficult years cautions Julie and me against doing the same.

Of course, old age isn't easy no matter where you are, and wider horizons bring with them agonizing decisions about where to go to feel at home, and thoughts about the people you would miss terribly. Julie and I have gotten to the age where we miss people terribly, even when they're alive and in the neighborhood, simply because they won't live forever.

The winters are easier here than they were when I was a kid. This is a statement of fact, not some walk-both-ways-uphill-to-school old man foolishness. We have electricity, and a propane furnace to keep the house above freezing if we leave for a week or a month or even longer. We have broadband, and Julie, with her college education, edits sales materials for HP, writes grants for nonprofits, and proofreads books for East Coast writers.

Between her paychecks and my savings, we keep ourselves in groceries, and, until this year, cheap airline tickets. Before the pandemic, we used to be travelers. We would get in the car and drive all the way to Boise on a plowed road, board a plane and walk out into the three a.m. heat of Bangkok or Saigon, wide awake and ready for adventure.

We're a long way from that scenario these days. This fall has taken us back 70 or 80 years, to a world where hunkering if not hibernation is essential for survival. It has put us in too-close touch with long-ago Sawtooth Valley adolescents, who spent miserable Januarys and Februarys trapped in too-small houses, stuck with carrying buckets of creek water to cows and horses in too-small barns, swamping out manure-choked stalls, re-reading *David Copperfield* for its shocks of recognition.

That's why the woodpile looks so healthy, and why we spent our stimulus checks on the new woodstove in the living room. That's why there are a couple extra cases of chili in the crawl space. But it's also why the vehicles in the garage have full gas tanks.

It's why the To Read shelf is packed with books, and why I'm halfway through *Anna Karenina*, Tolstoy's 1877 fine-print doorstop. If you'd like to leave the world you're in and enter fully into another, even if it's one full of gossip and intrigue and doomed people saying awful things to each other, a Russian novel will do the trick.

The winters are also easier because of climate change. We still see 20 below. It still snows enough some years that roofs need to be shoveled. We still ski the peaks in May if we're not tired of skiing by then. But it's been a long time since we've seen two weeks of 40-below nights and 10-below days. Fifty-five below, the coldest temperature I've experienced, hasn't been reached since the 1980s. It's been decades since I've watched a late May snowstorm come down over Williams Peak from the picture window in the Sawtooth Hotel dining room and listened while the cook padded out from the kitchen, looked at the same frozen view I was looking at, and muttered, "I'm sick of this shit."

Now, spring comes early. Fall comes late. We worry from July to October that a mega-fire will sweep through the valley, destroying everything.

Earth is close to 2 degrees Celsius warmer than it was in 1712 when Thomas Newcomen invented the steam engine. Recent headlines note that we've gone beyond the target set by the Paris Climate Accord, and a number of exponential feedback loops are in full swing. That means this climate phase change isn't the last one that will blindly transform our world.

Blind transformation is what phase changes do—they're a little like black holes, where if you get close to them time gets all wonky and the past doesn't make it intact to the future.

It still doesn't feel warm in the darkest 26 days of the year. It still doesn't dispel the feeling that sometime in the next few years, you might look at the world we're in now as a fat Russian novel, full of nasty doomed people who had no idea what was about to hit them.

*

Covid-19 is not the only plague to have hit Sawtooth Valley in the past few years. A blight of giant houses has appeared in spots that have iconic views of the Sawtooths.

The law that established the Sawtooth National Recreation Area specified that the rural/rustic/agrarian values of the valley be maintained as they had been since homesteading days. But what has infested the land of our vanished neighbors consists of great angled mansions, inspired, apparently, by airport terminal buildings. Walls of windows face the mountains. The spaces inside are designed for fundraisers rather than for small, intimate dinners. Who will live in them, and for how long?

Given the climatic, epidemic, and political variables in the air, it's an unanswerable question. I don't look to *Anna Karenina* for answers, even as our country permanently divides into what might be called nobility and what might be called serfs.

I don't think we'll have the kind of revolution the Russians had, and that's a good thing. If some future Trotsky were to lead a proletariat army out of the foreclosed suburbs of Boise, I'm certain that Julie and I would be mistaken for capitalist bourgeoisie and murdered, no matter how poor we are in relation to our new neighbors.

I hope, rather, that we'll have a revolution in ethics. At some point, people will start thinking that building 10- and 15-thousand-square-foot homes in a world where more and more people are homeless is flat-out tacky, ugly, selfish behavior. I can remember touring great mansions in Newport, Rhode Island, built the other time we had robber barons running the country. They had become what in the U.K. are known as *piles*, objects of architectural entropy that had become prisons for the heirs of the people who built them. They had begun as hopes for the future, but had ended as burdens from the past, in the form of vast echoing mausoleums for lives of questionable taste.

Meanwhile, in Sawtooth Valley, more of them are going up every time one of the old ranches changes hands. Of them, my friend Bruce says, "There must be *giants* living in those places."

"They're just trying to make a statement," I say.

"I'm not sure I'd make a statement like that about myself," says Bruce, "even if I was one."

*

I've read a big chunk of *Anna Karenina,* but still have 543 pages left. I hope to finish it by the shortest day of the year, and then start on something cheerier, like *The Pickwick Papers* or *Best American Science and Nature Writing.* I'll read on the couch for a month or so, until the sun stops sinking behind the southern horizon at four in the afternoon. When there's a little more daylight, and a little more snow, we'll start skiing farther out in the backcountry.

That's as much of the future as I feel confident to predict. In the meantime, I'm spending evenings with a bunch of Russian nobility. I worry about their ability to access French fashion, and who of them is sleeping with whom, and whether or not their serfs should be given land, and which of the Tsar's army officers are good for their gambling debts and which are not.

You can get caught up in these matters, especially when you remember *Anna Karenina* is a cultural artifact. It's not really fiction. It was based on real people, ones careless, pampered, and cruel. They ignored the signs of their times: the pain of the poor, the waste and useless luxury of their social lives, and the criminal injustice they were a part of. They turned away from anything unpleasant in their lives, even when they caused it, and the generations that came after them paid dearly for it.

We hope nobody has to pay for anything Julie and I did or didn't do. We didn't mean to end up in a world that is less just than we were told it was in high school civics class. We didn't mean to live in a country that has failed to take care of its least fortunate citizens. We didn't mean to end up in a small warm house with a pot roast in the oven and skis in the foyer, and feel guilty every time we see three-hour food lines on TV.

We didn't mean to end up in a valley full of third and fourth houses, but we did. In these dark days of December, with an election still threatened by martial law, with Covid vaccines still awaiting distribution, our valley seems meaner and colder than it did 60 years ago, a warming climate notwithstanding.

Cave Life

December 14, 2020

ALL THEIR LIVES, the prisoners have been chained facing a blank back wall in a shallow cave. They watch dim shadows of people, animals, and clouds passing the mouth of the cave, and they mistake these shadows for reality.

One prisoner escapes his chains, leaves the cave, and wanders amazed through the trees, farms, and cities of the outside world. When he sneaks back into the dark cave to describe to his fellows all that he's witnessed, they refuse to believe him.

Watching their sunburned escapee friend stumble around in sun-blinded confusion, the prisoners resolve to never try to escape.

This small story forms the core of Plato's *Allegory of the Cave*. It's a story useful to anyone who teaches critical thinking, because it's a handy way to explain that reality isn't always what it seems.

I used to mention the cave in journalism classes when I was trying to explain the need to verify news stories. "As a reporter, you need to know when something looks like what it isn't," I told them. "That requires time, effort, and a perpetual refusal to take things at face value.

"That's why you go into interviews having done some research. You find out whether the person you're interviewing has a reputation for lying. You interview more than one person. You consult experts on points of dispute.

"You can maybe start thinking a story is true once it's been verified by two independent sources, but don't stop at two. Keep looking, and never refuse to change your mind when new evidence contradicts old evidence. Don't ever mistake what you know for what's real."

It's been a while since I taught journalism, but Plato's Cave has stuck with me, especially this winter in Sawtooth Valley, where evidence of the outside world comes from an occasional pickup or SUV on the highway, plus aircraft contrails far above our heads, plus the internet.

In spite of what the internet tells us, the pickups do not appear to be full of right-wing militia members and they don't have anti-aircraft guns mounted in their beds. The contrails are too few and too thin to be chemtrails, and the aircraft leaving them don't look like military transports flying shock troops into cities run by Democrats.

The news stories and commentaries on my computer screen present themselves as reality. They're not. As a critical thinker, I don't need Plato to point out the internet presents a corrupt and incomplete version of what's really out there.

If anything is out there.

I've spent the morning reading people who expect Donald Trump to invoke the Insurrection Act and refuse to give up the reins of power on January 20. Almost all of these people think he should do this because he's been cheated out of the presidency by election fraud. They believe the military will back him up. They cite as evidence increased flights of troop-carrying C130s out of air bases, and the presence of aircraft carriers off our Atlantic coast.

It's assumed that Trump cannot take these steps without generating armed opposition from Black Lives Matter and Antifa protestors, but it's also assumed that these groups will be rounded up and shot shortly after the military takes control. Also, Covid-19 will be revealed as nothing worse than the common cold, and everyone will take off their masks and go back to work. The Dow Jones will take aim at 40,000. Industry will return to the Rust Belt. Women will return to kitchen and nursery.

On some websites, there are calls for traitors to be guillotined, except for journalists, who instead should be stripped naked and staked out in the desert over fire-ant nests. The ingrate justices Gorsuch, Kavanaugh, and Barrett, along with Attorney General Barr, are to be executed by firing squad.

You get the idea, reading the commentary on far-right websites, that over the next four years, a lot of people will be executed in ways limited only by their executioners' imaginations. You also get the idea that a lot of people aspire to be executioners.

I wish I was making this up, but I'm not. These are real comments on real websites, and real people are creating them. I think it's safe to say they're not critical thinkers. It's also safe to say their emotional lives are insanely violent and cruel and their confidence is unshakeable.

If the verification techniques I taught in my journalism classes had been followed by every voter in the country, Donald Trump's stories wouldn't have won him election in 2016. He wouldn't have become president if voters had demanded more than one source for their information, if they had insisted he release his tax returns, or if they had pondered the implications of his legal history.

He wouldn't have become president if an outright lie had been a deal-breaker for the average voter.

Now, we are asked to believe the story of a stolen election. Election officials, even in Republican states, are saying it didn't happen. Voting machine experts are saying it didn't happen. By any journalistic assessment, it's a lie. But it might keep Donald Trump in the White House.

Lies have put all sorts of people in power and kept them there. But the trouble with basing your power on a lie is that it requires more and more energy to maintain as time goes on. The energy that should have gone into, say, coordinating a response to a pandemic goes instead into making sure people still believe what you're telling them. Ultimately, nothing becomes as important as ensuring the real world doesn't impact your thinking or the thinking of your followers.

All that's required to paralyze these not-so-United States for the next four years is to keep Donald Trump in the Oval Office. There will be no energy left for anything but making up elaborate fictions to keep him there.

Sawtooth Valley is not a cave, but it has a cave's ability to substitute for the real. We who live here are not chained to rock walls, and we know that the images on our computer screens may be manipulated. We know the words we read on screens may be true, or partly true, or deliberate lies written by evil people, or by good people crazed by lives of disappointment and tragedy. Also, we here in the valley are free to drive over Galena Summit with our critical thinking caps on and do some good old honest fact-checking.

Most of us don't bother in these pandemic days. We know that fact-checking, for us, would only confirm that one Costco looks like another. Besides, we've got a nice wall here and we love it and its ever-changing shadows.

Even the news serves to convince us that other walls are worse. It's a recipe for complacency, which doesn't chafe like chains do, and is just as effective in keeping us from the world.

Plato suggested that if you want to escape the cave, you can dedicate yourself to a good, solid, eternal idea, like Truth, or Justice, or even Kindness. These ideas are more real than any faint shadow you could discern as a cave-dweller.

I sided with Plato. I told my journalism students that Truth was to be their highest and best goal, and although they could never completely reach it, there were ways of getting ever closer to it. It was worth going to jail for. It was worth dying for, even if it meant being staked out over a bunch of fire ants somewhere south of Tucson.

"Why can't you ever reach Truth?" they wanted to know.

"Sometimes your whole story is an artifact of your point of view," I said. "And deadlines always come before you're done. Some of your interviewees will have filled you full of happy lies. But the story will go to print with your name on it, and you'd better have done enough work and been perceptive enough that your readers know you've seen through the lies, accounted for any research bias, and admitted that you didn't have time to nail down everything you needed to. If you haven't done all that, you need to give up on Truth and become lobbyists."

None of my journalism students are, as far as I know, journalists. A number of them are lobbyists, however, which makes me think they were really paying attention when I described the ways journalists could be manipulated.

Sometime later today, the Electoral College is expected to certify that Joe Biden won the election. I have no idea if it really will do that. There may be enough faithless electors to give the presidency to Trump again. Or maybe the military will interrupt the proceedings and announce Trump is president for another four or eight years. Perhaps Trump will declare martial law for a decade. Perhaps Congress will refuse to accept the Electoral College results.

If any of these measures keep Biden out of office, all constitutional restraints on executive authority will be gone.

I know such things can happen, because they've happened in other countries, at other times. The Republican party has convinced me they won't let questions of conscience impede their vision of an Ideal Republic, no matter how shabby, avaricious, and ugly that republic ends up being in the flesh.

But I simply don't know what will happen. I can't know what will happen and I certainly, at this point, can't determine what will happen. I no longer can distinguish between what's real and what isn't real, especially on the internet. Uncertainty has become the gray stone wall upon which I watch the news.

Philosophers have been busy since Plato, and they've taken pains to logically undercut a lot of things that he took for granted, like ideas and mathematical axioms and even the natural world. Deconstruction has shown that if you change the context of an idea, you can change its meaning to anything—hence nothing—and that with a little tweaking, you can show that mathematical truth and the natural world exist only as artifacts of an oppressive culture. Plato's bedrock reality, the world of the ideal, is no longer believed to exist.

Plato's cave has been expanded to include its own outside.

Once people learned how to make reality itself into an artifact, there wasn't much that journalists and scientists and other believers in Truth could point to in its defense. Even if we could have pointed to Truth's solid service in World War II and in the civil rights movement, nobody was listening. Truth itself had already gone over to the enemy.

An astronomer friend has notified me that Jupiter and Saturn will appear as a point of light a week from now, on the solstice. They will be 400 million miles apart, of course, but from our perspective they'll look like they're almost touching. It's the best example I can give of our point of view creating the news these days.

The end of this process—and it is a process, one where each step seems inevitable once it's been taken—is that each of us becomes a world, and what each of us believes is true. That's not a good outlook for a country that hopes to arrive at a consensus on where to go, what to do, and what the national purpose should be.

Underlay, Underlay!

December 21, 2020

A YEAR AGO, Julie and I were in the last two weeks of a year without alcohol. We had decided to go an entire year without drinking, not because we were very often drinking a lot, but we were drinking a little, every day, and it was becoming part of our life, identity, and budget. On the occasions when we did drink a lot, we were waking up at three a.m. wide awake, cursing ourselves. So on January 1, 2019 we put all the wine and spirits in the crawl space and said goodbye to our social life.

Or so we thought. Our social life survived just fine, although when we got together with friends, we missed having a hot toddy after skiing, and we missed having wine with dinner. When summer came, we missed having gin and tonics on the deck. When we invited people over, we told them to bring their own wine, and on the rare occasions we had parties, the amount of alcohol people brought was far less than it had been. We no longer ended up with more wine at the end of a party than at the beginning.

The parties and dinners ended earlier. The conversations were less didactic, less loud, and, in my case, more intelligent. Six weeks into the exercise, we started sleeping better and longer. I began to remember my dreams.

I bring this up because I recently went in for a dermatology appointment, and the dermatologist's assistant, going over my chart, noted that I had quit alcohol. "Not anymore," I said. "It was just for a year. We've returned to wine with enthusiasm."

"Why'd you quit?" she wanted to know.

"It was time to reset the clocks," I told her. "It's a powerful drug and after a year without it, you notice what it does for you and to you.

Also, you spend less time thinking about all the shameful things you did in high school when you're not wide awake at three a.m."

"But you started drinking again," she said. It was an accusation, and I realized she wasn't talking about me, she was talking about other people, maybe people she loved, whose relationships with alcohol were not as benign as Julie's and mine have been. I was suddenly in a conversation I didn't want to be having. Fortunately, the dermatologist chose that moment to come in and start quizzing me about how many sunburns I'd had 40 years ago. I had a lot to confess. My relationship with the sun has not been a benign one at all.

This morning, the Johns Hopkins Covid map lists 17,862,876 U.S. coronavirus cases and 317,749 deaths. As a nation, we haven't let those numbers come to consciousness. We see tearful family members and devastated medical workers on TV, but congresspeople are still talking about herd immunity and why masks interfere with constitutional rights. Some of them are still insisting Donald Trump won the election.

Much of what we see on the news is deliberate distraction from what we don't want to think about, such as the pandemic.

We see people going into the valley's one open restaurant without masks, and we realize we cannot go there until we get vaccinated. When we've spotted maskless people in the post office, we sometimes have waited a day to get our mail.

It's a tyranny of the unconscious, although in our cases, we're facing more unconsciousness than tyranny.

Julie and I talk about the pandemic a bunch. Some days we have a glass of wine or a martini on the couch before dinner, and it becomes a pause in the day's occupation, one where we sit down, stare deep into each other's eyes, and talk about what's on our minds. We enjoy these conversations, despite their usually grim content. We're thankful that after 28 years together, we can still surprise each other with what we have to say.

That's not to say we're thinking radically different things. After 28 years, the surprise comes when one of us is struggling to put a thought into words and the other articulates it neatly, powerfully, and concisely. Julie did that last week when she said, "Thank God we quit drinking in 2019 and not 2020."

One or the other of us has also said, "Thank God we're still not teaching in Caldwell."

And "Thank God we're not homeless," and "Thank God we can still get out the door for a hike."

These statements sound blatantly obvious, but on the couch, they have the power of revelation. None of these things had to turn out the way they did.

We thank God for our good fortune, although if you go beyond the level of idiom, our theology turns out not to be connected to any organized system of values. God starts looking a lot like Mr. Dumb Luck, who rains his bounty on the good and bad alike, and who turns his face away from you when he feels dyspeptic.

When we look at what is happening in this country and in the world, Julie and I say, "Thank God we're still alive. Thank God we've made it this far." We never say, "Thank God all our tomorrows will be bright," because we're pretty sure that would trigger Mr. Dumb Luck's sense of irony.

My relationship with alcohol has not always been benign. When I bartended in Ketchum for a couple of winters, I served chronic alcoholics, drunk drivers, and young people whose IDs had been borrowed from grandparents. Ketchum is a resort town, and the cops—at least when I was bartending—tended to drive the town's paying customers home rather than hit them with a DUI.

I was a part of that dismal economy. Some of the people who got up from a barstool and walked out the door of Slavey's, keys in hand, were lucky not to kill someone. If they did and I didn't hear about it, I wasn't any less complicit. But no one has much incentive to change a system when they've got a starring role in it.

I did, on occasion, harangue my customers who were following alcohol down the road to jail or death. One of my regulars—once a professional-level athlete and business owner in Ketchum—had lost his house, his business, his marriage, and his non-alcoholic friends, all to alcohol. He told me all that on the chairlift in early December of my first year of bartending, when we had ended up next to each other in the lift line. His story affected me deeply, because he was a good skier, an intelligent conversationalist, and his ex-wife had been a teacher in my grade school. I still had a helpless crush on her. If I could have gone back to seventh grade and married her, I would have.

One afternoon that spring, when he sat down in late afternoon sunshine across the bar from me, I said, "Why do you keep drinking? It's not doing you any good."

If I hadn't just poured him a drink, he would have gone down the street to the Casino Club, where the drinks were cheaper and stronger. Nobody walks into a bar for a temperance lecture. But he looked at me and said, "I get bored. I get bored. I get bored, and then I drink, and then things start happening again."

A quick internet search reveals his last DUI was when he was 87 years old, and he spent a bunch of years in jail for multiple DUIs before that. Boredom must have been a bigger terror for him than jail. I don't know if he's still alive—that last DUI was close to a decade ago—but if he is, he must have a titanium liver.

I still have a crush on his ex-wife, at least his ex-wife as she was in 1962, her first year of teaching grade school.

Boredom has not been a terror for Julie and me this fall, even though the big snowpack we were expecting by now hasn't arrived.

We've substituted the grim terror of boredom with the exhilaration of plain old terror. The track we've put up above the Rocky Mountain Lodge has gotten icy and exciting, especially when Juno decides we qualify as herd animals and growls and snaps at our heels as we zip back to the car. Trees whiz by. Low branches threaten a bruised forehead when they don't threaten decapitation. We get back to our car about the time the sun goes behind the peaks, and the sudden cold reminds us to get home before we freeze solid.

This week we'll venture out on snowier slopes by Banner Summit, skiing around any mound of snow that might be hiding a big rock or a log we could get our skis under at speed. We will go with friends, in separate cars, and keep our distance, but we'll be glad to ski the same slope with them at long last.

Our indoor social life has not survived the pandemic, but Julie has her needlepoint projects and her editing work, which has been picking up after a quiet summer and fall. I have firewood to pack into the house every evening. The driveway needs to be snowblown and the deck shoveled. Clothes washed and folded. Dishes loaded and unloaded from the dishwasher.

Also, we have books. The ones we're reading consistently point out that social lives can be more problematic than fun.

Anna Karenina has gotten a bit millstony in its middle reaches— the Russian nobility *might* have died of boredom and spite if the Bolsheviks hadn't killed them first—but I still read a chapter or two now and then, and I'm pretty sure I'll be done with it by April.

Even if our day-to-day life, with its routine and its limitations, had us searching for something to do, we would have our memories. I can't speak for Julie, but I've been thinking about events I haven't thought about for 40 years. Embarrassing adolescent events have hit me with the force of hallucination. Most of them were incidents I have deliberately forgotten. It's a shameful business, but it keeps me occupied.

We have a joke when we're backcountry skiing: Hazards Exist That Are Not Marked. You find signs bearing these words at any ski resort, but they're much more appropriate in the unsigned backcountry, especially in a low snow year like this. The cushion of powder that all skiers have learned to relax and fall into sometimes obscures hard, sharp things, even when it's thick and soft, and right now it's neither thick nor soft.

Your biggest piece of safety gear is your outdoor social life. Your ski buddies will, one way or another, help you get to the car if you hurt yourself. If you don't have companions, you will probably die out there if you make a mistake.

*

Start thinking about maskless people in the post office or restaurants, or start asking addicts why they do things that destroy their lives and the lives of the people around them, and you'll see there's more than just surface to the world, and that things under the surface can be dangerous. Hazards exist that are not marked.

That's about as far as I want to carry this metaphor. Suffice it to say there's a complexity to this world we probably couldn't handle if we didn't spend most of our time skimming the surface of things. The writer Thomas Pynchon refers to "the concealed density of dream" that lives below our everyday existence, which is one of the better descriptions of reality I've read in literature.

The pandemic has begun to reveal the underlay. The election has begun to reveal the underlay. Dream and memory suddenly have a much bigger role in our lives than we thought they did. An action that looked like free will last year looks like the handiwork of Mr. Dumb Luck this year. We gaze—with some fear—at the past, as it rises from the deep.

Holiday Sermon

December 28, 2020

CHRISTMAS DINNER WAS a solemn affair this year, mainly because Julie and Juno and I were the only guests. Normally we have a houseful, or friends have a houseful and we're part of it. Laughter and kitchen noise and happy greetings make up our usual Christmas soundscape.

This Christmas, in what suddenly seemed like an empty house, we wished others were with us. Nobody among close friends and family has died in the pandemic, but our solitude reminded us that there are people—once close—we will never see again. In the absence of loud and happy conversation, people we hadn't seen or thought of for a long time crept into the silences. Several times in the past year, when I put the name of an old acquaintance into a search engine, I found an obituary. It was a shock, every time, even though I can read the actuarial tables as well as anybody.

Julie and I and Juno did do a Christmas ski into Redfish Lake Lodge during the late afternoon. We had to wait for Julie's pie to come out of the oven, so by the time we got on the snow, the day was already getting darker. When we reached the Redfish docks, a snowstorm was hovering over the peaks. The dark chased us back to the car. We had to take off our sunglasses or we couldn't see to ski.

Once home, Julie got serious with dinner. Juno went to sleep on the floor in front of the woodstove.

The menu:

Grilled Leg of Lamb
Roasted Garlic Potatoes

Kale and Arugula Salad with Pine Nuts
A '16 California Zinfandel
Port or Brandy
Apple Pie
Black Coffee
A Beautiful Day in the Neighborhood (movie)

We made it as far as the Zinfandel. I did get the dishes done before I fell into bed.

Although it's not listed, guilt was on our Christmas menu. This year has brought with it too many examples of lives ended, jobs and homes lost, careers destroyed, hopes dashed. We find ourselves dismayed that our country consistently ignores—when it doesn't deliberately harm—the poor people within its borders. We know that our Christmas dinner—all paid for, consumed under our own roof, with enough left over for Boxing Day—puts us among a fortunate minority of Americans. Our economy has become a zero-sum game, and this winter, if you watch the news, having enough can feel like a crime.

At the same time, we fear the sudden change of circumstance that could render our happiness into grief, our savings into worthless paper, our health into sickness, our world into ruins. Both of us absorbed the deep lessons of Depression Era parents and grandparents: work hard, save as much as possible, use it up, wear it out, make it do, never buy new. Both of us absorbed the even deeper lessons of the Cold War and of the AIDS epidemic and of nursing homes: in the end, other people make your life-and-death decisions for you. You can do everything you're supposed to do and still have no idea whether your virtuous, well-planned, well-deserved life will last the week.

Here's the mantra: It's not up to you. It's never been up to you. It will never be up to you.

That doesn't mean you can't feel guilty about it.

Julie and I have spent nearly 30 years in the muddy psychic terrain between the guilt of having a good life we didn't really deserve and the anxiety of losing it all through no fault of our own. Yet life remains interesting and full of joy. It's a contradiction we're in no hurry to resolve.

A week before Christmas, we cut a small skinny tree from a thicket of volunteer lodgepole out by the river. We decorated it with lights, strings of beads, and the ornaments that Julie's grandparents gave her over the years she was growing up. We attached red velvet bows to the ends of branches, wrapped the tree-holder in a brocaded cloth, and turned on the lights.

It looked just like all the other Christmas trees we've decorated over the years. Now and then we get a new ornament as a gift, and this year Julie made a needlepoint snowman that sits up near the top. But anyone seeing our tree this year would have trouble distinguishing between it and any of our other trees over the last 20 years. Dr. Seuss could claim them all as his own.

We called it good. We called it funny looking. We called it beautiful. In our house, all those things go well together.

We did finally watch *A Beautiful Day in the Neighborhood* on Boxing Day. It's a movie about Fred Rogers, whose television show for young children, *Mr. Rogers' Neighborhood*, was the subject of parody and ridicule for its general sappiness. But it was also a program that met tiny children on their own turf. It was designed to address what worried them, what made them angry or confused, and what made them happy.

Fred Rogers had figured out that few children, even ones raised in privileged homes, are allowed to have real selves in real time. They get damaged by families who love them for who they are expected to be, not for who they are. In every episode, though, *Mr. Rogers' Neighborhood* treated them like real persons. For many of these children, it was the first step on a lifetime project of realizing they were a person.

The movie made it clear that Fred Rogers, a Christian minister, lived as he believed. He practiced Christian charity, which simply meant that he genuinely loved his fellow humans and, when he had the opportunity, acted on that love.

The movie also made it clear that living a life according to the Golden Rule isn't easy. It takes time, sweat, tears, and pain, but it's likely the only path most of us have to any kind of earthly happiness. As for the people around you, you allow them to have real selves in real time. It's good for them, and the company of real people is good for you.

One of the lines in the movie referred to the idea—widespread across cultures and countries—that just about the time you learn how to live, you get old and die. It might be more accurate to say that when the evidence becomes overwhelming that you're mortal, you become open to the idea that life isn't all getting and spending, winning and losing, righting wrongs and making sure you've justified your life exactly as you've lived it. These things are crushing burdens for human beings, and any idea that counters them—such as the soul being a process, one that by definition will never be completed—comes as a happy and freeing revelation.

Every few years I reread Ernest Becker's *The Denial of Death*, an improbably cheerful book that details how human beings are creatures with divine minds trapped in mortal bodies. Becker says death is a reality we cannot face. Our lives, our bank accounts, our houses, our art and literature, and our children, if we have them, are all attempts to live beyond our mandated threescore and ten.

A pandemic is a near-death experience, causing us to even more emphatically deny we are subject to death. Becker says the same thing can happen when your football team loses a championship game, or your new car gets a ding in a parking lot, or a typo is discovered in your just-published book. Make any little thing into your immortality project, and it can be a near-death experience if you find a flaw in it.

Becker was a psychologist and social scientist. He was dying of cancer as he was writing *The Denial of Death*. His editors had to finish his book for him, which is delightfully ironic enough to get him into the Writer's Hall of Fame. He's immortal in my mind.

His editors also put together a posthumous volume called *Escape from Evil*. It consists of his notes on the problem of bad people. He, no doubt by habit, locates the dark side of the human psyche—our fallen nature—in our inability to come to terms with death. We kill people so we don't have to die ourselves. We hurt them so we don't have to feel pain. We leave damaging legacies so our descendants, in their suffering, won't forget us. We imagine that others want us to die, and that justifies any atrocity we choose to commit against them. Once they're dead and we're still alive, we've triumphed over death. But only if we're good at lying to ourselves.

Becker believes in science. He places his faith in the scientific method as a reliable way to know the universe we're in. He notes that organized religion owes existence to its offer of an escape from death, but he doesn't comment one way or another on an afterlife. An afterlife is not subject to scientific investigation in the same way as an all-too-present fear of death. Becker, with some wisdom, focuses on what he can explore in the world he still occupies, saving questions of the afterlife for after his life.

I used to tell my student advisees, usually when they had come back from a family funeral and were in their first away-from-home existential crisis, that regardless of what happens after death, death itself is a major lifestyle change. You can't expect to go through it and not have a period of serious adjustment, if you have anything left to adjust.

My students were oddly comforted by this view of things, mainly because religious dogma fails badly at funerals. Conventional certainties about eternal life, as Becker indicates, don't fare well in the face of an open casket.

My own view of the afterlife is not marked by any certainty whatsoever. At times I do speculate that everybody goes to hell after death, and hell is an indefinite period of examining, from a cosmic perspective, every evil thing you ever did. You get to relive every anger, every easy way out, every mean thought, every bit of sloth, avarice, self-righteousness, greed, envy, lust, and gluttony, all from a position of knowing better. I've been proceeding on the hope that you get time off if you start early.

Heaven springs into existence when you finally own up to your sins, understand why you committed them, and know that if you can help it, you won't commit them again. Not many people make it to heaven, at least on any human scale of time.

Science is a method of questioning reality, and as such it gives many more answers about what isn't than what is. It tends to destroy religious dogma on contact. Didactic images of the afterlife fall apart in the face of the Laws of Thermodynamics. Wine is much more likely to turn to water than the other way around. Walls do not tumble down when you blow a ram's horn at them. Snakes do not talk. People cast into fiery furnaces do not walk unharmed out of them.

Demonic possession is a real thing, but the demons turn out to be brutal ancestors seven generations removed, their sins cascading onto the heads of their descendants through time.

Resurrection and eternal life? Still awaiting scientific evidence.

Happily, you don't have to believe Christ exists to behave like him. You don't have to prove God exists if God is love. In the presence of love, the eternal starts edging into our lives. Also, questions of conscience spring up. They tend to banish questions about the afterlife into an irrelevant future.

If you're looking for certainty in this world, there's plenty of it on your own plate, in the choices you make to be kind or not.

Four hundred thousand more Americans died in 2020 than died in 2019. That number is evidence enough that business as usual will not occur for a while. We will never go back to what we were. A new generation has been forged this year, and it will have to live in a new world.

Four hundred thousand. No science of grief exists to quantify the effect those deaths had on the families fragmented by them, but none is needed. The grief is there, enormous and unmoving. There's no explaining it away. You can refuse to share it, but only at the cost of ignoring the truth that one of those grieving families could be yours.

Will be yours. Grief is woven into the fabric of human existence. Loss is the price of having love in your life.

Fred Rogers had the ability to value and respect little kids as they were when he was talking to them. For a lot of them, that was the moment they snapped into personhood. To have someone focus on who you are and what you're trying to express seems to be essential for human development, judging from the amount of people walking around who never became persons.

We owe it to ourselves to pay attention to each other, if only so we can live in a world where when you look at a human, you can expect somebody to be in there.

There's room for Christian ethics in our response to the grieving, even if it's only to say, "What you're feeling is real. I'm sorry this happened to you. I will grieve with you, so you won't be alone in your grief."

That sort of thing won't save the world, but it will make your part of it a friendlier place.

The Uncertainty Principle
and the New Year

January 4, 2021

ONE OF THE less-than-shining moments of my academic career was when I stood up in a faculty meeting at the College of Idaho and accused my colleagues of having it too easy. I was in my first semester teaching there. I was teaching four sections of English Composition and a journalism class, and spending my nights grading essays. I was also on a number of faculty committees, due to lack of seniority. New assistant professors get stuck with committee assignments, where they get to endlessly draft rewrites of the faculty handbook, write committee position papers, and keep the minutes of the committees they find themselves on.

Perhaps I was overwhelmed by committee work, or by the stacks of essays I was correcting, or by the line of students that formed outside my office every afternoon, demanding serious attention and care. On the one hand, I was listening to my advisees tell stories of family illness, grief, financial disaster, divorce, death, and incest. On the other, I was listening to colleagues moan about how overworked they were.

So I stood up in a late-November faculty meeting and said, "We're spending a lot of time talking about working too hard, but I put myself through grad school working on a cement crew, and you people [I used the phrase *you people*] don't work nearly as hard as the people who built the buildings you teach in. I'm teaching an overload and correcting 80 essays a week, and I feel like I'm in the best job I've ever had. Part of it is that I like the work, but part of it is that compared to being a cement worker, it's not that much work."

There was dead silence for a moment, and then people resumed complaining. I had committed one of those acts that is never acknowledged in polite company, no matter how bad its odor. After the meeting, the dean of the faculty came up to me and said, "Thank you for saying that. But you'll never get tenure."

You cannot plan the future when you've been told it's not going to happen. You also cannot depend on getting a job you've trained for, or assume you'll get vaccinated on schedule, or think your quick escape to Samarra will allow you to skip your meeting with Death. You can't even be sure you won't write a book, if some future Daniel Defoe decides to turn your notes into a Journal of the Plague Year.

Geneticists have computed the odds of you being you, and me being me, starting from one of our distant ancestors in the Pre-Cambrian, and they say your existence in any form is statistically impossible. Theoretical physicists tell us that to plan the future is to alter it, often in ways we can't plan for. Other theoretical physicists tell us we occupy one of an infinite number of universes, the endless writhing branches of a continuously bifurcating reality. Anyone we can imagine being, and a bunch of someones we can't, we are, somewhere and sometime.

In the universe where I was hired by the College of Idaho—after hearing from colleagues, people on the grounds crew, cafeteria workers and even the college president that I wouldn't get tenure—I ended up getting tenure. I was even promoted to full professor after 15 years.

In all, I spent 25 years on the College of Idaho faculty, but the last 10 of those years was as the College's writer at large, a position that didn't come with a salary or, it turned out, duties. During an institutional financial crisis, I had traded that expensive full professorship for a relatively cheap decade of medical insurance for Julie and me. It was more than worth it for all concerned, but yet more evidence that neither the College nor I was in a universe where tenure meant what it was supposed to mean.

Julie started editing for a company that produced sales literature for HP, and I started teaching in a low-residency MFA program. We moved to our house in Sawtooth Valley. We have lived here ever since.

*

New Year's Day, 2021: As we were getting ready for a Zoom call with friends in Illinois, Julie turned to me and said, "This time last year we weren't thinking about a pandemic. This time last year we didn't Zoom our friends, we got on a plane and visited them. We went out to dinner in Chicago. We walked in the lakefront park and stood under the Bean and looked at the picture of Dorian Gray in the Art Institute."

This time last year we were looking forward to a jubilee year, which would be marked by my 70th birthday, Julie's 50th, and our 25th wedding anniversary. I was planning to be reading in London on my birthday, but the other two occasions would be crowded celebrations at our house.

But the future we—and the rest of the country—thought we had this time last year is now a desert of expectation. The pandemic has put us all in a new place, and every day that it goes on carries us further from the old place.

That doesn't mean Julie and I and the country don't have a future. It just means that if a year ago we had predicted anything, we would have been a little wrong in February, a lot wrong by April, and completely wrong by now.

That's why, if you were today expecting me to provide a list of predictions for the New Year, you will be disappointed. I won't tell you every 70-year-old Idahoan will be vaccinated by May, or Donald Trump will be crowned Emperor for Life by June, or four Supreme Court justices will resign by July. I won't say in August the stock market will crash, or China will invade Taiwan and Shanghai and Taipei will be destroyed by nuclear weapons. I won't tell you 2021 will see an accident at a Russian bioweapons facility reducing the human population by 58 percent. I won't predict our country will be in a civil war, or that seven U.S. senators, three of them from western states, will be hanged for treason. I won't even tell you the College of Idaho will go bankrupt due to a permanent shut-off of foreign student visas and CTE lawsuits from brain-damaged football players.

According to some theories of physics, all these things will happen sometime, somewhere. It's a scary multiverse.

*

Sometimes the unknowable isn't all bad news. Julie and I, walking into a College of Idaho classroom in 1989, couldn't have known we would spend happy decades together.

Even if I had believed it was ethical to fall in love with a student and marry her, I would have said to myself, "If you do that, you'll never get tenure."

Julie and I have tried to figure out how we ended up together, and the best we can come up with is that hitting adolescence in vast non-civilized spaces (she on a ranch in the Eastern Oregon desert, me in Sawtooth Valley) deprived us of the kind of socialization we needed to become normal, non-alienated, tenured human beings. We both had a language invented over years of talking to ourselves, but neither of us expected to find another native speaker.

We both recognized socialization as a kind of covert violence we had never experienced.

My father was a trapper. Julie's father was a rancher. We knew what up-close violence looked like and knew when it was necessary for existence and when it wasn't. Socialization, when we figured out what it was, looked like a totally unnecessary detour to the slaughterhouse.

At any rate, the decades have flown by, as they do when you're having fun. I'm still in love, and Julie says she is too.

Julie has become a better cook, and she was a good one to begin with. I've become a better person, and so has Julie. Shows what good cooking can do for you.

This year I've been emailing friends New Year's greetings, wishing them, as a kind of mantra, good news from unexpected directions all year long. I've been sincere but non-specific, as I don't know what good news would mean to them.

But the other day I got some good news from out of the blue that was wonderfully specific. Jeremy Garber, an employee at Powell's, the great independent bookstore in Portland, put my *A Hundred Little Pieces on the End of the World* on a LitHub list: Best Under-the-Radar Books of 2020.

I've never met Jeremy, but I call him friend.

Literary Hub is a national book-focused website with hundreds of thousands of subscribers, and *Hundred Pieces'* ranking on Amazon jumped from down in the millions to up in the thirty-thousands. That may not sound like much, but it's a great leap in a universe where 2.2 million books are published each year.

Also, we went skiing New Year's Day on Banner Summit, and a slope that had been terrible skiing a few days before had received a five-inch layer of powder. The subsurface crust had softened up, and the snow was so good that you didn't even have to think to turn. We exhausted ourselves and the dog, climbing up and skiing down again and again, and got back to the car tired and happy. We were with our friends Liesl and Michael and Sean. Everybody remembered how to ski. Everybody was still in good enough shape to ski. It felt good for Julie and me to start the year off in the presence of other human beings.

On the suddenly reasonable assumption that what you throw out into your world comes right back at you, I'm wishing everyone reading these words even better news, from far more unexpected directions, for the entire upcoming year, and the year after, if you can stand it.

The day I received tenure at the College of Idaho, I became certain that I would die in the harness. I would teach long beyond my safe-to-consume date, and my students, used to waiting for long pauses while I collected what was left of my wits, would discover that my draped-over-the-lectern pose was due to death, not fatigue. It would not be a bad way to go, I decided. I loved teaching and I loved the College and couldn't think of a better way to get old.

That imagined future didn't happen. My imagination has gotten richer and deeper since then, and I've thought of even better futures. One thing I've stopped doing, though, is thinking the future has any relationship to the present. You can't count on cause-and-effect anymore, which puts a lot of guesswork in prophecy.

If you want to make the gods laugh, goes the old saying, tell them your plans. But that assumes a certain agency on the part of the gods, and further assumes you always plan what's best for you. In the presence of endlessly bifurcating realities, that's impossible.

Also, the gods—even the tiny quantum gods in charge of delivering us one future out of many—might be more benign than we give them credit for. They might gift you with nice surprises from unexpected directions. They might appreciate a little gratitude once in a while.

Good things can happen, and many good things are my 2021 wish for you, me, Julie, my former *you people* colleagues, everyone else within reading distance, and especially Jeremy who works at Powell's in Portland, who liked my book well enough to recommend it for a kind of tenure. If you see him there and you've been vaccinated, give him a hug for me.

The End of the Beginning

January 11, 2021

FOR A NUMBER of years now, I've tried to be a witness to the world from the outside rather than a mover and shaker on the inside. Start taking your witnessing seriously, and you'll live in a much bigger and more interesting and more terrifying world than you thought you lived in. You'll also give up any ambitions to be a mover and shaker, because, upon careful inspection, you'll see those people are miserable, and often enough, batshit crazy.

Julie and I witnessed the recent superspreader event in the Capitol with a deep sadness and an even deeper relief. The sadness comes from understanding that this country is divided into warring tribes who see each other as the embodiment of evil.

The relief comes from seeing video of Donald Trump looking old, sick, and not in control of himself. That may seem a cruel thing to say, but he's been a bad president, an incompetent administrator and strategist, and he's brought out the worst in the American people. The country will be a kinder and gentler place if he becomes incapable of politics.

He may be incapable of politics now. The people who know him no longer trust him. They watched him set his mob of supporters on poor old loyal Mike Pence—who foolishly thought he had been chosen as Vice President for his deep Christian incorruptibility—who had to be escorted out of the Capitol building by Secret Service officers responsible for his safety. Pence may see himself as a future Christian martyr, but like St. Augustine, he'd prefer not to transition just now.

We still worry the world is in danger of being destroyed if Trump decides launching a nuclear weapon toward Tehran or Pyongyang will let him stay in the White House for the duration of a national emergency. (It would be a national emergency all right, but of short duration. There's a reason it's called Mutually Assured Destruction.)

But nobody in the Pentagon will jeopardize their retirement by firing off a nuclear weapon. I suspect the military aide with the nuclear football has already been briefed not to let Trump near the codes, and they've been changed since the Russian hack anyway. Barring a suicidal chain of command, we all will live to vote another day.

What we will vote for will likely be a creature put together by a marketing team to appeal to exactly half of Americans.

It's important that we have contested elections. The Deep State exists, and it consists of millions of people dedicated to keeping Americans at each other's throats.

If this idea sounds far-fetched, consider who besides Donald Trump benefits when this country splits between opposing factions. There's Russia, China, North Korea, Iran, and Saudi Arabia, the news business, the ad agencies, the lawyers, the free-trade economists, the retailers of cheap Chinese goods, and the resource and energy companies.

In the case of other countries, a giant enemy paralyzed by infighting is safer than one that knows exactly what it wants. You also get an object lesson that helps sell your citizens on the advantages of totalitarian institutions.

In the case of corporations, equal opposing forces can be tipped one way or the other with a minimum of lobbying. For lawyers, it's always nice to have an unending supply of people in your waiting room who think they've been cheated.

For ordinary Americans, it's like rooting for one football team or another, which at least keeps our minds off rising sea levels, hurricanes, and economic collapse.

Get all these people giving what they can to right- or left-wing boys' clubs, and you can keep the pot boiling for another election cycle or two.

*

Yet the recent election was more honest than most. Safeguards were put in, ironically because Trump had insisted the last election was fraudulent.

Eighty-one million people voted for Biden against Trump's 75 million. The Republican Electoral College strategy worked until it didn't.

One of Trump's mistakes was telling a lot of people who had lost a lot and are set to lose a lot more that they would be winners, for once. They're probably disappointed at the moment, having finally seen that they still look like losers on TV.

Another Trump mistake was thinking he already had the election fixed. He made a typical political newbie's mistake, thinking people he had bought would stay bought. That's the reason he's so enraged at the Georgia governor and secretary of state right now.

Yet another Trump mistake was underestimating the level of violence he was generating in his followers, and how frightening yet familiar it was for the rest of us. Watching on TV, what happened in the Capitol generated not the Shock of the New but the Shock of Recognition. We had seen those expressions on those faces before, in supermarkets and gas stations and waiting at stoplights.

A problem arises with engineered chaos. It soon becomes the real thing, and refuses to stay within safe parameters in a world of declining resources and climate phase changes and pandemics. As Trump has discovered, trying to craft a little instability risks a collapse of the entire system.

In a worst-case scenario, civil war begins. Institutions that were supposed to last forever disappear. We are led by a series of military men dressed in civilian clothes if we're lucky. If we're not, we get a Stalin, a Mao, a Mussolini or a Hitler or a Franco. One thing we won't get is a Trump or even a Senator Cruz or Hawley.

The America we knew before January 6 is gone forever.

I expect more violence before, during, and after Biden's inauguration, more and more strident allegations of a stolen election from

Trump supporters, a gradually escalating war between police and people of color, multiple versions of the truth for everything, innocent people dead, a lot of once-nice people no longer innocent.

Sigmund Freud has been justly condemned for his misogyny, homophobia, pathologizing of outsiders, prurient Puritanism, his shoehorning of all human motivation into the Oedipus Complex, and his annoying compulsion to tell you what you're really thinking. But our own culture has, in cancelling Freud, thrown out a number of babies with the bathwater.

Among these are the ideas that the unconscious exists, and that its contents consist of what we know but refuse to think about, and that we project onto others those things we don't like in ourselves, and that any civilization has multiple traps and snares that cause deep pain to the people forced to follow its rules. The attack on the Capitol was carried out by people made unconscious by rage, who wanted to destroy a civilization that has, by Freud's definition, stunted their lives. They were looking for someone they could blame for making them destroy it. It was appropriate that they were called to action by a person who hasn't possessed conscious awareness for years.

One of the reasons Trump can tell lies and have them seen as deeper truths is because he operates largely on an unconscious level, and so can connect directly with the unconscious of his followers. It's like God talking to them, if God lives caged in the darkness within.

In such a situation, impulse substitutes for critical thinking, and impulse becomes the only reality. Impulse does not allow for self-doubt, nor does it allow for any distinction between truth and lies. It does allow for unrestrained violence against the people whom their God says deserve punishment.

Even if you're stuck hunkering down at home, dependent on screens for information, you're not completely at the mercy of people who tell you only what they want you to believe. You can start reading history.

Critical thinking has been around for 3,000 years, and it's teachable to anyone capable of reason and skepticism. You don't believe what you're told just because the person telling it roots for the same football team, is one way of putting it. You never look at the world through the fogged-over lens of ideology, is another. You approach new data knowing you'll have to work hard to make sure it's true. Once you decide it is true, you must be willing to renounce any cherished belief it shows to be false.

Critical thinking has been codified as the scientific method, and it's a powerful way to get at the truth. It's not perfect. Scientists, like any group of humans, can be stampeded into asking the wrong questions of the world, sometimes for centuries. And the scientific method is slow. Humans are sometimes too impatient to wait for solid evidence to base their actions on, especially if they've discovered the sheer exhilaration of acting on rage.

I have watched the Republican Party struggle with critical thinking since Richard Nixon was wandering the halls of the White House with a glass of scotch, talking to the portraits of his predecessors. From that time on, instead of subjecting their own doctrines to skepticism, they've doubled down again and again. Magical thinking has taken the place of honest observation of the world. Where reality intruded, reality has been blamed on Democrats. Where lies were needed to get elected, lies were told. Where votes needed suppressing, votes were suppressed.

When fighting for principles was called for, they fought for lies and called them principles.

When George W. Bush's advisor Karl Rove told a reporter, "We're an empire now, and when we act, we create our own reality," he was talking about a purely Republican empire. He was also talking about lies becoming the truth if you apply enough pressure. It's an assertion that devolves down to the ancient doctrine of might making right.

It has been a process of decades, and generations of lies and liars have culminated in the compulsive liar Donald Trump becoming president. To turn Karl Rove on his head (something I've always wanted to do), when you destroy a reality with lies, you destroy the empire that created it.

Trump's followers, in the aftermath of trashing the Capitol, suddenly find themselves in a world where wishes don't come true just because you want them to. There are warrants out for their arrest and termination notices in their corporate email. The Republican Party, which once trumpeted law and order, has corrupted the law and promoted disorder and defiled the temple of our democracy.

Trump's militias brought zip-tie handcuffs into the Capitol, looking for members of Congress. They erected a gallows and noose across the grass from the marble steps, which recalled the terrorism of the Jim Crow years. They tried to overthrow an elected government before it could be installed. They killed a cop.

Then they tried to blame their own actions on Antifa, their go-to scapegoat.

It's rare when an entire ideology collapses so completely into incoherence, but that's what has happened to Republicanism. I know the Democrats don't have a comprehensive and accurate vision of the world, but they're masters of realism compared to Republicans. They at least know that the hard work of critical thinking can discover reality, however slowly. It just can't ensure everyone will believe in it.

That would require all Americans to become critical thinkers. It's a nice thought.

The real masters of realism, of course, work at Johns Hopkins. From their Covid Map this morning: 22,410,609 U.S. infections. 374,348 U.S. deaths.

Winterpest!

THE STANLEY CITY COUNCIL has given the go-ahead for the annual Winterfest celebration, to be held February 12-14. It's usually a hopeful occasion, when Groundhog Day has come and gone, and the sun starts feeling warm again. For people who have made it through November, December, and January, another five weeks of winter is, for the most part, doable.

This Winterfest, Stanley is facing restrictions enforced by an honor code. Face masks and social distancing will be required, and the pub crawl and all live music will be outdoors. Stanley's mayor is concerned that if the weather is ugly, people will crawl into unlocked restaurants and bars. He's worried that honor alone won't be enough to keep them outside, especially if the wind is howling and snowdrifts are making it hard to swing dance in the middle of Ace of Diamonds Street. Also, it could be raining.

The mayor has a point. Winterfest is traditionally a time when the town drunk is a collective noun. Having, in the distant past, attended Winterfests and enthusiastically joined that collective, I have my doubts about anybody's honor holding up under the strain of copious alcohol, the after-sundown cold and dark, facefuls of wind-whipped sleet, the angry politicization of masks and distance, and the tendency of snowmobilers (right wing) and cross-country skiers (left wing) to form tribes and find defensible structures to cluster in.

Winterfest's traditional outhouse race is on. So is the traditional drag race—Stanley's nod to gender diversity—where heterosexual white males get to dress up in the clothes of mothers, wives, and girlfriends and run the length of Ace of Diamonds on snowshoes.

The fat-tire bicycle race is probably on unless the course is too snowy or too soft, or is solid see-the-grass-through-the-ice. The back-country figure-eight competition, sometimes held if the conditions are right, probably won't happen because right now our slopes are covered by an 18-inch layer of sugary snow under a two-inch rain crust. We'd need a foot of chilled, fluffy powder to get people to even sign up.

Julie and I won't be attending Winterfest. We're too close to having vaccines at the Stanley Clinic, and we don't want to be the last people to die on the morning before the armistice is signed.

As of this writing, a new, more contagious Covid variant (B117) has spread from the U.K. to Colorado, Texas, New York, Pennsylvania, Connecticut, Georgia, Florida, Oregon, and California. According to epidemiologists, its transmissibility ensures that natural selection will make it the most widespread viral variant by March.

Given that some people in those states are skiers, and wealthy enough to vacation or even have a home in Sun Valley, it's likely the U.K. variant is already 60 miles south of us. Somebody carrying it is likely to get bored with overly groomed slopes and long, spread out lift lines. They'll drive up to attend Stanley's Winterfest.

Even though the vaccines are designed to be effective for all sorts of strains of the virus, I'm worried that easier transmission will mean increased virulence. We've been told initial viral load is a prime factor in the seriousness of a Covid infection, so wouldn't the virus spread cell-to-cell more easily once it's contracted, and thereby increase the viral load *in vivo*? Just asking.

Julie and I did get a good ski in before it rained last week. We went up the north side of Gold Creek, a long ridge a mile north of us. It's a good place to backcountry ski because you have to cross a mile of flat before you get to the steep stuff. It's 2,600 vertical feet to the top, and unless you like a long slog through giant drifts and twisted trees, hiking around and through windswept piles of rocks, and watching for slab avalanches even in the best of conditions, there are easier places to ski. We like it because it's a steep and scenic tour, interspersed with some nice powder slopes. It's also isolated and a bit scary when you get all the way up there and see how far you are from your vehicle, should anything go wrong.

The route is usually empty of other skiers until we get a track up it, and even then, if we meet somebody, they're usually smart, deliberate skiers who won't need rescuing, there to savor the scenery as much as the skiing. You don't want to be on the same mountain with somebody who takes unnecessary chances. I've quit skiing Copper Mountain, the popular backcountry ski hill near Banner Summit, because I've seen too many people ski the chutes on its steep north side, and I've taken dead skiers down in toboggans before. That was when I was a ski patrolman on Baldy, not free-skiing on Copper. Not that the guys in the sled would have known any difference.

(It's a problem for ethics class. Q: Do you risk your life to rescue someone who skied down a couloir and got avalanched? A: Of course you do, as long as you're sitting safe in ethics class.)

Julie and I consider ourselves smart, deliberate backcountry skiers who err on the side of caution, but people who fit that description can still be found on avalanche fatality lists. You can reduce the risks out there, but you can't reduce them to nothing.

As it was, when we started across the flat from our car, we'd go 40 feet and the surface of the snow would drop an inch due to an airy layer of frost about halfway down. We'd go another 40 feet and it would drop again. Juno was with us, and if she got off the track her rear legs would spin out in the sugary base layer, and we'd have to pull her up on the track again.

"If the snow was any deeper," I told Julie, "we'd go home and drink tea on the couch."

"Where you go, I will go," she said, which has been our private joke ever since she refused to include that promise in her wedding vows. Now when she says it, I can hear the unspoken part of it, which is, "as long as you don't screw up."

Fair enough.

We cut a steep track up through the shallow snow of a wind-exposed ridge, for safety's sake. We didn't go all the way to the top, because we would have had to cross a slide area on the way. I didn't trust the deeper snowpack at that higher altitude to be anchored by the sagebrush.

It was a good thing. On the way down, we skied from tree to tree until we could get on a long hogsback that goes all the way to the bottom. We put side-by-side turns down through snow that was soft and deep in spots, wind-crusted in others. Sagebrush kicked our skis around a bit, but we didn't hit any rocks.

Our tracks looked graceful enough considering the conditions, until Juno came charging down through them, making them look broken and unskilled.

All along our descent, the snow kept breaking and settling. I watched fracture lines jump out from my ski tips and multiply upslope from me, which is never a good sign. Julie stayed at a safe distance until I'd get on the close downside of a big tree, and then she'd catch up. We didn't start any avalanches, but with deeper snow, we would have been wondering how to get out of there alive.

We kept our tracks on the very top of the hogsback. We avoided terrain traps. We didn't stick our skis under horizontal logs at speed. We all made it safely back to the car.

Outside Magazine has lately put out a flurry of cautionary articles about avalanches and backcountry skiing. It noted that the average age of people who get hurt or die in the backcountry has been going up. The complacency of long experience and the inevitable geriatric erosion of backcountry skills are taking their toll, according to one article, which sounded reasonable until I read that the casualties the writer was talking about were 35 to 40 years old.

In any event, the magazine has taken time out from its Ten-Best articles (a noxious sub-variety of journalism that has destroyed more beautiful places than any number of open-pit uranium mines and deep-water oil wells) to emphasize the trouble you can get into in the backcountry and the precautions you should take to avoid it.

Outside even published an avalanche poem that says avalanches don't care who you are or what you dream of doing with your life, but the people who love you do. That seems obvious enough, but upon reading the poem, I realized you could substitute coronavirus for avalanche and it would mean the same thing: it's a dangerous universe. It doesn't really care whether you live or die. For the sake of your own life and the happiness of the people who love you, you should do what you can to take care of yourself.

It occurred to me that I could do some work on the poem, translate its message and its metaphors into Covidese, and send it to the Stanley City Council. I realize they've approved Winterfest due to pressure from the local hospitality industry, which long ago designed and implemented the celebration to make money in a traditionally slack season.

But this year's event is a lot like skiing 18 inches of fragile windslab on a foot of rotten hoarfrost.

This pandemic has killed far more people than all backcountry avalanches put together. One can imagine the reaction of *Outside* if 400,000 backcountry skiers were buried by avalanches every year, even if most of them were over 35 and would die soon anyway.

If you're frightened of avalanches (we are), and you spend a lot of time assessing their risks (we do), and you avoid them when you can (like the plague), shouldn't you also be frightened of a variant coronavirus superspreader event this winter in Stanley?

You might think I've become a grumpy old fart. Guilty. I'm getting tired of watching people run around without masks in the local grocery stores. I'm tired of seeing people I know in the obituary columns. I'm tired of not seeing good friends because they're hunkered down just like Julie and I are, waiting for vaccination. I'm tired of having a week of 10-below nights followed by three days of off-and-on rain followed by 10-below nights again. I'm tired of Ten-Best lists, especially ones that mention Idaho, or Sawtooth Valley, or good places to go if you own a Sprinter van.

I've only seen one Sprinter van this month and I'm already sick of Sprinter vans.

All I can say in my defense is that being a grumpy old fart is an improvement over the person I was when I was skiing the northside chutes of Copper, thoughtlessly endangering myself and anybody who might be foolish enough to try to rescue me.

I wear my mask when I go to town. I think of friends and family that I hope to see on the other side of vaccination. When I see happy maskless people walking the streets of Stanley, heading for a bar with an open sign, I only mutter and snarl into my mask a little, and quietly, so I'm the only one who can hear what I'm saying. It's safer that way.

Trying to Remember a Future

January 25, 2021

JULIE AND I watched the inauguration last Wednesday. It was a sur-real experience, sitting in Sawtooth Valley and watching Joe Biden address the country from the same Capitol steps where lately rioters had swung Confederate battle flags, fought and killed police, and battered their way into the building.

As if by magic, the Capitol became a place where poetry and hymns were sung. It had become high enough moral ground that Donald Trump couldn't be there, for fear of altitude sickness.

It was a place where Joe Biden could say he wanted to be a pres-ident for all Americans, even the ones who had voted against him. For me, the best moment was when Amanda Gorman, a 22-year-old poet, embodied a brilliant hope as she read her poem detailing what it would take to finally lay down the burden of our country's history.

Julie was in tears of relief and joy for most of the ceremony, but I wasn't. The last inauguration that brought tears to my eyes was Bill Clinton's, and I remembered too well the way that turned out.

Clinton accelerated the move of U.S. manufacturing to China, Vietnam, and Mexico. He continued Reagan's destruction of labor unions, one of the main supports of the American middle class. He put the country's hopes and dreams in the incompetent but no doubt enthusiastic hands of Monica Lewinsky. Along the way, he showed us that an intelligent psychopath, one who had abdicated moral authority, could get re-elected to our highest office.

So even when Joe Biden called on Americans to live in a world ruled by Fate, one where our highest human defense against a brutal universe was to lend a hand to someone in need, I didn't cry. I just hoped that this time, our president wasn't a psychopath.

*

I taught college students for 20-odd years, and Amanda Gorman brought back memories of hyper-intelligent young adults in my classes. I remembered people for whom my biggest contribution to their education was to get out of their way. I remembered entire semesters where I had assigned a list of good if difficult books, and then watched what happened when 10 or 12 or 15 good if difficult minds grappled with life-and-death ideas. I had learned that when a professor started dictating answers instead of asking questions, mediocre students took a lot of notes and thinking students got terrifically bored. I saved my deep attention for the thinkers and learners and let the others keep up as they could.

Amanda Gorman interested me because she wasn't singing poetry that was cynical or enraged or bored. Those are popular choices for a lot of our young writers these days, especially ones who have been reduced to serfdom or paralyzing anxiety or dull resignation by educational loans. (Future historians, if there are any, will record that banks and colleges and universities reintroduced slavery in the United States with easily acquired and impossible to retire college debt.)

But Gorman's professors, her family, her fellow students, and her own clear ambition had brought her to this point, standing on the steps of the Capitol, reading her work to the president of the United States. A lot of people had helped her to get there. None of them, as far as I could tell, had convinced her that her horizons had limits.

She still has a long way to go. She wants to run for president in 2036. What had been Robert Frost's career peak, and Maya Angelou's, too, is for her merely a foothill.

To listen to someone that confident and still quite aware of the pain, terror, and danger the next four years will hold must have given Joe Biden a moment of genuine hope for his country. He's old enough to know that a human being, standing alone, doesn't stand a chance in this world. It was good to see so many young people's future given a chance, in the form of Amanda Gorman. It will be good to see them given many more chances.

*

Garth Brooks sang "Amazing Grace." His performance was in sharp contrast to the scenes of rioters in the halls of the Capitol. I had the thought that his singing would make for telling irony if done as a voice-over to all the scenes of mayhem videoed on January 6. As a performer, Brooks must have known he would enrage a plurality of his fans by singing a song of reconciliation and love and salvation at Joe Biden's inauguration. I've already seen a hit piece saying his fist-bumps with Democratic officials indicate his willingness to hang out with near-term abortionists and other friends in low places.

Brooks's performance sparked a good if ancient memory. Julie and I asked her older brother and two younger sisters to sing "Amazing Grace" at our wedding. For me, at least, it was a presumptuous request. On that day—August 17, 1996—I wasn't sure a wretch like me could be saved, or that Julie and I, pledging our union would last until death, would be blessed with the kind of grace that could keep that promise.

The future looked just as dubious then as it does now, and while my sins weren't as dark as those of John Newton, the reformed slave-ship captain who wrote the hymn, I wasn't at all sure I deserved forgiveness from God or my conscience or a series of angry ex-girlfriends. Also, I had colleagues in the English Department who had urged me, upon finding out I was dating a student, to date someone less innocent, less trusting, less intelligent, and less willing to give her heart than Julie.

I ignored their advice, and "Amazing Grace" has turned out to be a better selection for our wedding than we could have imagined, 25 years ago.

We'll ask her siblings to sing again at our 50th anniversary, if we all get there. I'll be 95. I hope we're in a more grace-filled and less dangerous world than we've lived in so far.

We're taking nothing for granted, not grace, not good works, not even our good friend Mr. Dumb Luck. But watching the inauguration last Wednesday, we began to feel that we could at least start planning our 50th anniversary party. We'll put Amanda Gorman on the guest list.

*

I have been sleeping eight or nine hours a night since Biden's inauguration. In the afternoons, I've been napping on the couch. A great relaxation has come over me, and I've realized it's because Donald Trump is no longer in the White House. I no longer scan the headlines, worried that some fundamental axiom of human decency has been violated, some self-aware, competent official has been fired, or another woman has revealed assaults physical and legal. I no longer have that small edge of anxiety that awaits each day's evidence that our government takes satisfaction from being cruel, that it pardons the guilty and executes the insane and takes children from their parents.

I hadn't realized the weight of the shadow of fear and anger the Trump Administration cast over the country, and the depth of the ugliness generated by its willingness to punish people of good will. I've always believed Solzhenitsyn's dictum that the line between good and evil runs down the middle of the human heart, but the last four years have shown that the line can move. A heart can contain far more evil than good.

Trump moved the line for us all. His anger and paranoia have been contagious. His lying has generated terror and rage in hearts where no terror or rage existed before.

Amanda Gorman suggested that we cannot lay down the burden of our history if we don't study it, know it, understand it, remember every year of it, and tell the truth about it. By extension, if we forget it, ignore it, lie about it, whitewash it—that burden will become heavy enough to break the mind of this nation. It nearly did so on January 6.

But the prohibition against remembering has been lifted. Buried images keep coming to the surface. They're not pretty, but once we see and acknowledge them, we no longer have to spend our energy making sure we don't think about them.

It will be a long time before the images of the Capitol riot fade from my mind. It will be a long time before I forget seeing a cop being beaten with a flagpole, or the retired Air Force officer in combat gear, carrying zip-tie handcuffs for captured congresspeople. I won't forget the broken windows or the furniture piled against doors. I won't forget the profanity, the threats, the murder of a man just doing his job. Fortunately, neither will the FBI.

Rumors are circulating that Capitol rioters were infiltrated by Antifa, and that no Trump supporter would destroy property or disobey a policeman. The video shows that they would, and did.

On January 6, our country very nearly lost its vision of itself. I have no doubt that had Trump succeeded in derailing the certification of Electoral College votes, he would eventually have ended up as the contemporary equivalent of Mussolini, hanging naked upside down from the marquee of a gas station. But millions of people would have died in the interim, most of them through no fault of their own. Trump would have happily sacrificed their lives and their happiness to his own ambitions.

These are strong words, but they're backed up by recent history. When a country gets as close as ours was to civil war, not much goes according to plan, unless the plan is for a lot of people to die by violence. As a people, we dodged a bullet. A lot of bullets. I'm relieved that what happened here didn't keep going like it did in Russia in 1917, Spain in 1937, or China in 1949.

Psychopaths will be with us always, and as a country we don't deal with them as we should. We don't always lock them up as incurably evil, even when they've destroyed lots of people. Often enough, we make them our leaders. That will get us in terrible trouble one of these days, more terrible than the trouble we're already in.

Here's a primer on how to recognize psychopaths:
1. They lie when they could just as easily tell the truth.
2. They're lazy unless they're working in their own self-interest. Then they can work tirelessly.
3. Their intelligence is cold-blooded, unless they're stupid. Then their stupidity is cold-blooded.
4. They remind you that reptiles once ruled the Earth.
5. They never accept responsibility for anything that goes wrong.
6. They never share credit for anything that goes right.
7. People they have been close to in the past will not go near them.

If you recognize any of these criteria in someone running for office, it's a good idea, for the country and for your family and for yourself, not to vote for them. If they're running in a mob toward the Capitol, get out of their way.

Amanda Gorman gave us a compass for right and wrong in her poem, and a moment of grace for a country that needed it. Watch her sing it again—it's easy enough to call up on YouTube—and you might start seeing a country we would vote for if it were on the ballot. I'm glad Joe Biden was listening. I hope we all were.

January is Dead. Long Live January.

February 1, 2021

TODAY WILL BLESS us with one hour, two minutes, and sixteen seconds more sun than we had on December 21. It's warmer and cheerier, too, thanks to a storm that dropped eight inches of snow in the past few days.

The storm came in with wind. Saturday, I spent a half hour blowing a big drift out of the driveway. Then I got the snowblower up on the deck and cleared it off. Then another squall came over the peaks and dropped two more inches of snow.

Juno had to be encouraged out into the drifts this morning. When the snow is deep, she tends to pee on the deck, which is one of the reasons we keep it cleared. Another reason is that sometime in February, the sky might clear between a couple of warm Pacific storms. We'll drag the deck chairs out of the garage and sit outside to watch the sun go down. It will be the first day of spring, equinox notwithstanding.

Big wind slabs line the gullies on the hill across the road, and even though it would be fun to ski them, we'll wait for the freeze-thaw cycles that begin in April. After a week of warm days and cold nights, the snow stabilizes.

In spots the hill is steep enough that you can skim the snow with an uphill elbow while you complete your turns. A deep exhilaration comes from making 40 or 50 windshield-wiper turns in two inches of new powder on a bulletproof base. Look back uphill and you'll see your mark on the world, at least until the next snowfall.

But not now. Now, we'll be getting windy storms all the way through March. The long vertical drifts that mark the hill will build up a few inches a day for 10 days or so, and then cut loose all at once.

The piles of snow at the bottom of the hill will last into June. I always keep an eye on them to see if anybody's skis or snowboard have melted out, or anybody's arm or leg, for that matter.

Julie and Juno and I did ski the hill before this last storm. Conditions were, in a word, difficult.

We had breakable crust and soft spots between the hard ridges of drifts, and we had to feel our way through four or five different kinds of snow on every turn. Julie got worried about falling, which in itself guarantees a fall. I've learned she can fall three times and still have fun, but after the fourth fall, fun isn't in the picture for either of us.

Nobody fell four times. One of us fell three times, but I'm not saying who. Nobody skied with the slightest amount of grace. (Juno displayed grace. She charged down the mountain in six-foot leaps, disappearing when she landed, exploding into sunlight when she jumped again.)

We all ended up on the highway, walking back to the house, tired but happy. If our ski tracks were our mark on the world, it looked like we've gone through life as rank amateurs.

This winter Julie and I have been arguing over living forever if we could. Here's what I want:

We get to live in the here and now. Eternal youth is part of the package. Both of us living in this house, in this world, skiing and hiking and reading books. Stacking fall woodpile after fall woodpile, forever. Writing journal entry upon journal entry, book upon book, until our hard drives rival the Library at Alexandria. One of us cooking fabulous meal after fabulous meal. The other loading and unloading the dishwasher, forever, fabulously. Planning a hundredth wedding anniversary every hundred years.

"I like living," I say to Julie. "I like this world. I like you. I'd stay in this life forever if I could."

She disagrees. "I'd hate living forever, here or anyplace else. I'd get bored. All our friends would get old, and sooner or later they'd all get Alzheimer's, and we'd have to visit them in nursing homes."

(This is a trap. She's trying to get me to say our friends could live forever, too, at which point she'll say which friends, and I'll say all of them, and she'll say what about their kids, and I'll say only if they behave, and she'll ask who gets to decide what good behavior is. Ultimately, I'll have to concede that everybody gets to live forever, which would, within a few generations, make for a Sawtooth Valley overrun with entitled, non-empathetic, and disgustingly immortal tourists in Sprinter vans. I don't take the bait.)

But I am hurt that she, a couple of decades younger than I am, would choose to leave me by dying. I wouldn't do that to her, if I had anything to say about it.

"Besides," she says, "life without death would have no meaning. Death gives depth to life. Take away death, and life would be static and lifeless. Everything would happen over and over again, even January. Alzheimer's would be a defense against the crush of memory."

"It *is* a defense against the crush of memory," I tell her.

A memory of a long-ago summer, no doubt brought to consciousness by the dark and the cold, and the mostly grim news of this discontented winter:

I'm five years old, and with my father, who is fishing for salmon on the river behind where our house is now, and he's hooked a big chinook salmon. The water is high and the fish has run downstream, and he's come to a place on the bank where the willows are too high to get his line over them. He looks at me and tells me to climb onto his shoulders. He kneels down, holding his fishing rod as high as he can, and I climb up and hang on for dear life. He walks out into the water, which with his first step rises to his waist, and he starts running with the current, trying to keep up with the fish so his line won't break.

The water reaches his chest—and my shins—before he can do an aquatic dance along the riverbed boulders to a gravel bar on the other side. He emerges with water-filled hip boots onto solid ground, sloshing with every step. I won't let go. He tells me to get down so he can land the fish.

The salmon finally stops its run. He plays it for another 20 minutes, finally pulling it exhausted into the shallows. He kills it by sticking the blade of his knife into the top of its head.

I try to lift the fish, but it's too heavy for me. My father takes a loop of baling twine from a coat pocket and threads it through the salmon's gills. He slings the fish over one shoulder. Its tail reaches the back of his knees.

We wander up and down the far bank, until we find a safe crossing. I again ride on his shoulders. When we get home, my mother, who spends her June days terrified she'll lose husband or son to high water, wants to know why my shoes and pants are wet.

"He went wading," says my father, not telling her I waded on his shoulders.

He picks up a fish scale from a shelf beside the kitchen stove, hooks it into the loop of twine, and holds the salmon high. It weighs 22 pounds.

This June, that memory will be 65 years old. I can still walk to the exact spot on the bank where my father hooked that salmon, although now where my father was chest deep in water there's 50 feet of gravel bar. Where that salmon died is now a deep swift hole. Where once the bottom of the valley flooded every spring, overflow channels lie choked with volunteer lodgepole. The river is empty of fish. My father is dead these 20 years.

I've changed a bit myself, but I still look at the big rocks on the other side of the river—their arrangement and their markings, unchanged for centuries—through the eyes of an unsurprised five-year-old, taking it all in. If I sit on the bank on a summer evening—this summer, if I'm alive—I'll see my father fishing across the river from me. He'll be backlit by the sunset, a happy man in the prime of his life, one confident enough to carry a small boy on his back and walk the bed of a raging river while reeling in a big fish.

*

I've told Julie more times than I should about Rutger Hauer's death scene in the sci-fi movie *Blade Runner*. Hauer plays a near-future replicant, an artificial human designed with superhuman powers and a less-than-human lifespan. Hauer's character starts remembering all the astonishing things he's done and seen in his allotted 30 years. Then he says, just before dying, "All those moments will be lost in time, like tears in rain."

That scene has haunted me ever since I first saw it, likely because tears in rain and ski tracks obliterated by new snowfall both evoke human mortality and its sheer indifferent waste of experience, of moments and images once bright in memory, of perfect turns, of eyes on faces and the touch of fingers on arms, looks of alarm or love or both—all gone, lost in time, never to be part of anyone's perception again. Of all death's terrors, the loss of memory is the worst.

But as Julie knows, and I am learning, memory has heft, and volume, and when enough of it piles on the slopes of your life, it can all slide down and take you with it. You'll end up buried, stuck in a terrain trap, unable to move or breathe, yearning to escape to sunlight.

Still, the next time I'm feeling like geologic time will erase me, memories, and everything else, I'll tell Julie again about tears in the rain.

Anti-mortality update: today I can sign up for my first vaccination jab, according to the St. Luke's My Chart web page. I'll do it on the advice of Amy Klingler, our friend who runs the clinic in Stanley, but I'm not happy about it.

Instead of what I hoped would happen—getting vaccinated in Stanley—I'll have to go to St. Luke's Wood River, between Hailey and Ketchum. It's a place I fear and loathe, partly because the St. Luke's organization has become a brutalist, malignant, administration-heavy, cyber-structured medical bureaucracy that has, Borg-like, gobbled up independent medical operations all over Idaho, and partly because my most recent memory from there is colonoscopic in nature. Resistance is futile in either case.

The Stanley clinic's health district is headquartered in eastern Idaho. The Stanley clinic will receive vaccine shipments in proportion to the population it serves. It's competing with Idaho Falls and Rexburg, the home of BYU Idaho, whose students, last fall, were caught conducting Covid-spreading parties so they could sell their antibody-laden blood for tuition. Stanley, with its official population of 63, will be far down the priority list.

St. Luke's Wood River is in the more tightly organized South Central District, but I'm not counting on getting vaccinated anytime soon. The Wood River Valley will get far more vaccine than we will, but it's a community where 75-year-olds outnumber children. There will be a long line, one full of people who have lawyers on retainers and whose only desire is for the process to be completely fair for themselves and their families. Vaccines can become metaphors of wealth and power, which means it can become literally hard to get them.

I've told Julie I'd wait until we could get vaccinated together, a notion she rejected immediately. But I think once vaccine production hits high gear, we'll go from famine to feast all over Idaho, at least as far as vaccines are concerned. In that case, we could still end up getting vaccinated on the same day.

Nothing is sure, I remind myself. We could die the day we're scheduled to get the vaccine, possibly by missing a curve on Galena Summit. I'd rather not, as I've explained above, but the irony of dying on the way to one's own vaccination—the irony of dying on the way to anything—has the effect of literalizing the metaphors we sometimes confuse with real life. The good news is that you don't always have to die to gain a sense of irony.

Conditions are Treacherous

February 8, 2021

I NEED TO begin this entry by noting that Julie and I have again skied the hill across the road.

Again, conditions were treacherous. I performed the season's first full-on face plant. Julie skied beautifully all the way down, not falling, not even once.

She wanted you to know.

Vaccine news: We have no idea when we'll get vaccinated. The St. Luke's My Chart appointment schedule was overwhelmed within a few seconds of eight a.m. last Monday, when it was opened to those 65 and above. No times were available when I could finally log onto their system. I am now on the waiting list at the clinic in Stanley. I will remain on the list until vaccination.

Today I got an email from St. Luke's, thanking me for my patience, noting that adjustments to the system were ongoing, and suggesting that I check with "the state, local health districts, pharmacies, or other health care providers about Covid-19 vaccination openings and to schedule an appointment."

Then: "THANK YOU FOR YOUR UNDERSTANDING. We know this is a challenging time for everyone, and your health remains our priority. Our goal is to get the Covid-19 vaccine to as many people as possible as quickly as possible. Thank you for your patience [again] and your partnership [*partner*ship?], in achieving that goal."

I understand that we have, in Idaho, hundreds of thousands of people wanting vaccines. We don't have the vaccine for them. We won't for some months. I also understand that here in Sawtooth Valley, due to our low population and isolation, we're far down the priority list. I understand we have to wait.

I don't understand St. Luke's calling me a partner. It's a bit too much like Amazon calling its warehouse employees associates.

In 1980, I was hired by a Ketchum, Idaho startup company, Health Data International, to write a layman's book on heart disease. My intended audience was composed of people who had survived myocardial infarctions and their families.

I was told to take the language of scientific studies and medical textbooks and turn it into writing that sixth graders could understand. By that time, I had taught junior high, and knew that sixth graders responded well to concrete, impossible to misinterpret language. After three months of interviewing cardiologists, reading studies, and translating medicalese, I titled my manuscript *So You've Gone and Had a Heart Attack*.

My manuscript was never published, because Health Data International went bankrupt before they could publish books and start distributing them. My words—concrete, impossible to misinterpret, hundreds of pages of them—rest in a law firm's archives somewhere in New York state.

If I had to sum up the meaning of those pages, I would say, "Everybody gets old and dies. No exceptions. If you've had a heart attack, especially if you've had heart-muscle damage, your life will become much more limited but will still be worth living. If you have a second or third heart attack, there are worse ways to go."

Health Data International went out of business because its target customers didn't like its language. They preferred the anesthesia of near-incomprehensible medicalese to the blunt-force trauma of plainly put truth.

*

Before my employer's bankruptcy, I was sent to Atlanta, D.C., New York, and Boston to interview people who had written seminal papers on heart disease. For two weeks, I navigated airports, hotels, and the maze-like corridors of research hospitals, talking to people who had taken time away from saving lives to answer my questions. The medical knowledge I acquired is mostly obsolete now, but I did take away lifelong common-sense lessons: stay in shape, stay away from cigarette smoke, moderate my alcohol intake, and don't get too angry at anyone or anything.

One of my interviewees was the dean of the medical school at SUNY Buffalo. He didn't want to talk about heart disease, though. He had been a bellhop in the early 1950s at the Sun Valley Lodge. He told me that when he saw I was from Ketchum, he cleared his afternoon schedule. "Those two years were the best of my life," he said. "If I could still go up a flight of stairs carrying a hundred-pound suitcase in each hand, I'd go back to it in a minute."

We talked about Ketchum in the 1950s, about Ernest Hemingway and his suicide, about Sun Valley and the changes it had gone through in 30 years. He asked me how old I was and I told him I was 30. I had been born in the Sun Valley Lodge—the hospital was on its third floor—about the same time he was carrying suitcases there. "I'll bet you're having a good time," he said.

I reminded him of the purpose of my visit. He told me to put away my questions. "Let me tell you about this industry," he said, and began describing a strike at a medical-equipment factory that had cut off the local teaching hospital's supply of pacemakers.

"We haven't installed a pacemaker in six weeks," he told me. "We've got a huge bunch of patients waiting. We've told them they'll die without one. So far we haven't lost anybody. We're over-installing the electronics, in case you don't know what that means."

I said I couldn't put that in my book.

"There's a huge bunch of things you can't put in your book." He put his fingers on his breastbone. "I've had bypass surgery. You know what most people who have had bypass surgery say? 'I'd rather die than have bypass surgery again.' We know what we're talking about."

If I had been a more experienced interviewer, I would have steered the conversation back to state-of-the-art developments in cardiology.

Instead, I listened as he said, "We've turned medicine into a soulless profit center in this country. We're squeezing more and more from our patients, and from our doctors, for that matter.

"I see our graduates go on to internships and residencies, and they get through them all right," he said. "They're waiting for the salary, and the Porsche, the family, the vacations in Paris. What they get is 80-hour weeks for the rest of their career, divorces, malpractice insurance. They lose patients they love. Their kids are strangers to them. They get bitter and angry, and it ends up hurting their patients. I think the system we've set up is causing more suffering than it cures.

"Look at Hemingway. His doctors could have saved that mind, that talent, if they'd sat him down after his last plane wreck and told him to quit drinking. Instead, they waited until he was in alcoholic dementia and then gave him shock treatment. It destroyed what little was left of him."

I couldn't put that in my book, either. But, as we say in the interview business, I was learning some shit. "You've thought this through," I said.

"Enough to be behind this desk rather than in an operating theater," he said. "Even here, I listen to a lot of cynical old people who were idealistic young people a couple of years ago. It's enough to make me wish I'd stayed a bellhop." He paused. "Not really. I'm proud of what I've done with my life. But I've got this fantasy that I'm carrying Hemingway's bags to his room in the Lodge when I have a heart attack and die. He puts me in one of his stories. It'd be like *Death in the Afternoon*. But no kitchen knives tied to a chair. Just too much baggage."

He grinned. The interview ended with me unable to tell where his memories ended and his relationship with death began.

Julie and I have an ongoing conversation about how the pandemic would have unfolded if the fatality rate was 20 or 30 percent, like hantavirus, and if it hit young people harder than us old folks. We have speculated that many of the people now demanding freedom from masks would start demanding prison for people who refused to wear them. The either/or nature of their thinking wouldn't change, but with a couple of dead children in every other family, mobs would demand curfews and lockdowns instead of unlimited church and sporting event attendance.

The trouble with our conversation is that it isn't hypothetical. The 1918 flu did hit young people harder than the old, and although the fatality rate stayed below three percent, a big fraction of Americans got it. Slightly less than three-quarters of a million died.

The downriver town of Challis, never overly welcoming to outsiders in the best of times, put checkpoints on the highways leading into town and stopped travelers at gunpoint. Still, the flu got in. I don't know if the infected were expelled to Stanley or Mackay, but I am sure that would have been the civic impulse.

The people of Challis had a point. Out in the wider world, cities that refused to lock down, or that opened too soon after lockdowns, paid for it in deaths. Cities that effectively ceased economic activity had fewer deaths and recovered their economies more quickly once the pandemic was over.

Millions of people who lived were disabled for months or years. The president of the United States got it, and it probably caused the severe stroke that eventually killed him.

The flu went on for two years before disappearing in 1920. Since that time, flu pandemics worldwide have killed millions every decade. Very few people, over the years, have conflated freedom with the flu.

Ever since my interview in Buffalo, I've been a student of industrial medicine. Nothing that I've learned contradicts what that former Sun Valley bellhop told me. If you combine the expensive and inhumane procedures performed to extend a life a week or a month, the malpractice industry, administrative bloat, the impoverishment and inequalities attendant to insurance, Medicare and Medicaid fraud, the deliberate addiction of millions, prescription cascades, diagnostic errors, abusive training practices—you can make the case that industrial medicine causes more suffering than it cures.

Should the tragedy Julie and I talk about come in 2022 or a few years later—and it will come, according to every epidemiologist I've read—St. Luke's won't be effective in fighting it. Industrial medicine is a system designed to fill hospital beds, not keep them empty. It's too big to respond quickly to a pandemic threat, too dependent on other institutions to take responsibility for life-and-death decisions, and too complex to have as its single purpose the prevention of disease and suffering.

When a pandemic comes along, a finely tuned financial mechanism that depends on a steady input of the sick stops working. Some of its profit centers get overwhelmed by oversupply, others cease to work because of shortages. Quick response to changing conditions becomes impossible, and first-line workers burn out, retire, or become sick themselves. Their lives become one long emergency. We call them heroes, but we don't demand that their employers treat them like heroes.

If all this sounds unfair, remember that not long ago, doctors and nurses didn't have the drugs, procedures, and infrastructure we have now. Their cure rate wasn't that great, but they did have their share of unexpected recoveries.

Their level of systemic harm was far lower. Their level of empathy was far higher, and I suspect patient quality of life was higher, too. I'm not saying we should get rid of the medical advances of the last 80 years, but we could administer them in a much more humane and human way, one that treats patients as something other than units of added value.

At the risk of sounding like the demented fascist Margaret Thatcher, let me assert that there is no medical industry. There are only patients and their families and the people who take care of them. As long as corporate medicine exists as a mechanism for extracting money from the sick, those patients and families and caregivers will suffer.

Saying so goes against the tide of corporate evolution. But to paraphrase Joseph Tainter's *The Collapse of Complex Societies*, any organization adds complexity in response to stress until it runs into diminishing returns. When the costs of complexity exceed the returns it delivers, the organization breaks down. Its choices are a return to simplicity or death. History suggests that death is more popular.

St. Luke's and other vast medical organizations do not exist in a vacuum. They are responding to an era of offshoring, just-in-time supply chains, pharmaceutical industry malfeasance, employee abuse, treachery toward clients and customers, and the financialization of everything. The difference is that lots of people within the medical industry have sworn an oath to do no harm. If they let themselves think about it, they may find their consciences at odds with corporate culture. Over time, that's a recipe for crazy.

I don't have a recipe to avoid collapse, but I can say that if we have a choice, returning to simplicity is better than death. If the way medicine is practiced in this country were simpler, smaller-scale, more humane and flexible, and less fragile and subject to disruption, we'd all have a better chance of living when the next pandemic hits.

A Little Writing Class Is Not the Same as Having a Little Class

February 15, 2021

LAST WEEK I gave a Zoom class for Jackson Hole Writers. Eleven people signed up. I asked for a thousand-word writing sample from them, taken from a work in progress that contained problems they hadn't yet solved. Given the nature of works in progress, it was a request they could easily fulfill, unless their problem was they hadn't written anything yet.

They had all written a bunch. I got eleven pieces of writing—good writing—and read them carefully, taking notes. Some people in the class were doing things with words I wished I could do. Everyone knew how to construct a scene and introduce a cast of characters. Everyone wanted to be a better writer, which made talking to them about craft a joy and a privilege.

I focused my class on the violence of everyday life, which almost never makes it into stories. Readers may not pick up a story for its violence, but they get bored when it's missing. They stop thinking the characters are real, because they're too nice to be real.

It's a rare story that keeps a reader's attention when it doesn't contain a bad person doing awful things to a good person, and a good person getting even or dying in the attempt. But it's painful to put those actions on the page. Often the violence is psychological, and it's even more painful to write than the physical kind.

I read the class a passage from my why-to-write book, *MFA in a Box*, which began by complaining that "Nothing much happens in many of the stories that I read. If the conflict needs to be solved by violence, often enough the writer leaves the scene."

I had prefaced the passage with an epigraph from the writer

272

Philip K. Dick: "Reality is that which, when you stop believing in it, doesn't go away." Later in the chapter, I had written, "The writer's most important function is bearing witness to what is real—to what hasn't gone away, even though you've stopped believing in it." I emphasized that writers need to have faith that reality exists, even though humans aren't very good about figuring out the difference between reality and wishful thinking.

Witnessing the truth takes care and hard work. You must never pretend you know what's going on when you don't, never pretend violence isn't there when it is, and never, ever run away from reality because you don't like it.

I write this as Donald Trump's second impeachment trial ended with his acquittal. I am not surprised at this outcome, because Trump has long experience in getting other people to commit violence for him. When the Capitol was breached and vandalized and the Vice President was threatened with hanging, Trump was safely back in the White House, watching it all on TV.

No one knows how close Mike Pence came to death, but he's a cautious man—cautious enough to never spend time alone with a woman who isn't his wife. He must have felt like he was spending time alone with death despite a lifetime of trying to avoid it.

Acquitted or not, Donald Trump remains a violent man. That fact won't go away, even though Republican senators wish it would. They also wish Trump's claim that the Democrats stole the election wasn't a lie, and that the Democrats really had managed a level of organization, discipline, and unified intent they haven't been capable of for 50 years.

What isn't a lie—what won't go away just because you stop believing in it—is that all humans are deeply violent beings. Violence is just under the surface for most of us, and all we need for it to come out is someone to tell us it's justified. Often enough, that justification is because someone has cheated us or stolen from us or is going to take our place.

Convince us of any of those, and most of us are capable of murder.

Get any of us in a mob, and the idea that Mike Pence might have ended his life suspended from a gallows on the Capitol steps isn't farfetched at all.

If you don't believe me, search your own heart for murderous impulses. Imagine having a button that, if pushed, would make someone disappear forever. If you can't come up with the name of a person you'd make disappear, you're a better human being than I am.

Or not. Maybe you would disappear whole political parties, occupations, economic classes, tribes, skin colors, and nations.

Watching the Capitol riot, I found myself wondering what would have happened if God had performed a miracle and placed the Chicago police force, as they were in 1968, in the halls of the Capitol, waiting for the mob to break in. Those were the police who forever darkened the 1968 Democratic convention by leaving hundreds of antiwar demonstrators brain-damaged, crippled, and broken.

The Chicago police may have destroyed the future of this country in their desire to punish people they saw as hippies and anarchists. They certainly destroyed *one* future of this country, the one that had President Hubert Humphrey and single-payer health care, and lacked Richard Nixon, Watergate, and Henry Kissinger messing with China and Chile and Iran.

Brought to January 6, 2021 by divine Uber, those same Chicago police would have held the Capitol steps against the rioters and killed a bunch of them. I'm ashamed to admit I would have cheered them on. Lots of people would have been injured and killed, but I would have thought it served them right for going up against a police force determined to make people behave in a civilized manner.

Did I really want to witness families missing parents or children, the grief attending to wrecked lives, the blood oozing from ears, the broken bones? Not really. But somewhere below my neocortex, primitive hardware exists. It hasn't had an update in a million years. It would have been happy if things had happened that way.

If I could get rid of the observing, empathetic, logical, kind, and human part of myself, the rest of me would be free to cheer on murder.

*

I'm worried the Democrats' muscle memory might come into play.

If this country gets contemporary equivalents of Chicago Mayor Richard Daly, Lyndon Johnson, Robert McNamara—to say nothing of Andrew Jackson, Woodrow Wilson, and FDR, Democrats all—we'll see what competent authoritarians look like, especially now that events have removed the constraints of compassion and decency.

If Republicans keep abusing Democrats with voter-suppression laws, lies about stolen elections, gerrymandering, scapegoating, and accusations of cannibalism and pedophilia, they'll awaken a sleeping giant.

For the moment, Democrats can pretend they don't have a dark side. Take away the obvious propaganda and QAnon conspiracy theories, and Democratic villainy takes the form of that too-nice-to-be-real Obama couple, Hunter Biden in rehab, OSHA regulations, the Clean Air and Endangered Species Acts, a 15-dollar minimum wage, and crippling the Postal Service.

But turn the Democrats into resentment-fanning populists, equip them with graphs showing the last two decades' worth of wealth transfer between classes in this country, wait for the inevitable fore-closures and bankruptcies and evictions as a debt-fueled economy reaches its brutal repayment stage, and you'll see what a mob of angry true believers, properly coached, can do to the people they're told to blame. A lot of people will have dibs on those weaselly little guys, Josh Hawley and Marco Rubio.

There's a good story in there somewhere, but it will require a better author than someone who leaves the scene when the furniture starts getting tossed around.

I've told a couple generations of writing students that they can send their characters into dangers they would stay away from, have their characters say things they wouldn't say themselves, and act on impulses they're too timid or too smart to act on.

One of my collections of short stories, *Sudden Death Over Time*, consists of first-person dramatic monologues. Every character I invented to tell those stories, except for the last, is a psychopath. I didn't have any trouble imagining them, which makes me a little worried about my all-too-active imagination.

People do mistake those bad, twisted, dysfunctional characters for the author. That's why I ended the book with a peaceful and maybe dull story told by a person deeply in love with his wife, who spends his days building fence because a good fence, with all its hard work and slow progress, grounds him in a good and honest and human-scale existence. His story manages to free him from his substantial anger at the evil he sees in other human beings. Most readers are relieved, by that time in the book, that the author finally has shown them somebody who knows the difference between right and wrong, love and hate, cruelty and kindness, violence and peace.

The readers have already seen what happens to people who don't discern those differences. A lifetime of amoral self-interest ends up as pathetic self-destruction, mainly because amoral self-interest looks pretty stupid from a deathbed.

At some point you have to start loving your fellow humans and doing what you can to help them, or your life doesn't mean shit.

All the psychopaths in my stories end badly. They die alone, staring into nothing, irrelevant when they aren't scorned, fools who thought they were wise.

I learned not to be a psychopath not just by seeing my characters' ends. Their whole lives are ugly, even in their moments of triumph. They are people who let their reptile brains construct their existences from the raw materials of laziness and stupidity and selfishness. The finished product is indistinguishable from pure evil.

I've learned a lot about people from writing books. Here's a tip: if you can't learn from real people, you should write fiction and learn from your characters. You should be able to learn from real people, however. Your fictional characters will be better. Classier.

In the end, writing is a program of self-improvement. Because it requires so much time and effort, writing glorifies the God of Hard Work, who is into self-improvement big time.

There are worse gods. The God of Hard Work always sticks with you and mostly keeps you out of trouble. If Christ had worshiped the God of Hard Work, he would have stayed a carpenter, and there wouldn't have been centuries of philosophers distressed about that episode of parental abandonment in Gethsemane.

I didn't tell my Zoom class, which contained a devout Christian or two, that last part. But they were all good writers, who had already learned that hard work is a solid, honorable way of life, if not a deity.

I did tell the class that everything they would ever write would be a necessarily imperfect artifact. If they were writing a memoir, they wouldn't be able to tell their own story just because they put an I on the page. Even when they tried to make those I-persons smarter, happier, more virtuous, and better looking than their authors, evil would creep into the mix. Readers would end up seeing things in authors that the authors themselves couldn't look at.

That's okay. Readers appreciate characters with faults, and even authors with faults. But they care about characters more than they care about authors. Readers know when you invest your life in your characters. They know when you care for them, empathize with them, and give them the dignity you wish you had yourself. Take care of your characters, and your readers will believe in them, even when they don't believe in you.

We have had, for the last four years, a not-very-conscious author writing our national narrative. Even his latest impeachment ended with a whimper rather than a bang. When conflict between good and evil threatened, he said there were nice people on both sides, which is no way to tell a story. He treated his characters with contempt, and nobody, least of all himself, believed in them.

We've had to bring in a new writer. He's got a new blank document on his computer screen. We hope he'll be better with the language, among other things.

We know he'll work harder than the last guy. We know he'll be more interesting than the last guy.

We think he has a sense of his own mortality and what a life lived in service to other people looks like.

We hope he'll be into self-improvement. We hope he'll respect and learn from his characters.

We hope he has a sense that whatever he does, it won't be perfect, but that won't stop him from trying to make it so.

We hope he writes a self-help book. We hope he writes a story with a moral. We hope, when he confronts the inevitable violence beneath the surface of every story, the good guys win, and that they don't take winning as permission to stop being good.

Death and Retribution

February 22, 2021

RUSH LIMBAUGH DIED last week. He was a man who had turned the sensibility and tactics of a grade-school bully into a job that paid 85 million dollars a year. His frequent targets were people of color, women, homosexuals, the transgendered, liberals, immigrants, Democrats of any stripe, Parkinson's victims, and seekers of social justice.

If you were white, straight, male, and angry, he welcomed you into his circle of admirers. He told you that you were smarter than other people. But he said you were victimized by affirmative action and a general prejudice against the successful. You were among a hardworking, honest minority that kept our nation going, but your tax dollars went to support dishonest parasites who sold drugs, were whores or pimps, and spent all day drinking 40-ounce bottles of Old English 800.

Upon hearing of his death, I thought if there is an afterlife, and if happiness there exists in proportion to the amount of kindness, understanding, mercy, and charity you've shown toward your fellow creatures during your earthly existence, Rush Limbaugh is, right now, deeply unhappy.

I never became one of Limbaugh's admirers. For one thing, I've always been smart enough to distrust people who told me I was smarter than other people. For another, I have hated bullies since I was old enough to be bullied.

Bullies were a playground fixture at Ketchum Elementary School. Early on, I learned to blend into the background so as not to attract their attention, all the while paying deep attention to them. I learned how to read the coded language of exclusion, that subcategory of English that designates some people in and some people out, and I got good at knowing when someone was about to get picked on. I tried to make sure it wasn't me, but I hated bullies just the same.

The biggest bully at Ketchum Elementary—not counting the hot lunch cooks, who must be forgiven because they knew not what they did—was Mrs. Mac, our third-grade teacher. As a third grader, I was terrified of her, and with some reason, because her favorite mode of discipline was to stand behind a child and administer hard and repeated slaps between the shoulder blades. My memory still retains an image of Ricky Day, nine years old, mouth open and moaning in terror, head snapping back and arms going in the air with each slap, while Mrs. Mac screamed at him to stop talking when she was talking.

It took me years to realize that Mrs. Mac was mentally ill, and that she should never have been allowed to enter a room filled with people smaller than she was. It took me more years to understand that bullies forget the pain and humiliation they cause others, but their victims remember everything the bullies did, and every detail about who the bullies were.

Once, 30 years after I was a third grader, a classmate told me a story that might have explained Mrs. Mac's cruelty. My classmate's mother had told her that Mrs. Mac had been a great beauty in her youth, with many admirers, and she could have married quite a few men who were far more successful than the man she had married.

When I was a third grader, Mrs. Mac was in her mid-to-late 50s, going through what in retrospect must have been one of the all-time Guinness World Records horrible pre-hormone-replacement menopauses, and suffering from depression, blind helpless rage, and nihilistic despair.

Much has been written about women disappearing from male consciousness after menopause, and how they find it a relief. For Mrs. Mac, though, in the time and the culture she was in, where female currency was counted in units of beauty, her mirror must have terrorized her like she terrorized her third graders. Her gray hair and wrinkles and jowls (and mad eyes, it must be said) must have convinced her she was being obliterated. Beating up little kids was reaching for another chance at existence. It worked. Sixty-two years later, she's still in this world, occupying space in my brain.

When I was in third grade, my father supplemented our family income by trapping mink, weasels, marten, otter, and coyotes. He supplemented our diet with wild game. Beef was a wasteful luxury, even in the form of hamburger.

He taught me to hunt and butcher elk and deer. I helped him check his trapline, and I watched as he killed the animals still alive in his traps. Early on, I made a fuss and wanted to take them home as pets, but my father spent a lot of time explaining the wild world to me, and how a predator made a living. "Humans are predators, too," he said. "We all have to kill to live."

When you learn this from a father, you make fewer cruel mistakes than when you have to learn it on your own. That's one good reason, if you're a kid, to make sure you have a father.

Over the years, I learned how to trap and skin animals, and I suppose, if I had to, I could pull a box of traps from the attic of the garage and start up a trapline again. I don't think that will happen, and not just because I don't want it to happen. If trapping is the only way Julie and I can stay alive, a bunch of other things will have occurred that would make our continued existence dubious anyway.

In the meantime, I much prefer that my killing be indirect. I tell Julie, when she asks me if I'm ever going to apply for an elk permit, that I will the day Costco closes its meat department.

If you're eight years old and your father is teaching you to kill furry little animals that look a lot like teddy bears and Easter bunnies and acrylic puppies, you become, of necessity, a philosopher. Fortunately, my father understood the process, and helped out. "Never cause unnecessary suffering," he told me. "There's too much suffering in the world as it is." It was sound advice, even coming from a man whose hands were covered in blood.

After a few years of trapping, I didn't need to be convinced that there was more than enough suffering in the world. I had also hunted enough to know that hunting usually guarantees a crueler death for an animal than a slaughterhouse.

Every year I find the remains of elk and deer in the hills above our house, shot and left to rot by people who didn't want to pack them out, or gut-shot and never found when they ran off and hid. Not causing unnecessary suffering takes skill and hard work, and there are better ways of not causing it than hunting or trapping. As soon as I got old enough to quit them both, I did.

These days I still see young men who try to make a living outside of the culture by trapping or guiding hunters. But it's brutal work, hard on the spirit over time, and over time pays less than working in a Burger King. Nobody I know has made a career of it. Even my father had to drive ski bus in the winter and work on road construction in the summer to make enough money to feed, clothe, and educate his kids. Fur prices have gotten worse since he was a trapper.

Without survival as a rationale, trapping becomes a cruel hobby. Cruelty shouldn't be a hobby.

I won't allow Rush Limbaugh to occupy a room in my brain. It's already crowded in there, and if I believe the gerontologists, the place is getting smaller and smaller. At some point you have to go through your hippocampus and throw out the squatters, the junkies, and the criminals. Limbaugh qualifies for eviction on all three counts.

I do have some sympathy for him. I've learned enough about the human psyche over the years to know that sadism is a part of everybody. That's because if you're hurting somebody, they have to acknowledge that you exist. Somewhere in Limbaugh's past, the self he was constructing got damaged enough that he quit trying to build on it and started trying to protect what was left of it.

Over time, it became a habit, and then a career. It was no doubt a process that involved one logical but cruel business decision after another. When his sadism got grotesque, as sadism always does, it was too late to change.

That he had so many fans suggests that plenty of people enjoyed his cruelty, and they used it to validate their own existences. If his fans weren't bullies themselves, they were at least akin to the kids who stand around a fight on the playground, chanting, "Hit him again. Hit him again."

I watched the ceremony where Limbaugh was given the Presidential Medal of Freedom by Donald Trump. Limbaugh was in the advanced stages of lung cancer by that time, and he must have known he wouldn't live long. He teared up. He might have been thinking of his own mortality. He might have been overcome by the honor of the occasion. He might have realized he would miss this world, maybe a lot.

But I don't think so. I got the distinct impression that he thought he had made the world a better place and was being rewarded for it. He was someone, finally. He was made so by order of the president. Those were tears of relief.

You cannot have your father tell you, "Never cause unnecessary suffering," and think that Rush Limbaugh made the world a better place. You cannot imagine Limbaugh's father ever telling him the world has enough suffering as it is.

I can remember every bully I have ever encountered. I can tell you their names, and, in most cases, where they live.

It's amazing what you can find out on the internet these days, and it's amazing how much comfort you can derive from a little personal information. It's amazing how much you can remember about people once you put your mind to it, and it's amazing what you remember about them that they cannot remember about themselves.

It's amazing how much information you can find between the paragraphs of an obituary.

I'm describing an utter waste of time, especially considering I'm not going to track down a bunch of third-rate people, one by one, and confront them with what they did, decades ago, to me and other people. It would be about as useful as confronting Rush Limbaugh, if he were still alive, because old bullies are well defended against remembering themselves as young bullies, or for that matter the bullies they were yesterday. You can't appeal to their consciences. You can't tell them they hurt you and expect them to feel guilty.

You can't call the cops on someone who sucker-punched you in a high school locker room. You can't confront the tattered little old lady who made fun of your clothes when you were twelve and she was thirteen and a foot taller than you and dating a ski instructor. You can't call out the guy who made his girlfriend wait in the car while he visited a whorehouse in Burley, Idaho in April of 1967.

It would be stupid and pointless and would increase the amount of suffering in the world. It might set off an exhumation of my own memories, ones where I hurt people weaker than me, and it might make me remember my father's voice, saying, "Humans are predators, too."

It might make me, God forbid, forgive bullies, just so I could forgive myself. I like to think my own sins were far less serious than any of the ones I've listed above, but I haven't consulted with the people I committed them against. They might remember things differently.

Mrs. Mac, long retired from teaching, died in a snowstorm, walking from the grocery store to her home in Hailey. She slipped and fell down and was covered up with snow, and, I heard, buried by a snowplow whose driver didn't see her. It was a day before somebody noticed her leg sticking out of a snowbank.

When I found out about it, my first thought was, "Good. Serves her right." I was old enough to know better than to think that, but I thought it anyway.

By then I had been a teacher myself. Even though I had tried to be a nurturer, not a torturer, I had made mistakes. I had made people cry when I gave them bad grades or showed them where their essays and stories contradicted themselves. I had made them angry when I caught them lying or cheating, and I had really made them angry when I stopped them from being bullies. I had a reputation for being sadistic to sadists, or at least to people I had decided were sadists. I was a shepherd protecting my flock from wolves, never thinking about where the flock was headed at the end of the summer.

No doubt there are people out there who will cheer if I'm ever found frozen solid in a snowbank, and who will say that if there is an afterlife, I'll soon be warm enough.

Ironic Juxtapositions

March 1, 2021

LAST WEEK I received my first dose of the Moderna vaccine. I woke up the next two days with muscles and joints aching, and a general lack of ambition. Could have been the vaccine. Could have been age. I am recovered—at least from the vaccine—and waiting for my second dose on March 25. By that time, we should know if Moderna's mRNA technology will have mutated my genetic code enough that I'll have a superpower. I'm betting on invisibility.

Getting the vaccine while Julie waited in the car was a difficult moment of conscience. It's hard to think I'll be protected when she won't be. That's not the way our marriage has worked, for one thing. For another, I would be lost without her, should she catch the virus and die.

Spending a year quarantining together without falling out of love is an accomplishment, I suppose, but it also reveals a terrifying weakness: whichever of us is left living after the other dies will live on in deep, possibly unbearable grief. Speaking only for myself, I don't think life would be worth living without Julie, or her cooking.

I'm not sure what she would miss most about me. I'm not about to ask.

Some other events of last week, in the vein of *Harper's Magazine,* the dark journal of ironic juxtaposition:

NASA's Perseverance Rover landed safely on a Martian river delta. Tiger Woods shattered both legs in a car accident. For the first time this year, Julie and I skied the hill a mile downriver—JPP, also known as Julie's Powder Palace—and it was better skiing than this year's weird temperature swings and intense winds had led us to expect. Ted Cruz discovered the science of optics and came back to a freakishly cold Texas from a warm Cancun. A Saturday *Daily Beast* article noted that Cruz's superpower is that he has no shame. CO_2 levels at the Mauna Loa Atmospheric Observatory were 416.52 ppm on Valentine's Day, higher than any time in the last three million Valentine's Days. Joe Biden launched the first air strikes of his presidency on Iranian-backed militia outposts in Syria, killing 22 or more. A snowmobiler was killed by an avalanche in the Smiley Creek drainage of Sawtooth Valley. Computer simulations have revealed that without humans on the planet, wooly mammoths would have lived another 4,000 years. No word on how long the mastodons would have lasted. We burned the last piece of firewood from the woodpile next to the garage on February 25. It had lasted three weeks longer than last year's woodpile next to the garage. We are now pulling firewood from the woodpile on the deck, which can be accessed while wearing slippers. In the Disney city of Orlando, Florida, attendees at the annual Conservative Political Action Conference unveiled a golden statue of Donald Trump, apparently unaware that their gesture lay in ironic juxtaposition to the *Book of Exodus*. Idaho became home to the California and British variants of Covid-19, which are more transmissible and possibly more lethal than the Wuhan original. Idaho's medical community has raised the possibility that second vaccine jabs should be delayed so more people can have their first. Julie and I successfully completed February Fitness Month, during which we abstain from alcohol, and exercise every day that lacks blizzards or vaccine side effects. Steak and red wine and postponed Valentine's hyperbole are on tonight's dinner menu.

We now return to our regularly scheduled programming.

Last week also saw pandemic deaths in the U.S. reach half a million. It was a number duly and solemnly noted by President Biden, who emphasized the tragedy the number represented. He urged Americans not to become "numb to sorrow," which sounds like good therapeutic advice, unless you're one of the many who grieve. Then you might require a little numbness just to live, because the loss of a parent, spouse, or child can be unbearable.

(Since Biden's speech, 11,300 more people have died of Covid-19. It's tempting to think you're at the shank end of history when the death toll reaches big round numbers, but you're always in the middle of it.)

We say time heals all wounds, but we all know people who never got over their grief. They died of it, or they embraced the fog of dementia, or they retreated into denial or paranoia. Families manage to forbid their members to even think about dead children, and grandchildren grow up not knowing about a dead aunt or uncle, or stillbirths or miscarriages. It's true that grief can act as growth hormone for the soul, but it's a rare soul that can allow itself the full embrace of sorrow and not come out the other side saying it's had way more growth than it can stand.

The sheer number of family members, co-workers, friends, lovers, and fans of the dead has turned us into the United States of Grief, a nation of PTSD victims, led by a grieving president, a therapist-in-chief whose life has been filled with irretrievable loss. If, as the evangelicals assert, God anointed Donald Trump as president for a reason, He has anointed Joe Biden for half a million reasons.

Perhaps the cohort we need to model ourselves upon is the American veterans who returned from the Second World War, who came home having lost friends, innocence, opportunity, youth—everything that made up their lives before the war—and got to work. They dropped their burden of grief and went to school and got jobs and raised families. They didn't complain, didn't talk about their war experience, didn't shirk from hard and lengthy tasks. They became tough in the best sense of the word.

Only toward the ends of their lives did the horror come back to them, in the delirium of hospice drugs or the loneliness of a hospital bed, revealing that you can live a life while being numb to sorrow, but the sorrow is still there when the anesthesia wears off.

If Americans could become a tough (if numb) people and, post-pandemic, build a nation the way we did from 1946 to 1963, I would have more hope for this country and this world. But this country and the world have, in the most literal sense, fallen apart since that time. The pandemic has exposed widening divisions between rich and poor, between people who read science and people who don't, between conservative and liberal, creditors and debtors, white and Indian, white and Black, white and Asian, white and Hispanic. We are divided into employed and not, religious and not, well-nourished and not. We are QAnon or not, addicted or not, armed or not, psychopathic or not.

The term *American* used to hold us all together. It doesn't anymore. There is no sense that we might be stronger as a nation if we had the courage and intelligence to partner with the fellow Americans we see as enemies.

I'm a person who has written an end of the world book, so it will come as no surprise when I say that America is over, more or less. I've written that the year 2030 will see us destroyed as a nation, with our formerly United States "a moonscaped radioactive desert where the survivors are confined to caves and ruins and drink ash-fouled water and don't look too closely at the meat they're eating, and knowledge and technology diminish with each burned book and broken machine and dead battery."

It doesn't have to be that way, of course. All it would require is courage and superhuman effort and constant brutally honest self-assessment as to whether or not we're contributing to the whole. Also, generosity. Also, temperance. Also, justice. Also, kindness. Also, sacrifice. Basically, we all have to put ourselves in the position of an ICU nurse during a pandemic.

Probably not going to happen.

2030 it is. Plan on having to get tough, and not in the best sense of the word. Bring the hot sauce. Don't expect that if there's a virus going 'round, you'll get vaccinated against it.

Rosa Luxemburg, the early 20th century economic theorist, is credited with inventing the slogan "Socialism or Barbarism," which has been stuck in my head lately.

I'm not advocating one or the other, because I can't. In fact, my reaction to the slogan is, "Like we have a choice."

I do know that capitalism is a temporary phenomenon, one dependent on free resources and the ability to pollute without cost. That's why energy companies—the prime example of contemporary capitalism in crisis—resist clean-air laws and restrictions on extracting oil and gas from public lands. If these companies aren't subsidized with public resources, they can't produce a product at a price their customers can afford.

It's worse than that. Capitalism has to expand and keep on expanding, because it depends on debt. Interest rates generally reflect how much an economy is growing, plus whatever the financial class takes for its own sustenance and amusement. That's why super-low interest rates indicate a non-producing, non-expanding economy, one headed for a crash once its debts come due. At that point, capitalism becomes barbarism, if barbarism means starvation in the midst of luxury, Orwell's "boot stamping on a human face—forever," or simple old Might Makes Right.

Socialism holds out the promise that a country or a culture can last a little longer than it would if it stuck with pure capitalism. You can argue this country still exists because of the socialistic reforms that tamed the trusts or brought Social Security to a generation of starving grandparents. Great Britain would be lacking its gentry if its returning soldiers hadn't chosen the ballot over the gun in 1946.

Julie and I are too old and too averse to violence to do well under barbarism. That's not necessarily true of the neighbors. Even now, absent the rule of law, there are people in Sawtooth Valley who would supply the boot if we would supply the face. That sounds paranoid, but it's more like the watchful waiting of a cautious oncologist.

Anyway, it's in our interest to return to as much of the world of 2019 or earlier—1955, say—as we can. But I'm old enough to have witnessed what millions of Americans call free will morph into a lemming migration, one heading in a rush toward the cliffs, and below them, the sea. 1955 won't come again, and neither will 2019.

The pandemic has delivered a body-blow to the American economy. In effect, it's sped up the process of economic decay, and increased the unavoidable costs of energy, health, food, and shelter at a time of extreme unemployment. 2030 doesn't look as far away as it used to. I think Joe Biden's got his heart in the right place, and he'll try to keep the suffering to a minimum, even if it means raising taxes on the rich. Because of that, this country will last longer under him than it would have under Donald Trump. But Biden's an old man, and the barbarians are at the gate.

Now that we're in a month when we're free to drink alcohol again, Julie and I will return to a sunset ritual that has us sitting on the couch with glasses of wine, eating hummus and crackers and kalamata olives, and conducting ongoing conversations about the many ironic juxtapositions that mark our lives. One of those juxtapositions stems from the fact that Sawtooth Valley, especially during tourist season, resembles a carefully constructed diorama, and we locals have a tendency to become part of the exhibit.

We note that we have done what we were supposed to do with our lives, mostly. We went to college, got jobs, bought a house in a rising market, saved our money, kept learning new skills, refused to buy snowmobiles or Sprinter vans, and lived as frugally as we could in the world of fragile privilege our parents' hard work had given us. As a result, we have had a good life, but it may have come at the cost of being the last middle-class couple in America, soon to be extinct. At least that's what it says on the plaque on the other side of the glass.

Smells Like Spring Spirit

March 8, 2021

WHAT HAD BEEN a cool, windy, and cloudy winter finally eased last week. The sun came out. The sky turned blue. Temperatures got above 40 in the afternoons. In places, the spooky wind crust on the hill across the road softened and achieved the predictable consistency of soggy corn flakes. Going skiing seemed like a mostly good idea.

Skiing down, you had to read the hill, but parts of it were written in an unknown language. The long deep drifts on the north sides of ridges acted as cold storage for the three inches of powder from the last storm, so you could make tight quick turns until the terrain or downed trees forced you out on the south-facing slope and into three inches of slush.

If you started too late in the day, you could, even skiing the tops of drifts, punch through to the bottom foot of snowpack—last fall's dry and cold powder, now a hollow blend of air and fragile flowers of frost.

If the tails of your skis dropped into that layer at the end of a turn, it was easy to fall backward and discover you were stuck in a hole, with the snow under you collapsing further every time you tried to get your skis under your center of gravity.

Your backpack turned you into an upside-down turtle. You had to wriggle free of shoulder straps, take off your skis, struggle upright in crotch-deep snow, and slowly boot-pack a platform you could stand on. In ten minutes or so, you were skiing again. Traverses and kick-turns, mostly.

These are avalanche conditions. In the late afternoons, the top foot of snow softens and compresses downward. It can get dense enough to collapse the bottom layer, especially if you're skiing over it. Then an entire hillside's snowpack can begin floating on a layer of trapped air. Once it gets going, it pushes more air under the snowpack below it. Given room, 10 acres of snow can start moving at highway speeds, breaking trees and ripping up brush and rocks along the way. If you're caught in a spring avalanche, you're more likely to die of trauma than asphyxiation.

You ski the ridges, where you're likely to be at the top of an avalanche if it starts. You keep an eye out for terrain traps, and you remember that people can die when their arms and legs are caught by deep wet snow and their heads are jammed into a drift or tree well. You don't ski alone.

I'm making skiing sound dangerous, but it's less dangerous than going to Stanley without a mask these days, now that Idaho has decided it will ignore the new, more contagious Covid variants. Snowmobilers are coming into the valley from towns that have eased all restrictions on masks and distancing, and they crowd into the bars and restaurants, treating Stanley like a sanctuary city for aerosol droplets.

We locals mask up for the post office and the grocery store. We do our best to stay out of the restaurants, although Julie and I have gotten takeout three or four times this year. When we've had to wait for our order, it's been less than comfortable. Our masks draw what look like hostile stares from the maskless. You find yourself feeling guilty and defensive in your own town. After years of trying not to upset the tourists, you've upset the tourists.

This tourist season is starting out like last tourist season, with an influx of people who believe the virus doesn't exist. Or if it does exist, it's no worse than a cold. If it's worse than a cold, it's no worse than the flu. If it's worse than the flu, it won't kill you. And so on. Tourists get together in Stanley, infect each other, and return to their homes. We locals, possibly because we have getting caught in an avalanche as a handy metaphor for catching the virus, try to maximize our odds of survival in a situation where there's some risk no matter what you do. In that way, a mask is like an avalanche beacon, a kind of talisman that—if the worst should happen—tells the people who find your body that you weren't being an idiot. Even dead, you were being as careful as you knew how to be.

*

Vaccination will arrive too late for most tourists to have what they remember as a normal summer. But they'll be back, anyway. Sawtooth Valley will seem less dangerous to them than wherever they live, if only because they don't know people who died here. For those of us who have lived here long enough to have seen whole generations come and go, the tourist industry's implied offer of a vacation from death rings hollow, especially in the face of CDC-predicted surges in infection.

For those of us who have been vaccinated, plague-year habits will die slowly, if at all. Our days of casual, non-special-occasion restaurant dining are gone forever. Weddings are now in the same hazardous category as gender-reveal parties. Shaking hands is out. Costco on weekends is out. Even if it's just a cold, saying, "It's just a cold," is out.

Going to see Steely Dan and Pink Floyd tribute bands in crowded basement nightclubs is a thing of the past.

Also, we fear getting on a plane and getting off in a city half a world away. The pandemic has shrunk our world, and where Julie and I once talked of flying to Vietnam or London or Portugal, we now talk about driving to Portland or Albuquerque or Seattle. We worry about the economic horrors coming as whole nations lose the ability to buy plastic shit to make themselves feel better, and as housing bubbles collapse when people find that no matter where they go, there they are. We've imagined ourselves in the situation of the folks who got stranded across oceans when the pandemic closures hit. We comfort ourselves that we're stranded at home.

Bad as they are, these scenarios assume that 2021 won't deliver anything worse than 2020. No new and more lethal plague. Our damaged world economy will have enough resilience to rebound and keep a majority of humans alive and functioning. No major climate disaster. No earthquake a magnitude greater than the one last March. No screeching halt to the Gulf Stream and the subsequent icing of what's left of Great Britain. No nuclear war. No Second Coming of Christ, or of Donald Trump, for that matter. No world leaders revealed as space alien lizards in lifelike rubber human suits.

In short, we imagine that the place where we're stranded—physically and culturally—won't change beyond all recognition.

Would that that were true. Our home has already changed beyond any happy recognition, and not simply because of this summer's expected mass in-migration of Sprinter van owners in lifelike rubber human suits.

I don't think there's a human alive that doesn't know, somewhere below the level of conscious thought, that things post-pandemic will never again be the same. But a lot of effort is being expended to keep that realization unconscious.

Rational human decision-making this summer will be constrained by a near-unanimous denial of humanity's undeniable crises: economic inequality, racial conflict, climate tipping points, starvation-and-torture inspired migration, the triumph of right-wing dictators, the malignant machine intelligences of Facebook, Twitter, and Amazon, the decline of Energy Return on Energy Invested, a global corporate culture that has put an Inc. behind every country's name—all manifestations of a world civilization whose mainspring has come unwound. When the energy that motivates civilization starts to flag, the everyday becomes the grotesque, the lethally imbalanced, the best of intentions gone wrong, the best of human beings gone bad.

The bottom layer has gone out of things, is another way to put it, and what looked like a solid structure can't even hold itself up. The only thing left to do is pretend that memory is more solid than reality. It's an exercise we're doing a lot these days, and not just when we're skiing.

Maybe you're doing it, too.

I did get two big days of memorable skiing in last week, warm temperatures notwithstanding. Both involved long climbs with long approaches, and both left me exhausted at the end of the day. Julie, who had to work while I went skiing with our friends Michael and

Liesl and Sean, was remarkably tolerant about my coming home and immediately going to sleep on the couch.

I am discovering that, at 70, you don't bounce back from a day of intense exercise. It takes more than a night's rest to restore muscles, more than a day or two to get excited about climbing another two or three thousand vertical feet. Aches and pains that used to vanish in the presence of blue skies and powder snow now persist through the long uphills. Climbs that used to take an hour still take an hour, but the hours are way longer than they used to be.

It doesn't help that my ski partners are youngsters in their 50s, who have spent this year hiking and skiing and otherwise getting in excellent shape. Still, I keep up the best I can, and they wait for me at the top. I'm grateful to be able to get there, but I've realized that big ski days won't last forever, nor will my existence. Some of the futures I'm worried about, I won't have to suffer through.

Last Saturday, anti-maskers held a demonstration on the Idaho statehouse steps. They built a fire in a barrel and had their kids— their young kids—throw masks into it. They made national news. Commentators pointed out that Idaho didn't have a mask mandate, so it was a demonstration against a regulation that didn't exist. I told Julie that some of those parents might regret dragging their kids to a mask burning once their kids turned into sullen adolescents taking high-school biology.

Julie said she didn't think they would regret anything, because they were all insane. Looking at the photos of people tossing masks into the flames, it was hard to disagree with her. I said that we, as a civilization, have deliberately forgotten that all humans have an unconscious death wish. "What you refuse to bring to consciousness, you have to act out," I said. "They're acting it out."

Judging from the things people are refusing to deal with consciously, we're in for a lot of acting out over the next few months. I would advise staying away from crowds, because we all will do things in a group we wouldn't do alone.

It's easy to get caught up in the bad craziness of others, especially as the mob mentality takes you far away from the things you don't want to think about.

Spring is the season of migratory mass movements, and sure enough, traffic on Highway 75 is increasing. After the snowmobilers will come steelhead season. Early season campers, usually with trailers, will come next. By July, tourism will be in full swing, and the roads and campgrounds will be choked with people until school starts in September, if it starts. Our visitors will once again act like there's no pandemic. Maybe by September, there won't be.

As mass movements go, the ones we'll see this year will be relatively harmless. We may have superspreader weddings, a few thousand acres of forest burned from unattended campfires, and roadsides littered with beer cans and Styrofoam, but we don't yet expect rioters breaking into Stanley City Hall, or marching soldiers on Ace of Diamonds Street, or rifle-toting people bicycling out of the cities with bug-out bags on their backs, children in tow.

But one of these years, the spring equinox will see masses of people who aren't here for recreation. When that happens, we hope they won't be bleeding from their pores. We hope they won't be in tanks. We hope they won't be acting out death wishes.

We hope they'll just be traveling through on their way to Canada to see Banff and Jasper Parks, not fleeing a country and a culture and a climate that has turned them into refugees who cannot remember peace, or health, or snow.

The End of a Tough Year

March 15, 2021

A YEAR AGO, Julie and I were scheduling a book tour. My collection of apocalyptic essays, *A Hundred Little Pieces on the End of the World*, had just been published by the University of New Mexico Press. It had been a long winter, and we were looking forward to getting on the road. I was practicing my signature for signing books, and my smile for delivering bad news about the future of civilization.

We had reservations at the elegant, entropy-ridden Riverside Hotel in Lava Hot Springs, Idaho, on March 19, 2020. Our plans included a soak in the hot pools next door and dinner at the excellent Riverside restaurant. The next day, after another soak in the early morning, we would head for Salt Lake, where I was reading at The King's English Bookshop. From Salt Lake, we would drive to Durango, Colorado, where I would visit writing classes and give a reading at Fort Lewis College.

We were scheduled to arrive in Albuquerque on March 25. I looked forward to meeting the fine folks at the University of New Mexico Press, and an evening reading at Albuquerque's Bookworks.

Over the next two weeks, we would make our way back home, starting with Santa Fe and Taos. I was planning to flog my book anywhere in the American Southwest that would have me. In between appearances at bookstores, book clubs, and college classes, Julie and I would visit national parks and monuments, hit any other hot springs resorts on the map, and wine and dine like there was no tomorrow.

There was a tomorrow—365 of them, as of today—but no book tour. On March 11, a Covid pandemic was declared by the World Health

Organization. Very quickly, the country started shutting down. On March 13, Idaho had its first officially confirmed case.

We began cancelling reservations. Our 2020 calendar is marked with cross-outs through April. Starting in May, there are blank spaces where once there would have been birthday get-togethers, solstice parties, more road trips, and visits from friends.

On March 22, the *Los Angeles Review of Books* published "On Having One's Book Tour Cancelled by the Coronavirus Outbreak," a piece I had written at the suggestion of Stephen Hull, the director of UNM Press. In it, I said a cancelled book tour wasn't the end of the world, but it was the end of a certain type of world, a world where you could get in the car and head for new territory, give in-person readings, and talk about economic collapse in the abstract.

Soon after the *LA Review* piece was published, I decided to write a journal, along the lines of the one Daniel Defoe's uncle had written during the Great Plague of London in 1665. Defoe took his uncle's work, researched its details, edited it, and republished it as *A Journal of the Plague Year* in 1722. Defoe had the advantage of a 57-year perspective on the events he was writing about. He knew what would happen next, and so did his readers. His uncle's primary source became a well-crafted history, which only lost a little of its authority due to Defoe's previous fame as the author of the fictional *Robinson Crusoe*.

I didn't have the luxury of a 57-year perspective on Covid, so I set out to write primary-source material.

I started publishing 2,000-word entries every Monday at ten a.m., often focusing on the week's headlines, or my thoughts on the dismal politics of the world and the country. I kept track of state and national Covid deaths, and the flood of tourists that hit the valley last summer. I meditated in print on the human tendency to act in self-destructive ways.

The journal made the year whiz by. There's nothing like a Monday deadline to make the rest of the week seem like a too-short break. It took at least a day to write 2,000 words, but I had gotten used to the length while writing for *Travel and Leisure* and the ski magazines.

Then another day to edit and rewrite. Then Julie would do another, more professional edit, and I'd enter her corrections. Julie would give one more reading, alert me to any lapses in fact or taste, and post it on my website.

I adopted an anecdotal, elliptical style, one where I could throw seemingly unrelated topics together and see how they jelled. I threw in jokes where I could. I charged my readers with the responsibility of making sense of my writing.

Thankfully, they rose to the challenge.

The final manuscript is long enough to make a book, written at a time in my life when I thought I was done writing books. I don't know if anyone will publish it. At the least, I can have a few copies made up and pass them out to the CNAs when I move into the memory ward at the First Hard Frost Assisted Living facility in Stanley, if it's ever built and if I win the contest to name it.

I did not anticipate that we would have vaccines so soon, and I had no idea the pandemic, masks, and vaccines would be politicized. I didn't envision that after a year and more than a half-million deaths, people would still be saying the virus didn't exist.

I didn't predict Biden would be elected or that he would be as competent as he has been so far.

I did insist we were living in a radically different world.

Biden seems to understand that the situation requires massive changes in the role of the American government, akin to FDR's programs in the 1930s. He has quickly pushed through a bill that begins the transfer of the country's wealth to poor people, something that will let the country last a little longer than it would have otherwise. He has begun work on an infrastructure bill that will put people back to work. He gave a speech that proved he's not as demented as the last guy.

The Republican half of the country, in a kind of ghost dance, reopened bars and restaurants and eliminated restrictions on large gatherings. They declared the pandemic over. As ghost dances go, this one won't have any better results than the ones that inspired Wounded Knee.

In my first post, I wrote, "With luck and wisdom, we will carry on," a sentence that qualifies as prophetic if you leave out the wisdom part.

When I was teaching fiction workshops, I told my students that now and then when you are working on a story, you can suddenly feel the whole thing drop into a deeper and more solid reality. If that happens to them, I said, they have found the real story, and they should live there for as long as it takes to see how it turns out. More than once in the past year, I've had that sudden loss of altitude in the middle of one of my journal entries. A story was beginning, and I could feel the pull of its suddenly real soul. But to follow it into a fictional world would have taken too long, and I had to finish the post I was working on, which was usually about something else entirely.

I've spent a lot of time writing about the dehumanization of my world, and I want to write about a world where the trend is in the opposite direction. That will probably require that I start making things up. I hope when I make things up, they turn out to be true. If they do, I'll probably continue writing despite the difficulty of making meaning in what looks to be an increasingly meaningless universe.

This journal of the plague year is over, but the plague is not. The world has had a tough year, and from what I can anticipate, the next few years won't be much easier. Covid will have a long tail, and the damage it inflicts on its survivors may last for decades. There will almost certainly be other plagues. The world economy will not get any better without huge increases in the production of goods and energy, and those increases will run hard into climate and vital resource limits.

I have written elsewhere that all we need is cheap fusion reactors that can be loaded on a flatbed and delivered to the city they will power, and cheap briefcase-sized batteries that will power a car over 500 miles. Then we could have the 20th century all over again, if we had another Earth to have it on. I think the reactors and the batteries will be just as hard to come by as the extra Earth.

*

I want to thank my readers. Your presence in the world made writing a real-life activity for me. When I got stuck in the middle of a piece, all I had to do was visualize one or two or a dozen of my readers, and I could feel the momentum of thoughts pick up again. It was a conversation, and it continues. Thank you all.

Epilogue

April 24, 2021

YESTERDAY, JULIE GOT her second vaccination shot. Today, she is feeling generally malaisy but is functioning well enough. She's been reading all morning, and we took a walk out to the river to see if we'll have high water this year. It doesn't look as though we will, not without Biblical-level rains in May. We're not counting on it raining at all.

We're not counting on much these days, especially the future.

One notable exception: we believe Julie will be her usual cheerful and healthy self by tomorrow. That may be wishful thinking, but friends who reacted badly to their second shot told us they felt fine after a day, and better thereafter. I started feeling better after my second shot, but it could have been the placebo effect. It could have been the small feeling of safety, although I didn't really feel safe until yesterday, when I could finally stop worrying about Julie's vaccination status. Maybe other old men felt fully vaccinated when they got the shots but their spouses had to wait. I didn't.

I've heard of people bursting into tears when they were declared vaccinated, but neither Julie nor I felt that kind of unadulterated relief. For too long, we've been imagining what it will be like to be around people again. While it will be good to see friends face-to-face, it will also feel reckless and weird.

We have been careful so long that it seems like careful is all we know how to do. Masks and hand sanitizer and hunkering down indoors have shaped our lives for over a year. We have grown used to it. We like it. We feel vulnerable without it. Even if new cases of Covid stopped tomorrow, we'd find other microbes to mask against, other reasons to become agoraphobic.

Pfizer's CEO went on record a week ago about the need for booster shots six months after a first full vaccination, and yearly thereafter. He was just trying to sell stock, but it was not welcome news for us non-stockholders. The CDC immediately pushed back, stating that nobody knows how long the Pfizer or any other vaccine will be effective. The CDC, as usual, emphasized what we don't know over what we do.

The CDC knows what it's talking about. Nobody knows what the future will bring. Count on that.

Also, the Minneapolis police officer Derek Chauvin has been convicted of the murder of George Floyd, the man whose neck he knelt on for nine-and-a-half minutes, cutting off his air. I did feel a great moment of relief when I heard the verdict. If the jury hadn't convicted Chauvin after viewing that video, I would have lost all faith in the rule of law in this country. So would a lot of other people who are a lot more violent than I am.

I've tried to hold onto that faith in the face of too many uniformed murderers being let off in the past decade, but a lot of people have stopped believing in justice, on both the left and the right. Taking the law into their own hands seems like a good idea.

When the jury delivered its verdict, it felt as if the country backed away—a little—from the end of civil authority and the beginning of the end of our country.

Since the end of my weekly journal entries, I've been reading a lot, mostly science fiction stories from the 50s and early 60s. You can get a hundred of these stories for 99 cents on Kindle. True, these were stories published in poorly-proofread pulp magazines with bug-eyed monsters chasing half-naked women on their covers, but they are useful object lessons in cultural anthropology.

Your 99 cents will buy you a lot of unconscious racial bigotry, a lot of semi-conscious misogyny, a lot of adolescent boy fantasies about the perfect girlfriend/wife/mother (a sort of Holy Trinity for adolescent boy science fiction authors). But you also get a presumed future, a future that could actually happen, that has some relationship to the past and the present, that is susceptible to the occasional educated guess. That's something you can't have at any price these days. But it once existed, if these stories are to be believed.

They tell of a future where people survive nuclear war, at least to the extent they can huddle in ruined basements and snag the occasional dog or cat for a meal. They can survive on an Earth that has 350 billion people (not a misprint, just a couple of hundred years more of an exponential curve on a graph). Absent biowarfare and hydrogen bombs, they live in a techno-Utopia, with faster-than-light travel, vat-grown chicken, free energy, underwater cities, asteroid mining, robots and androids, all-knowing computers, talking aliens—the list goes on and on.

Contrast these worlds with ours, and you'll see that a hundred stories of pulp science fiction for under a buck is a bargain.

It's a bargain for me, because I don't think Julie and I can presume a future that has any connection to the present. That's because the present we're in doesn't have any connection to the past. You can make predictions, of course, because that's what human brains are wired to do, but then you have to wait around for results.

You might think you're able to predict the present, but the year 2020 has shown that it takes us a long time to even grasp what happened yesterday.

It may be that we have a future. It's just that we won't realize we're in it until we get there, and probably not even then.

My other reading has been Marcus Aurelius's *Meditations*, which gets around the question of having a future by saying that a human life, whether it lasts for a hundred years or less than a day, is so small relative to Eternity that its length doesn't matter. He also says our lives are the struggles of a little soul carrying around a corpse, which, if I understand it correctly, means we are creatures of Eternity rather than of Time. It takes a leap of faith to believe in that little soul, and

Eternity, but right now they're looking considerably more resilient than the rule of law.

I find Marcus Aurelius comforting, in spite of his insistence that life is hard, vanishingly short, and lacking in free will. He says there is joy in fulfilling one's fate, doing one's duty, recognizing that fighting evil is a losing but worthwhile endeavor, and accepting one's defeats with grace. He advocates being as kind as possible to one's fellow beings, within the confines of fate.

Meditations is free on Kindle. Read it, take it to heart, and even if you haven't just read a hundred science fiction stories for a buck, you'll know the value of literature is seldom related to its price. Also that the wisdom of human beings can live long after them, if they're willing to write it down.

In the last week, I've had two inquiries about my memoir *Traplines*, which was published in 2003. The reason for the interest—that far post-publication—is the possibility that the lower Snake River dams will be breached to restore salmon runs to Central Idaho.

Passages in *Traplines* describe my father's guiding business and his clients, who paid him 10 dollars a day to hook chinook salmon and then hand them the pole so they could pull the fish to shore. I wrote about salmon thick in the rivers and a valley bright with high water and new willow leaves and sunshine. People wanted to quote my words in books and articles that supported dam breaching.

I declined to give permission, because I no longer believe in breaching the dams or restoring the salmon runs. I've become a heretic. I tend to see salmon restoration as a kind of ghost dance, an attempt to bring back the world the salmon left. That world is gone forever.

Also, tourism—given as one of the reasons for breaching the dams—has become a force for evil, a phenomenon of surface that destroys everything authentic it touches. Plus, the proponents of breaching see nuclear power as a substitute for hydropower, and if there's one thing worse than tourism, it's a world with a Fukushima/Chernobyl-level event every 25 years or so, over the projected half-life of plutonium.

The salmon that we used to fish for in the back yard are extinct. In their place is an artificial species, one that can substitute for the real thing, enough that magical thinkers can pretend things can be put back to what they were 60 years ago.

For me, the value of the salmon is in their absence. We can look at our empty rivers, slack water reservoirs, barren spawning beds, and fish trucks spewing six-inch rainbow into tourist-lined fishing holes, and we can see how little substance magical thinking gets us. If we bring the salmon back, it will be expensive camouflage on an utterly denatured world.

I don't believe you can go back into a warm and comfortable past, whether it's 1960 or 2019. Humans, at least during their time on the planet, are stuck in the present. Geologists talk about Deep Time, evoking a past that encompasses millions and billions of years, against which (thanks, Marcus Aurelius!) our lives are as nanoseconds. Perhaps we should start to think about the Deep Present, the place we can live if we pay attention to the Now, a place just as full of good and evil and wonder and possibility as the past, but one that we can actually live in, as long as we run to keep up.

About the Author

John Rember was born in Sun Valley, Idaho, and grew up in the nearby Sawtooth Valley. He was educated at Harvard and earned his MFA at the University of Montana. He has worked as a ski patrolman, wilderness ranger, technical writer, concrete and construction worker, high school teacher, bartender, journalist, and professor. John taught for many years at The College of Idaho in Caldwell and in the Pacific University MFA program in Forest Grove, Oregon.

John's memoir *Traplines: Coming Home to Sawtooth Valley* was named Idaho Book of the Year. His other books are *A Hundred Little Pieces on the End of the World*, *MFA in a Box: A* Why *to Write Book*, and three short story collections: *Coyote in the Mountains*, *Cheerleaders from Gomorrah: Tales from the Lycra Archipelago*, and *Sudden Death, Over Time*. *End Notes* is the first of three volumes in his *Journal of the Plague Years* series.

John lives in the Sawtooth Valley of central Idaho with his wife, Julie.